PHILOSOPHICAL ETHICS

PHILOSOPHICAL
ETHICS

Stephen Darwall

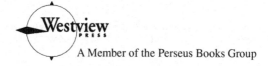
Westview
PRESS
A Member of the Perseus Books Group

Dimensions of Philosophy Series

Copyright © 1998 by Westview Press, A Member of the Perseus Books Group

Published in 1998 in the United States of America by Westview Press, 5500 Central Avenue, Boulder, Colorado 80301-2877, and in the United Kingdom by Westview Press, 12 Hid's Copse Road, Cumnor Hill, Oxford OX2 9JJ

Library of Congress Cataloging-in-Publication Data
Darwall, Stephen L., 1946–
　Philosophical ethics / Stephen Darwall.
　　p.　cm. — (Dimensions of philosophy series)
　Includes bibliographical references and index.
　ISBN 0-8133-7859-1. — ISBN 0-8133-7860-5 (pbk.)
　1. Ethics.　I. Title.　II. Series.
BJ1012.D33　1998
170—dc21　　　　　　　　　　　　　　　　　　　　　　　　97-40578
　　　　　　　　　　　　　　　　　　　　　　　　　　　　　　　　CIP

The paper used in this publication meets the requirements of the American National Standard for Permanence of Paper for Printed Library Materials Z39.48-1984.

To my students—past, present, and future

CONTENTS

PREFACE

This book is intended for use in undergraduate courses in ethics that approach the subject from a philosophical perspective. I have taught much of this material over the past thirteen years in an introductory ethics course for students with some prior philosophy. But the book may also prove useful in a second course for students whose first ethics course was less philosophically intensive.

I have sought to anchor issues in the context of contemporary debates as well as the enduring works of Western ethical philosophy: Aristotle's *Nicomachean Ethics*, Hobbes's *Leviathan*, Kant's *Groundwork of the Metaphysics of Morals*, Mill's *Utilitarianism*, and Nietzsche's *Genealogy of Morals*. Although reference to these works is not crucial, the book is likeliest to be effective in conjunction with substantial selections of at least some of them. All are widely available in various editions. Electronic versions can be accessed through my Web page: www.umich.edu/~sdarwall.

In coming to the ideas expressed here, I have had the great benefit of learning from many students, both here at the University of Michigan and at the University of North Carolina at Chapel Hill, and from many colleagues, including Elizabeth Anderson, Richard Brandt, Sarah Conly, Allan Gibbard, Arthur Kuflik, Adrian Piper, Jerry Postema, Peter Railton, Don Regan, Laurence Thomas, Gregory Velazco y Trianosky, David Velleman, Nicholas White, and the late Jane English, W. D. Falk, and William Frankena. I am indebted also to my former teachers Kurt Baier and J. B. Schneewind.

Michael Slote and Don Loeb read the manuscript for Westview and provided many useful suggestions. Sarah Warner and Melanie Stafford of Westview helped greatly with the production process, and Christine Arden gave invaluable editorial advice. Finally, I thank Spencer Carr for his persistence in convincing me to write this book and his generosity in allowing me so much time to do it.

Stephen Darwall
Ann Arbor, Michigan

Part One

INTRODUCTION

1

WHAT IS PHILOSOPHICAL ETHICS?

Ethical Opinion and Human Life

Ethical thought and feeling are woven throughout our lives in ways we rarely appreciate. We all have some implicit ethics, whether we know it or not—even if we deny that we do. We may occasionally fail or refuse to acknowledge our values, of course. Or avoid developing them into a coherent ethical outlook or philosophy. But we cannot live without values. Those who think we can should consider that without values we would lack such feelings as pride, admiration, respect, contempt, resentment, indignation, guilt, shame, and a whole host of others. Would a life be recognizably human without any of these?

Take pride, for example. To be proud of something is to see it as something *to be proud of.* This is an ethical thought—namely, that something is *worthy* of pride, that it has **merit** or **worth**.[1] When we take pride in a thing, therefore, we commit ourselves to its value. If we come to think of it as worthless, we can no longer see it as an appropriate source of pride.

It may seem surprising that pride should have this ethical dimension. The point, however, is not that pride has value but that it reveals the values of the person who feels it. If the composer of a nihilistic rock lyric denying all value takes pride in his composition, we may conclude that he doesn't really believe what his song proclaims. Or that, if he does, there is a conflict between his **nihilism** and the thoughts we must attribute to him to make sense of his feeling as one of pride.

Analogous points can be made for the other emotions I mentioned, **guilt** and **shame** being the most obvious examples. The very nature of these feelings involves standardly accompanying thoughts or beliefs: respectively, that we have done wrong or that something about ourselves warrants shame. Similarly, resentment is the feeling of having suffered an undeserved injury. Admiration is a response to something as having value or merit, as worthy of emulation. And so on. Those who claim to lack ethical beliefs, therefore, are likely to be proven wrong by their own feelings.

And refuted, as well, by their conversation. Talk with others, no less than internal "self talk," is laced with ethical categories and convictions. Gossip provides particularly good examples. Terms such as 'jerk' or 'creep' would lose interest for us if they weren't tied to the idea of warranting disapproval, disdain, contempt, or censure. The same is true of 'cool' and other terms of positive evaluation. Imagine someone muttering angrily to himself. What do you imagine him saying? I'll bet it's something evaluative—something like "I can't believe what they want me to do," something implying an evaluation, such as that an expectation is unfair or otherwise inappropriate.

Nor is it just in emotional response and conversation that we reveal our values. Anyone reading this book is an **agent**: a person who chooses to act for **reasons,** and whose choices commit her to views about what choices are worth making. To see this point more clearly, consider the contrast drawn by the eighteenth-century German philosopher Immanuel Kant (1724–1804) between **actions** and other occurrences that do not involve self-directed thought and **agency.** Kant said that although all events happen for reasons, only actions are *done for reasons.* Only actions can be explained by reference to the **agent's reasons**—that is, considerations the person herself took to be **normative reasons** weighing in favor of her choice.[2]

Suppose, for instance, that you drop a ball to illustrate to a child how gravity works. Consider the difference between two events: your letting go of the ball and the ball's dropping. There are reasons for both events, but only your letting the ball go was *done for a reason.* Only you *had* a reason for so acting. The ball had none. Nothing was *its* reason, and dropping was nothing it did *for* a reason.

To act is to take some consideration as a normative reason to act and to act for that reason. And this, again, involves an ethical thought—namely, that there are respects in which the choice is **desirable,** or worth choosing. In letting go of the ball for the reason you did, you must have thought that the fact that it might help the child to learn about gravity was a reason *to* drop it, that this was a respect in which that option was choiceworthy. Otherwise, you wouldn't have dropped it in order to illustrate gravity to the child.

We can see this point even more clearly from the **agent's perspective** in deliberating about what to do. Imagine that you are considering how to spend your evening. What do you do? You look for reasons, the pros and cons of what you might do, in the hope of finding something worth doing and, ideally, finding the best choice. In deliberation we try to make up our minds, but not arbitrarily (as by flipping a coin). Rather, we seek reasons or grounds to determine our choices. And when we act, we commit ourselves to views about normative reasons. Any being entirely lacking in ethical opinions, therefore, could not be an agent. Hence anyone who claims to lack ethical views or attitudes will be proven wrong by his own choices, whatever he chooses to do.

Ethical Inquiry: Normative Ethics

By this point, I hope you are prepared to accept that you have ethical convictions, or at least to grant this as a working hypothesis. However, I haven't said what makes a belief or an attitude an *ethical* one (i.e., as opposed to a *non*ethical belief or attitude, not as opposed to an *un*ethical one). I have given examples: taking something to be worthy of pride, believing an action to be wrong or an injury to be undeserved or something about oneself to be shameful, or thinking that there are reasons for doing one thing rather than another. A central, perhaps *the* central, ethical notion running through these examples is what philosophers call the idea of the **normative**, or **normativity**. Each example concerns what a person *should* or *ought* to desire, feel, be, or do. Let us, then, provisionally define **ethics** as the *inquiry into what we ought to desire, feel, be, or do*.

Ethical Versus Nonethical Disagreement. Suppose two people disagree about whether the law should permit doctor-assisted suicide. This seems to be a clear case of ethical disagreement. However, it could be based on a further disagreement, and we may wish to consider (especially in trying to understand and perhaps resolve the issue) whether that further controversy concerns ethics or not. Suppose that the only relevant matter on which the two people disagree is whether vulnerable individuals would likelier be taken advantage of if there were such a law. They agree that *if* the law would have this consequence, it should not be passed and that this would be the only reason against such a law. Moreover, they agree about what "taking advantage" amounts to. In fact, the only thing they disagree about is *whether* vulnerable individuals would likelier be taken advantage of if there were such a law. Their ethical disagreement concerning the law is thus rooted in a further controversy that is not about ethics at all. They simply have a difference of opinion about what would happen if the law were passed. Here, then, are two people with identical ethical premises who are drawing different ethical conclusions because they disagree about the nonethical facts of the case.

Now imagine a third person who is also opposed to the law, but for a different reason. She thinks that it is morally wrong to assist in suicide and that the law should not permit such immorality. Although she agrees with one of the first two in opposing the law, she disagrees with both in her reasons, since neither of the other two believes that assisting in suicide is immoral *in itself*. This third person has a deeper ethical disagreement with both of the first two, although she agrees with one of them in opposing the law.

Consider, finally, a fourth person who agrees with the third in opposing the law and in doing so because she thinks assisted suicide is intolerably immoral. Imagine, however, that these two disagree about *why* assisted suicide is immoral. The third person believes that we are God's creatures and that He has a proprietary interest in our lives such that it is wrong for anyone else to determine their end point. The fourth person holds no such view. She believes that human life is intrinsically valuable and that killing is always wrong. Is this disagreement ethical or nonethical?

The answer may not be immediately obvious. If we suppose that the fourth person agrees with the third that *were* there a God we *would* be His property, and that this fact would make assisted suicide wrong, but simply disagrees about whether God exists, then the two have no fundamental ethical disagreement. The real issue between them would be theological, not ethical. If, however, the fourth disagrees also about whether God's creating and sustaining His creatures would make them His property, then this would be an ethical disagreement, since it would concern what rights and obligations follow from such a creative act. Or if the fourth person holds that life has intrinsic value whether it is created or not, and the third holds that its value derives entirely from its creator, then, again, we have a disagreement in ethical belief.

Reasons and Normative Ethical Theory.   I have gone into these matters in some detail for two reasons. First, it is only by considering the difference between ethical and nonethical considerations at the margins that we can gain an intuitive grasp of the distinction. Second, thinking about the interrelations between our ethical convictions helps us see how they must fit together into a coherent structure, whether in an individual's mind or in the moral culture of a community. Our ethical convictions are not simply an aggregated set of unrelated items. Some are deeper than others, providing reasons for and supporting the others in much the same way that the third person's conviction that our lives are ultimately owned by God supports her belief that the law should not permit assisted suicide.

What accounts for this phenomenon? The seventeenth-century British philosopher John Locke (1632–1704) once remarked that no "moral rule" can "be proposed, whereof a man may not justly demand a reason."[3] Why should this be? Why, when someone says that some action is wrong, or that something has value, do we naturally feel entitled to ask *why* (if only silently, to ourselves)?[4] The beginnings of an answer are contained in the insight that ethical propositions concern *justification*, and that whether something is justified depends on whether it is supported by *reasons*. If, for example, I admire the way a colleague interacts with her students and think it estimable, then I must regard features of the interaction as worthy of esteem, as *reasons* for its merit or value. Perhaps these reasons include the respect she shows and elicits, the humor and light touch she adds while expressing and encouraging a serious interest in her subject, the way she draws out her students' best efforts, and so on. I take the value of the interaction to be *grounded* in these features. These reasons warrant or support my admiration or esteem, not just in the sense that they are signs or evidence of value but also in the sense that these features *make* the interaction valuable. They are what its value depends upon. Similarly, when a person morally disapproves of something, and expresses this disapproval by saying it is wrong, she commits herself to there being reasons that *make* it wrong. Someone who disapproves of permitting assisted suicide is thus committed to there being reasons to proscribe it.

I can restate the point underlying Locke's demand in what philosophers call **metaphysical** terms: No particular thing can be *barely* good or bad, right or wrong. If a particular thing has some ethical property, it must be by virtue of other properties it has—either "intrinsically" (in terms of its being the kind of thing it is) or "extrinsically" (in terms of its relations to other things, including its consequences). For example, if you say to me, "You shouldn't have done that," that commits you to thinking there was something about what I did that makes it something I shouldn't have done—that there was a *reason* why I shouldn't have.

Discovering what grounds our ethical emotions and choices is simultaneously a process of self-discovery and of developing a deeper understanding of what, as we believe, really is good or bad, right or wrong. For example, I may find myself admiring my colleague's way of teaching but not be initially clear about what I admire in it, about what I am seeing as its value-making properties. By reflecting on its various qualities and analyzing my responses, I may come to a clearer understanding of just what I find admirable about it. And, in so doing, I may come to a more articulated comprehension of the values of good teaching. I learn something about myself and about certain values (at least, as they seem to me). Similarly, someone may be, as we say, "uncomfortable" with the idea of legalizing assisted suicide, but not be sure why he feels this way. Only by thinking through and analyzing his feelings, ideas, and opinions—especially in conversation with others—can he come to see what really concerns him.

These are cases where one has an ethical conviction but wants to understand what reasons support it. Alternatively, one may lack a conviction on some matter, or have a conviction but doubt or wonder about its validity. Here again, we look for reasons. But now, if we are open and genuinely desire to come to a supportable conviction, we do not restrict ourselves to ethical convictions we already hold. The object, after all, is to find out not what we already think but what we *should* think. So we have to take seriously the possibility that there are reasons that we have not thought of or that we are aware of but have insufficiently appreciated.

The branch of ethics that inquires into specific ethical issues and the general ideals and principles underlying them is known as **normative ethics.** As we shall see, there are disagreements about how general and systematic **normative ethical theory** can be. At one extreme, we find philosophers who believe that ethical truth can be summarized in a few, highly general propositions. According to **act-utilitarianism,** for example, there is only one principle of right conduct: An action is right if, and only if, it will produce no less happiness overall than any available alternative. At the other extreme, we find thinkers who hold that there is such an irreducible multiplicity of goods and evils, virtues and vices, obligations and prohibitions, that it makes little sense to try to articulate general ideals or principles. Still, virtually everyone who has thought seriously about normative ethics respects Locke's demand for reasons in some form or other. By its very nature, normative ethics aims at comprehensive and systematic answers to ethical questions, even if the most defensible answers are very complex.

The search for reasons gives normative ethics its direction. Since no particular thing can be *barely* valuable or right, normative ethics seeks to uncover the *grounds* of value and obligation—the features that are **value-** or **right-*making*.** And it attempts to do this in a systematic way, with as much generality as the subject admits of.

Philosophical Inquiry About Ethics: Metaethics

I hope it is now evident that both ethical conviction *and* normative ethics are firmly rooted in ordinary human life and, therefore, in *your* life. We all have some drive to uncover more general ethical reasons, whether in seeking to understand our own convictions or in trying to answer the ethical questions that confront us. So not only do we all have some implicit ethics, we are all also to some extent normative ethicists. As a formal subject, normative ethical theory simply extends and develops an impulse that is already firmly planted in human experience. It attempts to articulate the grounds of value and obligation in a way that is maximally systematic and maximally sensitive to genuine complexity.

Normally, when we ask questions of normative ethics—"What has value?" "What are our moral obligations?"—we more or less take for granted the categories in which these questions arise. We implicitly assume that there are such things as value or right and wrong, and ask what, if anything, has these properties. But we can step back from these questions and ask also about their presuppositions. Just what *is* value, or moral obligation, itself? Are there really such things? Here we are no longer asking a question of normative ethics. Our question is not about what *has* value or is morally obligatory. Rather, we are asking about the nature of value and of right and wrong *themselves*. What does it mean, if anything, to *be* valuable or morally obligatory? Not: What is valuable (and why)? But: What is value? Not: What is morally obligatory (and why)? But: What is moral obligation? These are questions of **metaethics** rather than of normative ethics. They arise, not within ethics, but when we step back and reflect on the nature and status of ethics itself. Metaethics consists of *philosophical questions about ethics.*

As an analogy, consider the contrast between two kinds of questions we might ask about numbers. If I ask, "Is there a prime number between 11 and 17?" my question is straightforwardly mathematical. If, however, I ask, "Are there numbers? Do numbers exist?" and make it clear that an answer like "Yes, there is 1, 2, and so on" simply will not do, my question is no longer a question of the same kind. It is not a mathematical question but a philosophical one about the nature and status of mathematics and mathematical "objects." Metaethics is the philosophy *of* ethics, and it stands to (normative) ethics as the philosophy of mathematics stands to mathematics. Or consider the analogous distinction between questions that arise within science—for example, "Is this biological theory preferable to that one?"—and philosophical questions about science—"What is a scientific explanation?" "What is a theory?"

When we have a pattern of this kind, involving a primary subject area and philosophical speculation about (philosophy *of*) that subject matter, philosophers sometimes refer to the questions that arise within the primary subject as **first-order questions** and those involved in philosophical inquiry about it as **second-order questions**. In ethics, the first-order questions concern normative ethics; and the second-order questions, metaethics.

The foregoing might suggest that normative ethics isn't really part of philosophy. And, indeed, perhaps it wouldn't be if it could be completely divorced from metaethics. But it can't. What is distinctive about a philosophical approach to ethics—**philosophical ethics**, as I call it—is its integrated treatment of normative ethics and metaethics. More on that in a moment.

Metaphysics.   Metaphysics is the branch of philosophy concerned with the fundamental nature of reality, with what there is. Questions like "What is value?" are metaphysical questions. All of us raise metaphysical questions about ethics at some point. Who hasn't wondered, for example, about the relation between ethics and religion? Some of us, indeed, *proclaim* metaphysical views about ethics—for example, that the only truth in ethics is "relative," or that ethics simply concerns matters of taste. To see how metaphysical issues about ethics arise, recall our example of a law permitting doctor-assisted suicide. And imagine that someone favors the law because he believes that everyone has a *right* to autonomy, that this right includes the right to end one's own life, and that in order to adequately establish this right, society must not prohibit doctors from assisting in suicide. What, we may want to ask, is a **right**?

I assume that most readers of this book believe they have rights. Appeal to experience may help to confirm this assumption. When we feel resentment, for example, we naturally express our feeling by saying or thinking such things as "He can't treat me that way" or "I have a right not to be treated that way." In this context, 'right' means not a legal right but a moral right. After all, we can resent injuries resulting from an oppressive political order that lacks the relevant legal rights. But what is it we believe we have when we think we have a moral right?

As a beginning, we might try to translate ethical propositions concerning rights into other ethical propositions. We might say, for example, that for someone to have a right against assault is for it to be wrong for anyone to assault her, for anyone to be morally justified in defending her against assault, and for compensation and punishment to be warranted if she is assaulted. When we believe we have a right to something, our belief may take this complicated form. But our question can still persist. What, if anything, would make that complex set of ethical propositions true? And by virtue of what, if any, features of reality would it be the case that someone has a moral right to something? Here we are asking a question about the metaphysics of rights.

Especially when we are faced with what seem to be intractable ethical disagreements, those concerning the boundaries of life (abortion and assisted suicide), for instance, it is difficult to avoid more philosophical questions about the very nature of ethics. Is there such a thing as truth in ethics? Is ethical truth somehow "relative"? If there is ethical truth, whether relative or absolute, in what does it consist?

Philosophy of Language and Mind.   Metaphysical questions of this sort are closely related to issues in the philosophies of language and mind concerning the *meaning* of ethical language and the states of mind we express when we use it. When a person says it would be wrong to permit assisted suicide, what does she mean and what state of mind does she express? We can, of course, rephrase her ethical statement—for example, by saying that a law permitting assisted suicide should not be passed. But the real question is what *any* of these ethical statements mean or express. This, too, is a question of metaethics. These statements *appear* to assert that passing the law would have a genuine property, wrongness—that included among the extant facts is the ethical fact that passing the law would be wrong. In this century, however, some philosophers, called

noncognitivists, have argued that such appearances are misleading. There are no ethical facts, they contend, and when a person makes an ethical judgment, she is not really saying that there are; she is not making a genuine statement that is either true or false. Rather, she is expressing a state of mind that is more like a feeling or a desire, one that cannot, unlike a belief, be either correct or incorrect by virtue of matching or failing to match the way things actually are.

Epistemology.   Another set of metaethical issues is **epistemological,** concerning what, if anything, we can know or justifiably believe. I've said that when we consider what to believe on some ethical issue, we look for *reasons*. So if we come to the conclusion that reasons exist not to permit assisted suicide, we will, of course, regard these as evidence that there should not be such a law. But this process goes on *within* normative ethics. The question we are now asking raises a further epistemological issue that is *metaethical:* What entitles us to count what we *take* to be reasons against such a law as really being such reasons? What is our evidence for that? What, as we might also put it, are our *reasons for believing* that there really are such reasons against such an action?

I mentioned at the outset that many of our emotions are laced with ethical thoughts and beliefs. May we then take these emotions as evidence of the truth of these beliefs? Is, for example, the admiration I feel for my colleague's respectful, encouraging style of teaching evidence of its merit in the same way that you naturally take the sense experiences you are currently having as evidence that you are reading a book? And if so, what is the relation between merit and esteem or admiration? Is it possible that value might exist without anyone being able to appreciate it, in the same way that it seems possible for a physical substance to exist without our being able to perceive it?

Sensory experience gives us evidence of the way things contingently happen to be in the world. But are ethical truths similarly **contingent** (as opposed to necessarily true, in the same way that, for example, mathematical truths seem to be)? Does the gratuitous torture of innocents merely *happen* to be wrong, just as it happens to be true that objects are subject to gravitational force? The world *might* have been such that there was no such thing as gravity. Might it also have been such that gratuitous torture of innocents was not wrong? This is a metaphysical question. But if we answer it by supposing that fundamental moral truths are **necessary** rather than contingent, this supposition would have epistemological implications. If gratuitous torture could not be anything but wrong—if it is *necessarily* wrong—then it seems that this could be known only in some way other than through experience, since experience is the result of our sensory encounter with the way things merely happen to be. If ethical truths are necessary rather than contingent, then how is ethical knowledge possible?

Philosophical Ethics

Normative ethics and metaethics can be, and often are, pursued as distinct enterprises. In fact, some philosophers believe that they must be kept entirely separate. Noncognitivists hold, for example, that their metaethical theory that ethical convictions express noncognitive attitudes lacking truth value says nothing about which ethical attitudes we can sincerely avow: It leaves normative ethics entirely unaffected.

A separation between normative theory and metaethics is also reflected in the way that ethics is usually presented to students. Courses generally divide attention between these areas, and only rarely consider potential interactions. But this separation is unfortunate, because it ignores one of the most exciting aspects of philosophical thinking about ethics. In the works of the great figures in the history of ethics, we rarely find this separation. On the contrary, thinkers such as Aristotle, Kant, and John Stuart Mill all attempted to *integrate* metaethics and normative theory into a coherent systematic view. Their normative theories about what has value invariably depended on their philosophical theories about what value *is*. Even Nietzsche's radical critique of morality, his "transvaluation of values," depended on his philosophical views about what value and valuation could be. All these philosophers bring their most deeply probing philosophical thinking about ethics to bear on their normative ethical thought. For these thinkers, philosophy has ethical consequences—it matters.

As noted earlier, philosophical ethics is what I call this project of *integrating* normative ethics and metaethics. In particular, philosophical ethics aims to discover which normative ethical claims and theories are best supported by the most adequate philosophical understanding of what ethics is itself fundamentally about. Inevitably, philosophers disagree about this latter issue. It is a sign of their philosophical ethics that, when such disagreement occurs, they frequently disagree in their normative theories as a consequence.

As an example of how a philosophical theory can shape a normative position, recall Locke's dictum that we can demand a reason for every "moral rule." We interpreted this as an uncontroversial commonplace, but what Locke actually meant was (and remains) quite controversial. Locke thought that no action can be morally required or forbidden simply in itself, just because it is the kind of action it is. If an action is wrong, he held, that is so only because its being socially proscribed would have beneficial effects. So far, this is a thesis in normative ethics. It is the normative ethical theory called **rule-consequentialism:** An action is wrong if, and only if, the existence of a rule proscribing it would have the best consequences. What lay behind this normative theory for Locke, however, was a metaethical view, a philosophical theory of morality.

For Locke, morality just *is* a set of rules that God commands us to follow because, if we do not, we will fall into conflicts that are worse for all. Locke believed that God has created human beings, given us a generally self-seeking motivation, and placed us in circumstances of sufficient scarcity that mutually disadvantageous conflict would inevitably result unless He had also benevolently commanded us to act on certain rules and, by creating eternal sanctions, given us reasons to follow them. Moral rules, then, consist in those universal prescriptions and proscriptions having the property that universal conformance would be mutually beneficial. And their moral **authority** derives from their having been commanded by God, who has the right to our obedience because we are His creatures. (If at this point you ask "What makes it true that a creator is entitled to the obedience of his created subjects?" you are getting the knack for philosophical ethics!)

It follows from Locke's metaethical theory of morality that no act *could* be right or wrong in itself. So Locke regarded himself as entitled to deny the normative thesis that, for example, lying is intrinsically wrong. Anybody who holds this normative belief, Locke thought, is simply confused about what morality is. Thus Locke's normative rule-consequentialism is grounded in his metaphysical theory of morality.

Although it may seem odd from our perspective, some of the first attempts to advance **consequentialist** and **utilitarian** normative theories in the seventeenth and eighteenth centuries were based on similar metaethical arguments. The normative thesis that right and wrong depend entirely on the goodness of consequences was considered by many writers to flow from the philosophical idea that God *creates* morality as an instrument (there were different theories about how this is possible), together with the thought that, since God is omniscient and omnibenevolent, morality's inherent, instrumental goal must be the greatest good or happiness of all His creatures. In the last two centuries, consequentialists and utilitarians were far likelier to have been secular thinkers than nonsecular ones. But generally speaking, their normative consequentialism has remained rooted in an instrumentalist philosophical theory of morality's nature, situated now in a secular framework.

Philosophical ethicists who oppose consequentialism have also frequently tried to support their opposition philosophically with a metaethical theory. **Rational intuitionists** have argued on epistemological grounds that the intrinsic wrongness of torturing innocents is no less necessary and self-evident than the arithmetic fact that 7 added to 5 makes 12, and so must be capable of being known by reason alone, independent of sense experience. And Kant, who is famous for the normative doctrine that actions such as lying and promise breaking are wrong even when they lead to beneficial effects, based his rejection of consequentialism in a philosophical theory of morality as essential to the **deliberative standpoint** of a **free moral agent**.

A Plan of Study

This book's main goal is to introduce the reader to philosophical ethics. We shall begin in Part 2 with a first pass at the basic questions of metaethics, along with a brief discussion of responses that philosophers have given to them. Then, in Parts 3 and 4, we shall turn to a more extended examination of some of the major alternatives in philosophical ethics. Rather than considering abstract positions, however, we will find it more illuminating and interesting to encounter thinkers actually *doing* philosophical ethics. Thus we will be able to see ethical philosophizing as a living activity, one that results when an individual human being, or a group, tries to think through the ethical and philosophical questions we all face in a unified way—in short, tries to see whether philosophy can matter.

Morality Versus Ethics?   Part 2 concerns philosophical and normative moral theories. When contrasted with ethics more generally, **morality** refers to universal norms of right and wrong conduct that are held to obligate all persons. **Philosophical moralists** such as Hobbes, Mill, and Kant sought to develop a unified normative and philosophical understanding of this notion. They sought to understand what morality is (metaethically) in order to support a conception of what morality requires (normatively).

But morality does not exhaust all of ethics. In fact, the idea of a universal *law* of conduct plays no significant role whatsoever in the ethical thought of some thinkers, Aristotle being a notable example. And others, starting with Nietzsche in the nineteenth century, rejected the very notion of morality as philosophically insupportable. They regarded it as the misbegotten inheritance of a philosophically flawed Judeo-Christian theological tradition that continues only for disturbing reasons we are loath to acknowledge. For these latter thinkers the central ethical notions were not **right** and **wrong** but worth, merit, or excellence, on the one hand, and a **person's good** or benefit, on the other. Accordingly, Part 3 examines some cases of philosophical ethics that provide counterpoints and alternatives to theories of morality, both Nietzschean and post-Nietzschean critiques of morality and moral theory and ancient Greek philosophical ethics to which these critics frequently look for alternative models.

In the end, what united all these thinkers was their relentless pursuit of a human project in which we are all engaged. They pressed forward to striking conclusions a process of ethical and philosophical inquiry that is to some extent unavoidable for any thoughtful human being.

Part Two

METAETHICS

2

METAETHICS: THE
BASIC QUESTIONS

This book's major aim is to introduce the reader to some of the ways in which major thinkers have tried to support differing normative ethical outlooks *philosophically*. In seeking to understand what is valuable and morally obligatory in human life, they have sought to grasp what value and obligation themselves are. These latter questions are **metaethical**. To begin, then, we need a clearer picture of what metaethics is. What exactly do metaethical questions ask? And how do these questions arise?

The Objective Purport of Ethical Conviction

It will be useful to start by thinking about how things seem from the perspective of someone holding an ethical conviction. To make this exercise vivid, let's suppose that person is you, and that the conviction is one you hold strongly, stably, and confidently. Imagine that you read about an incident in which a children's hospital has been attacked by a contending group in a civil war. The assailants have dragged the children out of their hospital beds and tortured and brutally massacred them and the hospital staff in an effort to terrorize and intimidate and thereby gain tactical advantage in the war. How do you think you'd feel as you take in the grim details? You might feel horror, disgust, sadness, perhaps a profound sense of discouragement at the human prospect, maybe a desire to look away, and so on. Among these reactions, however, you might also feel a sense of indignation or outrage—a feeling you might express in some such way as this: "What a vile and despicable thing to have done." Let's suppose you would.

Now imagine you encounter someone else who is also familiar with the case, but who has come to a very different conclusion about it. This person takes the view that although it is certainly regrettable that so many innocent, defenseless people had to suffer such horrible deaths, the attack was nonetheless justified because it was a necessary means to the right side's prevailing in the war. How, then, might you view your conviction in relation to this other person's?

There would appear to be a definite issue between you and this other person. You think the attack was despicable, but he thinks it was justified. Knowing this, wouldn't you think that you cannot both be correct? Wouldn't your respective convictions appear to vie for a space that, logically, no more than one can occupy? If, consequently, you continue to hold to your conviction, having heard everything the other person can say in support of his, would you not think his mistaken? And would he not, presumably, think the same of yours?

Ethical Opinion Versus Taste.   Compare this with what is sometimes called a "brute difference of taste." Some people strongly dislike eating okra, others like it a lot, and still others can take it or leave it. Suppose you are in the first group and I am in the second. How are we likely to view the disagreement between us? Well, we *might* think there is a genuine issue—something about which no more than one of us could be correct. Or we might see our different responses as a mere difference of taste—not the kind whereby a taste can be cultivated and a value appreciated, but a brute difference. If we were to see things in this way, we would no longer be treating our difference as a disagreement concerning some objective matter. In fact, we would no longer see our responses as either correct or incorrect at all. Once we see the disagreement as one of brute difference, we can then agree that eating okra is an experience I like but you don't, and that's the end of it.

But is this the way things would seem to you in feeling indignation at the massacre? Would you be likely to think that there is, in the end, nothing about which you and a person who thinks the massacre justified really disagree? Could you see your disagreement as a brute difference in taste, such that you simply lack the stomach for such tactics whereas others apparently do not?

I think it unlikely that this is the way things would seem to you. Perhaps after some (exasperating) argument you might be prepared to say something like: "Well, the massacre is wrong *to me*, but obviously it's not wrong to you." However, although this may look like the okra case, it really is not. You and I may be prepared to conclude that the experience of eating okra is good for me but not for you because we are prepared to understand it as amounting to no more than that I like the experience and you do not. But would you be prepared to believe that you simply dislike massacre more than the other person does? In this context, saying it's wrong to you but not to him amounts to saying something like you *think* it is wrong, but he doesn't—or that it *appears* or *seems* wrong to you, but not to him. *What* you think and *what* he thinks remain in conflict; the way it seems to you is still at odds with the way it seems to him.

Ethical Opinion "From the Inside." Let me emphasize that this is how I think it would seem to you from *within* your feelings and ethical convictions. Of course, you might also accept a philosophical theory according to which ethical convictions or attitudes cannot *properly* claim any more objectivity than preferences and tastes. My point is that there will be some tension between any such theory and what philosophers call the **phenomenology** of ethical experience and judgment—the way things seem when we experience a feeling like indignation or hold the belief that, for example, something is gravely wrong. And so the philosophical theory will have to explain away this appearance as misleading or confused. It is not unusual to hear people say, in one moment, that ethics is no more than opinion, taste, or preference and then vehemently express, in the next moment, some strong ethical view. In the latter instance, it certainly *looks* as if they are committed to the correctness of their view. Surely it looks that way to their interlocutors.

Fallibility and Objective Purport. At this point, I hope you are prepared to draw the conclusion that to hold a moral opinion, at least one such as I have been describing, is to take that opinion to *purport* or *aspire* to objectivity or truth. This is not to say that having ethical opinions means assuming that one is infallible. Nor is my point that we have to deny our own subjectivity in the sense of denying that we are impervious to the influence of perspective or bias. To the contrary, that we take ourselves to be fallible and never fully able to transcend our own subjective standpoints is itself evidence of the **objective purport** of ethical opinions. If we think ethics to be something on which we are not immune from error, we must think it to be something we can be in error *about.* Or if we regard our own perspective in ethical judgment as unavoidably subject to bias and idiosyncrasy, then, again, we must suppose that ethics is an area where it makes sense to speak of bias, where actual judgments can be more or less subjective or objective—more or less reflective of our own subjective perspective or of the way things really are.

If I simply like eating okra whereas you do not, we cannot speak of bias or fallibility. Neither makes sense in that context. The kind of moral conviction we've been considering, however, is a state of mind purporting to represent the way things really are—that something is really right or really wrong. It is a sign of this phenomenon that we naturally speak of having a *view*, conviction, or belief in the latter case, although not in the former.

Agreement, Disagreement, and Objective Purport. I've purposely picked an example that is apt to strike you as uncontroversial. I've done this in the hope of finding a resonance in your feelings and judgment, so that you can consider vividly what it is like to have the feeling or conviction yourself. However, you may want to object that in doing so I have prejudiced my case and, perhaps, that I have compounded the problem by underdescribing the conflicting view. Just what *would* be the consequences if the "wrong side" won in this conflict? Can we assume that everyone shares the belief that terrorism is wrong no matter what the consequences? Or that everyone would do so on reflection?

However, the important thing to see is that, for my present point, nothing turns on whether this belief would be universally shared or not. On the contrary: If there were disagreement, this, too, would prove my point, since the disagreement would be about whether or not something was really so— that is, about whether the massacre really was wrong or, as we might also put it, about whether it is *true* that the massacre was wrong. Even if we consider an example where disagreement is likelier, the same point could still be made, although for either side there might be many readers who would have to exert some effort to think themselves into the perspective of someone holding that view. From the viewpoint of someone who opposes legalizing doctor-assisted suicide, for example, it seems as if such a law would really be wrong. And similarly, it seems that disagreements with those who favor the law are about which view is correct.

I've also purposely picked a *moral* conviction—one concerning right and wrong, rather than an ethical conviction about, say, what experiences are desirable—because I think readers will more readily agree that such convictions purport to be about something objective. But a similar line of thought can be pursued with respect to other ethical beliefs. When I admire my colleague's teaching, regard it as good, and see her interactions with her students as having worth, I am hard-pressed to see this stance as being merely a matter of taste or preference. And were someone to disagree about its merit, I would likely think there is an issue between us on which we cannot both be correct. Or, to take a less academic example, suppose I have a bad headache and see that as a reason to take a pain reliever. If someone denies that pain is a reason for acting, it will again seem that there is a genuine issue between us. *Maybe* she could say she has no reason to relieve her own pain without our convictions directly clashing. There might be relevant differences between us or our situations. If, however, she says that pain is no reason for me to take a pain reliever, then it seems we can't both be correct.

Finally, consider the following poignant illustration. In 1983, Wei Jingsheng, a leading democratic dissident, was imprisoned by the Chinese regime and denied permission to speak to anyone, even his prison guards. His health failing, Wei was offered medical care if he would write to China's leader, Deng Xiaoping, disavowing his democratic convictions. Wei did write to Deng, but this is what he said: "If you're asking me to change my basic values, well, my ideas are the fruit of long-term . . . reflection, and you're asking too much. . . . You think I can lie so lightly?" Knowing he was risking his life, Wei nevertheless refused to disavow values that seemed to him so clearly true that to deny them would be to lie.[1]

What Is There for Ethical Convictions to Be About?

But if ethical convictions purport to reflect something objective, we must ask, What objective ethical reality is there for them to reflect? We should be careful here, since it is easy to miss the real force of this question. Consider the judgment that the hospital massacre was despicable. It seems clear enough that in one sense this judgment is about the massacre and the qualities that make it despicable, and that, regrettably enough, such incidents and qualities really do exist in the world.

But it may also seem that although a full description of these qualities includes the grounds or basis for our ethical judgment—namely, the qualities we take to be despicable-*making*—this description will not itself amount to an ethical judgment. Only when we judge not just that the massacre has these qualities but that these qualities *make it despicable*—that the action is, for these reasons, despicable—do we make a judgment that seems genuinely ethical. Before that point we just have reportage about which there can be agreement between two people who disagree in their ethical assessment of the incident—one judging it despicable, the other judging it a regrettable but justified tactic. But if that is so, then what ethical convictions *distinctively* purport to concern and reflect are *ethical* properties such as being despicable, morally justified, and so on—or perhaps, more complicated properties such as being despicable-making, morally justified-making, and so on. It is one thing, it can seem, to believe that the attack involved the torture and violent death of innocent children and staff, and another to judge that these qualities make it despicable. After all, the person who considers the attack to be justified agrees that it has all the former qualities.

But we can now ask, Are there really any such properties as being despicable for ethical convictions to reflect? Or, perhaps equivalently, what could make *true* the judgment that the attack was despicable? In what could its truth consist? In addition to all the facts on which we base our judgment, and which are unproblematically, if depressingly, real, is there an *ethical fact*—namely, that these other facts make the act despicable or, as the other person thinks, morally justified? Is there a further ethical *property* of despicableness?

When we contemplate the massacre, we feel indignation. And we express this by attributing to the massacre the moral quality of despicableness. Are we actually responding, then, to this quality—in the same way that, say, our experience of visual shape is a response to a thing's actual physical shape? It can well seem that we are not, that all we are responding to are the facts on which we base our ethical assessment, the ones we perceive as despicable-making—for example, that innocent children were tortured, and so on. But if we then attribute this further property, despicableness, what could make this attribution correct? Where, in reality, is despicableness? What is there for ethical convictions attributing it to reflect?

The same sort of question was sharply formulated by David Hume (1711–1776) in a famous passage:

> Take any action allow'd to be vicious: Wilful murder, for instance. Examine it in all lights, and see if you can find that matter of fact, or real existence, which you call vice. In which-ever way you take it, you find only certain passions, motives, volitions and thoughts. There is no other matter of fact in the case. The vice entirely escapes you, as long as you consider the object.[2]

Call this "Hume's challenge." The qualities of a wilful murder that we perceive as vicious are what Hume termed "matter[s] of fact in the case." These include qualities such as disregard for human life, a willingness to treat others as mere instruments to one's own ends, and so on—qualities that are plainly part of the objective situation. But what about the further property of being vicious? This property, Hume wrote, appears not to be *in* the object in the same way that the qualities on the basis of which we attribute it are. So "where" is it?[3]

A Related Problem Concerning Evidence in Ethics

More recently, Gilbert Harman has pursued a similar line of thought, arguing that when it comes to ethics there is a problem concerning what we can reasonably treat as *evidence* for our convictions.[4]

In science, and more generally when we are testing general empirical conjectures about the world, we confirm theories by seeing whether their predictions correspond to experience. For example, current physical theories predict that black holes will exert a profound gravitational effect on the motion of bodies in the area surrounding them because of their extraordinary mass. Accordingly, when scientists using the Hubble Space Telescope observed data indicating motions of a kind around the core of galaxy M87 that could be explained in no other way, they took this observation as evidence of the truth of the theoretical prediction about black holes. They took their (telescope-aided) experience as confirmation of the truth of the theory.

Now, this example might already seem to involve a contrast with ethics. For there may seem to be nothing in ethics to play the role that experience plays in confirming scientific theories or ordinary common-sense beliefs about the way things are. Granted, we might think, people have ethical feelings and beliefs, but we can't use these as evidence for or against any ethical theory because people may already be presupposing some theory or other when they have these feelings. In science, on the other hand, it may seem that experience provides us with an utterly unprejudicial or "theory-neutral" forum in which to assess theories.

The latter contention betrays a mistaken view of the relation between experience and scientific theory, however. The idea of an entirely neutral court of experience before which scientific theories stand to be judged is a myth—the "myth of the given," as it is called. *All* experience is "theory-laden," already involving a rich array of implicit concepts and categories whose meanings are determined by the theories in which they are situated. To paraphrase Kant again, "experience without theory is blind" (just as "theory without experience is empty"). Only because experience is already structured through assumed theories (including those implicit in our language) can it confirm any beliefs at all. Purely inarticulate and inarticulable sensory impressions would be, in William James's vivid phrase, a "blooming, buzzing confusion" that couldn't count as evidence for or against anything. So if ethical feelings and convictions are theory-laden, the same is true of experiences that we take to confirm theories about the way things are.

Scientists take their Hubble observations as confirming current theory about black holes because this theory best *explains* their observations. What would be analogous in ethics? Given that observations of individual, specific phenomena are evidence of more general, universal theories in science when (and because) the latter explain the former, the question must instead be whether *anything* analogous holds in ethics. Is there a sense in which more general, universal ethical theories can explain "observations" or "experiences" of individual, specific ethical phenomena?

In one sense, at least, it seems there might be. When we consider the massacre, the individual incident, we find ourselves having an ethical feeling, indignation, and a belief or "observation" that it was despicable or, more simply, wrong. But if, as I argued in Chapter 1, something can have such an ethical property only if it has features or qualities that make it wrong—features that are reasons not to do it—then it follows that our feeling or conviction can be correct only if there are such reasons. But this will be true if, and only if, there is some such universal truth as that anything with those features would be wrong, other things being equal. In particular, the general proposition that it is wrong to torture and violently kill innocents, perhaps especially those who are most vulnerable, in order to gain tactical military advantage would seem to "explain" the more specific observation that this massacre was wrong. Theoretical generalization explains specific observation in the sense that if the former were true, the latter would be also.

So if what licenses us in taking observations of individual phenomena as evidence for (more general) theory is that the latter explains the former, then it might be asserted that this same relation can hold in ethics. And, therefore, perhaps we *can* reasonably take our ethical feelings and intuitive convictions about individual cases as evidence for ethical generalizations or, more grandly, for ethical *theories*.

Harman argues, however, that there is an important remaining difference between ethics and science. Scientists take their observations as evidence for a theory about black holes because the theory would explain not just *what* they observe—that is, the behavior of surrounding bodies—but also *their observing it*. The theory helps explain their *experience* in the more robust sense that it explains why they have the experiences they do and see the motions they seem to see when the telescope is pointed toward galaxy M87. The theory hypothesizes the existence of a general physical phenomenon that initiates a causal chain culminating in their having the experiences they do when they view data from the telescope. And so they properly take their having this experience, their observing what they do, as evidence for the truth of the theory, since, if the theory is true, they should be having the very experiences they are having.

Harman argues that nothing similar is true in ethics. When we feel indignation at the massacre and form the conviction that it was wrong, it may well be true that the theory that it is always wrong (other things being equal?) to torture and violently kill vulnerable innocents to gain military advantage explains *what* we observe, in the sense that if the theory were true, then what we observe, that this massacre is wrong, would be true also. But does it explain our *observing* it to be wrong? It would, it seems, only if the wrongness of massacres were a real property of them that could initiate something like a causal chain terminating in our ethical feeling or conviction. But whereas we generally think our experiences of the physical properties that things seem to have are best explained as the result of a causal interaction (sense experience) with physical properties that things actually have, should we believe that our ethical convictions and feelings are similarly explainable as resulting from some kind of causal interaction with ethical properties? Should we think of our ethical sensibilities as faculties for detecting ethical properties that are triggered when we turn our attention in their direction—similar to, say, our sensory abilities for detecting size and shape?

It can certainly seem, on reflection, that nothing like this is so. When we turn our attention in the direction of the massacre, it can seem that all that is there are properties about it that we take to ground or justify our reaction and conviction—namely, that the massacre involved disregard for human life, torture and violent killing of innocents, and so on. To put it tendentiously, all that is there to notice and respond to are facts about what *is* or was the case (what properties the combatants' conduct actually had), not what *should* have been the case, or what properties their conduct *should* have had. As Hume argued, a gap appears to open up between 'is' and 'ought', between fact and value. (I hasten to add that there *seems* to be this gap. As we shall see, ethical naturalists argue that there really is no such gap and, as well, that there are explanations in ethics of the kind Harman denies.)

If, however, Harman were right, then there would be a significant disanalogy between the relation between experience and scientific theory, on the one hand, and that between ethical feeling and conviction about individual cases and ethical theory, on the other. What justifies taking experience as evidence for scientific theories would seem not to hold in the ethical case. In itself, this contention raises an epistemological worry; it concerns the possibility of ethical knowledge and of evidence for ethical belief. The worry arises, however, from a reflection about metaphysics. In particular, it derives from the thought that although we take our attribution of ethical properties to things to be grounded or justified by their real qualities or, alternatively, by the facts about those things, ethical properties and facts seem themselves not to be included among these. As Hume said, the "vice" of wilful murder seems nowhere to be found among the "matter[s] of fact" about it. There we find only those features or facts that we take to justify our holding it to be vicious (its vicious-making qualities), not the further "fact" of its vice (i.e., that these qualities are vicious-making and, therefore, justify us in regarding it as vicious). The metaethical question is, What is there to which our *taking these facts as justifying* can be adequate or inadequate, correct or incorrect?

A Fundamental Dilemma of Metaethics

What looms before us, then, is what is sometimes said to be a gap between *facts* and *values*. When we think along Hume's and Harman's lines, it can seem that there is a fundamental divide between what *is* (facts) and what *should be* (values). Viewed this way, values are no part of reality but, rather, are something we add or project through *valuation*—that is, by valuing and having values. But this assertion conflicts with the way things seem, from the inside, when we do value. In feeling indignation at the massacre, and judging it despicable, we see our judgment as portraying an objective fact.

This divide between the way ethical thought seems to be from the inside and from the outside raises what can be called the **fundamental dilemma of metaethics**. Ethical thought and feeling have "objective purport." From the inside, they apparently aspire to truth or correctness and presuppose that there is something of which they can be true or false. But it is not clear, from the outside, what the truth of an ethical conviction could consist in. Ethical convictions are apparently unlike empirical beliefs in that they seem not to arise through a process whose function is to detect the real features of things by causal interaction with those features. Whether an empirical belief is true or false depends only on whether the world really has the features that the belief represents it as having. And we take ourselves to have evidence for such a belief (and hence for thinking the world really has those features) when we can explain the belief as having arisen through a process of interaction with those very features. But if nothing like this happens in the case of ethical belief, then we must ask, What, if anything, can make such beliefs true? And what can count as evidence for our ethical convictions?

Metaethics confronts us, then, with two basic questions, which follow from those just stated:

1. In what can the truth of an ethical conviction consist?
2. If nothing can make an ethical conviction literally true, then why do we think and talk as though they can be?

And these lead to a fundamental dilemma: Either there are real ethical properties and facts or there are not. If there are, the problem is to say what these properties and facts might be like, how there could be such properties and facts. But if there are no such properties and facts, the problem is to explain why we think, talk, and feel as though there must be and to explain, moreover, how ethical thought is not undermined by the lack of such properties. Our normative ethical thought and feeling seems to commit us to something like objectivity, correctness, and truth in ethics. The philosophy of ethics, therefore, must explain how ethics can admit of objectivity and truth, explain how ethical thought and discourse can justifiably proceed without these, or, somehow, explain ethics away.

Suggested Reading

Frankena, William. *Ethics*, 2nd ed. Englewood Cliffs, N.J.: Prentice-Hall, 1973. See especially Chapter 1.

Harman, Gilbert. *The Nature of Morality*. New York: Oxford University Press, 1977. See especially Chapter 1.

Hume, David. *A Treatise of Human Nature* (1740). Second edition edited by L. A. Selby-Bigge, with text revised and variant readings by P. H. Nidditch. Oxford: Clarendon Press, 1978. See especially pp. 455–476.

Mackie, John. *Ethics: Inventing Right and Wrong*. Harmondsworth: Penguin Books, 1977. See especially Chapter 1.

Moore, G. E. *Principia Ethica*, rev. ed. Thomas Baldwin, ed. Cambridge: Cambridge University Press, 1993. See especially Chapter 1.

3

NATURALISM

In Chapters 3 through 8 I briefly discuss a variety of possible responses to the basic metaethical issues raised in Chapter 2. By this means I hope to provide an initial sense of the alternatives available in metaethics before we turn, in Parts 3 and 4, to an examination of how different philosophers have developed and elaborated these ideas—and how they have related their metaethics to distinctive normative views within a comprehensive philosophical ethics. At this point, I'll be sketching abstract positions with a broad brush. Later, however, we shall see in more detail how these ideas can come to life when a philosopher tries to think through ethical and philosophical issues in an integrated way, attempting to discover whether philosophy can matter ethically.

Metaphysical Naturalism and Ethics

An important strain in ethical philosophy since the rise of modern science in the seventeenth century has been the desire to achieve an understanding of ethics that is consistent with the worldview of the empirical sciences. **Empirical naturalism** is the general metaphysical doctrine that nothing exists beyond what is open to empirical investigation. It is frequently called **naturalism** for short. I will generally follow this practice except when discussing other forms of naturalism, such as Aristotle's **teleological naturalism**, in Chapters 17 and 18. For the (empirical) naturalist, all facts are "natural facts"—facts about the natural realm with which our senses causally interact—and all substances and properties are natural substances and properties. Naturalism thus denies that anything supernatural exists, that minds or souls exist independent of physical bodies, and that metaphysical essences or forms, or Aristotelian purposes or "final causes," are any part of reality.[1]

This general position is especially influential in our own time. Modern science has made impressive advances in understanding the world, and although human psychology and behavior have proven especially complex, it is now hard to deny that we are natural, physical creatures. It would seem, therefore, that such central parts of our lives as ethical conviction, feeling, and choice must also be natural aspects of the human condition that are open to empirical investigation. In saying that we are natural beings, however, I am not denying that we are social creatures, or that much of human life depends on invention, artifice, and convention. Although the "natural" sciences—physics, biology, and chemistry—are standardly distinguished from the "social" sciences, such as economics and sociology, all of these disciplines study natural phenomena in the sense in which we are currently interested.

Thus **metaphysical naturalism** (as we might also call this general view) holds that nothing exists beyond what is open to empirical study and, consequently, that ethical thought and feeling are empirically ascertainable facts about the world. But what about the *content,* or objects, of ethical thoughts and feelings? This is what matters for the philosophy of ethics. If you are indignant upon reading about a massacre, and judge it to be despicable, your having these thoughts and feelings are natural facts about you, a human being in a specific natural social context. But these facts are not what you have in view when you feel indignant; they are not the content of your ethical feelings and convictions. Observed from the inside, these feelings seem to present you with a view of an *ethical fact* that is not about you at all—namely, that the massacre was despicable. This phenomenon is what sets up the metaphysical problem of metaethics. From the inside, from the perspective involved in having an ethical feeling or conviction, there seem to be ethical facts. But are there really? By itself, metaphysical naturalism does not dictate an answer to this question.

Ethical Naturalism.   A metaethical, or ethical, naturalist is a metaphysical naturalist who believes that there are ethical facts that are facts about the natural order and no less open to empirical investigation than are the objects of other, more obviously empirical disciplines such as psychology, biology, and anthropology. Ethical convictions that accurately represent these aspects of the natural order are thus true in the same unproblematic way that it is true that you are now reading a book. Our main aim in the chapter is to explore this possibility, and we shall turn to it presently. But first I want to make some preliminary remarks about the relation between ethical naturalism and metaphysical naturalism.

Nihilism.   Metaphysical naturalism does not entail ethical naturalism. For example, it might be that although ethical convictions and feelings are familiar aspects of the natural realm *and* that such natural states of mind *appear* to have ethical facts as their objects, these appearances are nonetheless invariably mistaken, since there are no ethical facts. Perhaps it's that feeling indignant involves the *projection* of a property of despicableness onto the object of one's outrage, rather than that the feeling is a response to that property. Maybe all ethical beliefs are like that. Under the influence of emotional reactions, we project (ethical) properties onto things that do not actually have them.

The position that there are no ethical truths is sometimes called **ethical skepticism.** But since 'skepticism' strictly means lack of *knowledge,* and since that could be true even if there were ethical facts (that we couldn't know), a better name is **nihilism** or, as it is sometimes called, the **error theory.**

Suppose you are deeply impressed by the thought that the natural realm exhausts reality, but you are unable to see how ethical properties could be natural properties. Some form of nihilism would seem an inevitable conclusion in this situation. Although Hume was not himself a nihilist, his thought experiment (discussed in Chapter 2) of scanning the natural properties of wilful murder, trying unsuccessfully to find its viciousness, is indicative of a line of thought that sometimes leads to nihilism. The nihilist must, of course, accept that we have ethical thoughts and feelings, but she holds that the way things seem when we have them is always illusory. She thinks all ethical beliefs are false.

Noncognitivism. There is another position that both accepts metaphysical naturalism and denies ethical naturalism, but that also rejects nihilism—namely, **noncognitivism.** Ethical naturalists and nihilists are united in taking ethical convictions to be genuine *beliefs*—that is, states of mind that aim accurately to represent reality, and that are mistaken when they fail to do so. They take the "objective purport" of ethical thought and feeling at face value. Noncognitivists, however, deny that ethical convictions really are genuine beliefs, as we shall see in Chapter 8. What we call ethical beliefs, they think, are really more like feelings or attitudes that have no truth values at all. Ethical attitudes are ways of being for or against things—more complex, perhaps, than mere tastes or preferences, but like them, nonetheless, in being incapable of truth or falsity. They do not have "objective purport" in the same way that ordinary beliefs about the world do.

Noncognitivists thus agree with ethical naturalists and nihilists in holding to metaphysical naturalism. But because they believe that ethical convictions cannot be literally true, they deny ethical naturalism. And because they believe that ethical convictions cannot be literally false, they also deny nihilism.

Other Possibilities? Morality and Freedom?   Are these the only metaethical positions that are consistent with metaphysical naturalism? Not necessarily.

One can accept metaphysical naturalism and argue, as did Sartre and Kant, that the ethical perspective differs radically from the perspective of the empirical sciences (just as it differs from any standpoint that aims to understand how things actually are) because it is the **practical perspective** of an agent deliberating about what to do. Ethical norms, Kant argued, are norms of **practical reason** that are implicit in the deliberative standpoint of a free rational agent. So ethical judgments are made true or false, not by virtue of how well they represent some independent order of ethical fact (natural or supernatural), but by virtue of their relation to norms to which any agent is committed in the activity of rational deliberation. As we shall best appreciate in Chapters 14 and 15, an **ideal deliberative judgment theory** or **practical reason theory** such as Kant's rejects nihilism and noncognitivism, since it insists that ethical judgments can have objectivity and truth, and it also denies ethical naturalism, although it may be consistent with metaphysical naturalism.

Ethical Naturalism

What distinguishes ethical naturalists among metaphysical naturalists is their belief that value is an aspect of nature. When we first considered the example of your indignation at the massacre, we distinguished between the facts about the killings on which you based your conviction and the ethical property (despicableness) that you attributed to the killings. The former—the "despicable-making" facts as they seemed to you—uncontroversially concerned natural phenomena (for example, that the victims were children and other defenseless noncombatants, and so on). The ethical naturalist makes the additional claim that *despicableness* is also a natural property (and that the fact that killing and torturing innocents is "despicable-making" is a natural fact as well). The ethical naturalist thus believes that ethical convictions are about the natural world in a sense beyond their being evaluations *of* natural occurrences. She also asserts that, if true, the ethical properties they attribute are also aspects of nature. And that, when true, they are made true by natural facts concerning those aspects. But *which* aspects of the natural world are ethical properties?

Goodness and the Desirable.   Many ethical naturalist theories of value take their cue from the (natural) properties of *valuation*. What is it, for example, to think that something is good? There seems to be an intimate relation between holding something good and *desiring* it. If so, then perhaps what it is for something to be good just *is* for it to be an object of desire. This is not a *logical* consequence (make sure you see why), but it might seem a natural progression of thought nonetheless. On this simple naturalistic theory, the goodness of health, say, just consists in the fact that people want to be healthy. No more, no less.

A Person's Good.   But *whose* desire? What if people have different desires (as they certainly do)? A frequent naturalist response is to say that it depends on *whose good* is in question. The naturalist can argue that there is a kind of value, being **good for** a person or part of a **person's good,** that is determined by his desires. This is what we refer to when we speak of a person's welfare, benefit, or interest. A simple naturalistic theory of this kind, then, might hold that what it is for something to be good for someone is for it to be something that person desires.

Of course, this is only a very crude form of naturalism, one that seems defective even in its own terms as a theory of welfare. Is everything we desire good for us? And aren't there things that are good for us that we don't desire? To take account of objections like these, naturalists who pursue this line often hold that what makes something good for a person is not the mere fact that he happens to desire it, but that he would desire it (or, perhaps, that he would desire *himself* to desire it) were he under ideal (though naturalistically specifiable) conditions.

Maybe being desirable for a person is the same thing as being what that person would want if he had experience and knowledge of it. Mario, in Michael Radford's *Il Postino* (The Postman), begins the film with no knowledge or experience of poetry but ends up loving it after he has learned what poetry is. Here we might say that reading poetry would have been good for Mario even before he had a desire to read it because he would have had this desire if he had known what poetry was like. Obviously, we can't say that value consists in what a person would want if he knew it was valuable. That would be viciously circular. Rather, we must say something like this: Something has value (for a person) if he would want it if he knew, was experienced with, and fully appreciated all the nonethical aspects of it.

A view of this sort is a species of another general metaethical approach—the **ideal judgment theory,** which is discussed at length in Chapter 6. (An alternate name for this approach is the **ideal observer theory.**) We will also see how a naturalist view of this kind works when we explore John Stuart Mill's philosophical ethics in Chapters 12 and 13.

Alternatively, a naturalist can argue that welfare need not be defined in terms of valuation or desire in order to be a natural phenomenon. When we think of a plant as *flourishing* or *prospering* and of various things as being good or bad for it, the properties we attribute to the organism are certainly natural, even though they obviously do not depend on any attitude such as desire. The same might be true of a person's good. Human welfare might also consist in natural facts about a person's condition and prospects that, although they are not reducible to any fact about her desires, nonetheless frequently serve to explain them. Such an approach could regard various empirical disciplines, such as psychology, medicine, psychoanalytic theory, and so on, as concerned with different aspects of the good life for human beings.

Merit and Esteem.   Perhaps a naturalist can give a convincing account of a person's good or welfare in one of these ways, but what about the rest of ethics? How, for example, are we to understand values such as the kind that I said (in Chapter 1) my colleague's way of teaching exemplifies? Value of this sort is not the same thing as benefit or welfare. We can assume my colleague's teaching benefits both her and her students, but it does so partly because of their appreciation of its intrinsic *merit*, a kind of value that is different from benefit. This is the sort of value that is involved when we are proud of something, when we admire or are inspired, or, in the negative direction, when we feel *shame* or an emptiness or lack of meaning. Holding something to have merit or value of this sort is less to desire than to *esteem* it.

However, this difference suggests a form that a naturalistic theory of the *estimable* might take. It might identify merit with the psychological property of being esteemed. Or with the property of being such as would be esteemed if the person were fully informed and experienced. These would be naturalistic theories of the *estimable,* analogous to the naturalistic theories of the *desirable* that we considered earlier.

But, again, *whose* esteem? The question has greater bite this time because the idea of merit is not relativized to individuals in the way that the idea of *a person's* good or benefit is. In admiring and being inspired by my colleague's teaching, I esteem it and take it to have merit. But whereas that is certainly *my* view of it, the *content* of my view is not that it has merit for *me* but that it has merit, period. How is this phenomenon to be understood naturalistically?

One possibility would be to hold that although such values may present themselves as absolute, they are not completely unrelativized. But neither are they individual-relative in the same way that a person's good is. Rather, worth might be held to be a kind of **intersubjective** value. Whether something has intrinsic merit might depend on whether esteem for it is in fact shared among all persons (of a certain species? of a certain society or community?). Or, more plausibly, on whether esteem would be shared by all under ideal (again, naturalistically specifiable) conditions. My belief that my colleague's teaching has merit would thus be true if, and only if, anyone (suitably specified) would esteem her teaching were they in (suitably specified) ideal conditions.

Morality.   But what about the idea that some actions are morally obligatory and others are morally wrong? How can we hope to find a referent for this idea in nature? There are various possibilities for the naturalist here as well. Nietzsche believed that a sensible naturalism should simply reject the idea of morality as a vestigial holdover from a Judeo-Christian theological tradition that can be given no empirical naturalist basis. However, many naturalists deny this. They argue that morality can be vindicated naturalistically.

A common way of trying to do so is to define morality by a distinctive perspective (the **moral point of view**)—namely, that of equal, impartial regard for all human (or perhaps all sentient) beings. A naturalist can then hold that what it is to be **morally desirable** or **morally good** is to be desirable from this point of view—for example, that it would be desired by any person were she to be both fully informed and viewing things from this perspective. What, then, about the ideas of moral **right** and **wrong?**

Moral Obligation. When we think or feel that something would be *wrong*, we typically feel that we are *bound*—under an **obligation** or some kind of necessity—not to do it. What is wrong is not just morally undesirable. It is what we *ought* not or *must* not do. Morality presents itself as a kind of law, a **moral law,** by which we are inescapably obligated and whose **authority** is **categorical**—independent, that is, of our desires and interests. If torturing innocents is wrong, we are apt to feel, then people should not do it, even if it serves their interests or is called for by local customs or authorities. How are these ideas to be accounted for naturalistically? Merely noting that the moral point of view is one of equal regard for all does nothing to explain the authority, or **normativity**, of morality. How is *that* to be explained?

Normativity and Moral Obligation. Actually, there are several different problems for the naturalist here. One is wholly internal to the moral sphere: It is a matter of explaining the difference between being morally undesirable and being morally wrong. Unlike undesirability, being wrong seems to involve a violation of some kind of rule or law. How, then, can this difference be explained naturalistically? *Descriptive* laws are a staple of natural science. But how could there be *prescriptive* natural laws?

In Chapter 13, we shall see how Mill addressed this issue. Mill's idea is a secular version of Locke's view, which I mentioned at the end of Chapter 1. Like Locke, Mill saw morality as a set of rules that serve a useful purpose; but Mill viewed these rules as *our* instrument rather than God's. We enforce moral rules in our social practices, and these rules define right and wrong when their existence is desirable from a moral point of view (when, that is, they promote the general happiness). An action is wrong, therefore, if it has the following complex natural property: being a violation of a (perhaps hypothetical) rule that, *were* it established in our social practice, *would* promote the greatest general happiness. Needless to say, complex empirical investigation will be required to discover whether or not any given action actually has this natural property.

Morality is unlike just any set of rules, however, in that we think it is not up to us whether to "play" or not. The rules of chess define violations also, but they make a claim on a person only if he wants to play. So a second problem is to explain naturalistically the apparent fact that morality binds persons *categorically,* whether or not it serves their interests or aims, whether or not they want to play. Yet a third is to explain the further (apparent) fact that morality makes not only *some* categorical claim on a person but one that appears to *override* all other claims. What natural fact can vindicate the thought that if it is wrong for me to cheat on my income tax, then I really shouldn't do so, even if I want to and it is in my own interest?

Of course, a naturalist may not think she should try to account for all these moral appearances. Even without rejecting morality wholesale, as Nietzsche does, she may believe that only some aspects of our common-sense view of morality can be provided an adequate philosophical basis. Like Mill, she might accept the burden of trying to explain the difference between moral undesirability and moral wrong, but hold that the most that can or should be done in establishing the bindingness of moral rules is to show people how large a stake they themselves have in the social practices these rules establish. Even if moral obligation is then conditional on their own ends or desires, and not really categorical, it may nonetheless be quite strong and enduring.

Problems for Ethical Naturalism

Moore's "Open Question" Argument.   Ethical naturalism has powerful arguments in its favor and many adherents on the current philosophical scene. At the beginning of this century, however, G. E. Moore (1873–1958) advanced an argument that persuaded many philosophers that its prospects were quite bleak. Moore asserted that for any proposed naturalistic property, N, we may know that something, X, has N, and yet whether X is good will still seem an **open question** to us. That is, whether X, which is N, is also good will still seem to us a sensible question. If goodness were *the very same property as N*, however, and if we know that X is N, we should not be able sensibly to ask whether X is good. That question should be closed by the knowledge that X is N.

As an analogy, consider the property of being a bachelor. This is the same property as being a never-married, adult male. And because it is, if we are given the knowledge that Eric is an adult male who has never been married, we cannot sensibly ask, "But is Eric a bachelor?" Since the two properties are identical, that question is closed by the knowledge that Eric is a never-married, adult male. However, when it comes to the property of goodness, Moore challenged, for *any* naturalistic property, N, whether X, which is N, is also good will remain an open question.

For example, consider the suggestion that something is good (for a person) if it is what she would want if she were fully experienced and informed. We may know—as may the person herself—that something has this property and still *sensibly* ask whether it is good for her. There is nothing incoherent in the thought that what I *would* want, even if I'm fully experienced and informed, is not what I *should* want. So being good for me cannot be the very same property as having *this* natural property. And, Moore argued, we will get the same result for *any* ethical property/natural property pair. We will always be able sensibly to ask whether something that has a given natural property has the ethical property. Therefore, no ethical property can be identical with any natural property.

Analytic Versus Synthetic Identity. It has been known for decades that Moore's argument strictly depends on the assumption that two terms 'N' and 'G' can refer to the same property only if 'N' and 'G' have the same meaning. It is synonymy that closes the question in the bachelor example. 'Bachelor' means the same as 'never-married, adult male'. And as technically defined by philosophers, 'If X is a never-married, adult male, then X is a bachelor' is an **analytic** truth. It is a proposition whose truth is guaranteed by the meanings of its terms. 'Never-married adult male' is said to be an analysis of 'bachelor'. It "unpacks" the latter's meaning.

Naturalist philosophers often argue, however, that two terms can refer to the same property even if they differ in meaning. For example, the term 'gene' got its meaning when it was coined within genetic theory to refer to whatever it is that carries genetic information. Mendel did not know what genes actually were when he hypothesized in the nineteenth century that there must be such things to explain the heritability of traits. Only much later, in the twentieth century, was it learned that what genes actually are, in nature, are segments of DNA molecules in chromosomes. Naturalist philosophers argue that this amounted to the discovery that a particular **synthetic** (i.e., not analytic) claim of property identity is true—namely, that being a gene is identical with being a segment of a DNA molecule, that the properties are the same. However, before this discovery was confirmed, we can well imagine the following question having arisen: X is a segment of a DNA molecule in a chromosome, but is X a gene? Obviously, the openness of that question did not foreclose the very possibility that scientists later discovered to be true.

Thus one response that naturalist philosophers make to Moore's open-question argument is to argue that, for any natural property, N, it remains an open question whether something X that is N is good because 'N' and 'good' differ in meaning, *but* that it does not follow from this that 'N' and 'good' cannot refer to the same property. 'Being a gene' and 'being a segment of a DNA molecule' differ in meaning, but they refer to the same property. And just as that was an empirical discovery, so there might also be an empirical discovery, for some 'N', that 'N' and 'good' refer to the same property. And similarly for other ethical properties. In both cases, the identification of properties is a synthetic rather than analytic matter.

Reductive Versus Nonreductive Naturalism.   Ethical naturalists who make this response are sometimes called **reductive ethical naturalists,** since they hold out the hope that goodness can be "reduced" to properties we can refer to by terms already having a place in the natural and social sciences or by terms of a naturalistic common-sense "theory" such as 'desire'. Another naturalist response is to argue that even if the advance of empirical theory never puts us into a position to refer to ethical properties with terms already having a developed use in (other) empirical theories or common sense—even if we can never identify some *other* empirically applicable term 'N' that refers to the same property referred to by 'good'—still, the open-question argument would not show that 'good' does not itself refer to a natural property. It would just show that no *other* term in any *other* empirical theory refers to the same property that 'good' refers to. But, for all that, 'good' could still refer to a natural property, and ethics might itself be an empirical discipline. This is what **nonreductive ethical naturalists** believe.

Normativity and the Open Question.   Despite the availability of these responses, the open-question argument continues to exert a powerful influence. Why is this? Why do many philosophers find it a compelling argument against *ethical* naturalism even though they wouldn't give it a second thought in other areas (as when showing that genetic properties cannot be identical with molecular ones)? The explanation, I think, is related to what philosophers call the *normativity* of ethical properties and the difficulty of seeing how any natural properties could have this feature.

The reason why genuinely ethical questions seem to remain open when we know all we can about something's natural properties is that ethical questions concern what appropriately *regulates* choice, desire, and feeling—what we *ought* to choose, want, or feel. Ethics is **normative.** And how any natural property could have that feature can be difficult to see. Whatever naturalist account of the desirable we take, it can seem a genuinely open question whether a person *ought* to seek or desire something with those natural features. And similarly for the estimable. It can seem one thing to know that something is *in fact* esteemed, or even that it *would* be esteemed if someone were fully knowledgeable and experienced, and another to know that it *should* be esteemed, or that esteem for it is warranted.

This is the upshot of another version of the open-question argument.[2] It would seem that we can imagine, say, two people who are in complete agreement about all the natural properties of a particular action, but who disagree about whether the action *should* be done. The normative disagreement concerning what should be done cannot then be a disagreement about the action's natural properties, since we have stipulated that the two agree about that. No empirical discovery, it would seem, can settle a disagreement of this sort. What remains at issue in such a radical normative disagreement, consequently, cannot be a matter of natural property or fact. And if that is right, it would seem that the normativity that is an essential aspect of any genuinely ethical property cannot consist in any natural property or properties. As we shall see in Chapter 8, the open-question argument is sometimes put forward in this form to support noncognitivism.

Explanation and Normativity.   Recall the possible disanalogy between science and ethics that was discussed in Chapter 2. In the scientific case we comfortably take our observations as evidence for hypothesized states of the world because we believe these states to best explain our making these very observations. If ethical naturalism were true, this relation would also hold in ethics. Suppose that being good (for me) were the same thing as being desired by me. Presumably, my thinking that something will satisfy a desire I have is often an effect of my actually desiring it. If, consequently, being good for me were the same thing as being desired by me, then my "ethical observation" (my thinking that something is good for me) would be the effect of the obtaining of this (ethical) fact—namely, my desiring it.

Even if ethical properties cannot be reduced to properties referred to by terms in some empirical science or naturalistic folk theory, they might be natural properties nonetheless. And, if so, an analogy between scientific and ethical observation might still hold. It might be true in ethics also that the best explanation of our making the ethical "observations" we do is that they respond to the natural ethical facts. After all, the naturalist argues, there seems to be a direction to ethical thought that is not entirely unlike the convergence we see in science. Despite remaining ethical disagreements of various sorts, something approaching a consensus among thoughtful people would seem to have emerged over the centuries concerning, for example, the moral equality of humankind. How is this to be explained? The naturalist answer is that convergence in ethical thought is explained in the same way that convergence in scientific thought is—namely, as the result of continuous interactions with the natural world, including, of course, those we have with one another.

Now, Harman has argued that this analogy does not hold, that we do not, in fact, take our having the ethical convictions we do to be best explained by the holding of some (natural) ethical fact. If you agree with Harman in resisting this analogy, it may be because you are impressed by ethics' essential *normativity*. Ethical propositions, by their very nature, concern what there is reason to do, feel, or desire—what we *should* do, feel, or desire.

In the scientific case, we take our observations as evidence for our hypotheses because we believe our observations to be **world-corrected**. That is, we see them as responding to the world they aim to represent. Only if we can regard them as arising in this "world-corrected" way can we reasonably take them as evidence for hypothesized states of the world. In the ethical case, however, our convictions concern not how things are but how they *should be*—how we should desire, act, or feel. They are normative, and because they are, we view them not as world-correct*ed* but as world-correct*ing*. Their object, as Lenin might have said, is not to understand or represent the world but to change it. Our confidence in normative ethical convictions, accordingly, may not depend on our seeing them as resulting from any process of correction by the world. Nor would our taking them as evidence for the truth of any ethical fact seem to depend on our regarding them as having resulted from any such process. Rather, confidence in ethical convictions may be a matter of seeing them as embodying appropriate standards for correcting the world—our own actions, desires, and feelings included.

If this reasoning is sound, then what underlies both the remarkable staying power of the open-question argument and Harman's claimed disanalogy between science and ethics is the same thing—namely, the difficulty that naturalism has in accounting for the normativity of ethics. The challenge for naturalism, then, is either to explain normativity or to explain it away. We will see the naturalist John Stuart Mill grappling with this very issue in Chapter 13.

Suggested Reading

Boyd, Richard. "How To Be a Moral Realist." In *Essays on Moral Realism*. Geoffrey Sayre-McCord, ed. Ithaca, N.Y.: Cornell University Press, 1988.

Brink, David. *Moral Realism and the Foundations of Ethics*. Cambridge: Cambridge University Press, 1989.

Moore, G. E. *Principia Ethica*, rev. ed. Thomas Baldwin, ed. Cambridge: Cambridge University Press, 1993. See especially Chapters 2–3.

Railton, Peter. "Moral Realism." *Philosophical Review* 95 (1986): 163–207.

Sturgeon, Nicholas. "Moral Explanations." In *Morality, Reason, and Truth*. David Copp and David Zimmerman, eds. Totowa, N.J.: Rowman and Allanheld, 1985.

4

THEOLOGICAL VOLUNTARISM

Permit me to begin this chapter with a short sermon. You may have ended the last chapter a bit confused and discouraged. As I discussed in that chapter, there are powerful reasons in favor of any metaethics that can show how ethics fits into a naturalistic picture of the world; then I pointed to other arguments, also powerful, against ethical naturalism. When we encounter metaethics for the first time, it is not unusual to be disappointed upon discovering that attractive theories also face strong objections and that things are far from clear-cut. Impatience is understandable. After all, we want to know which theory is true!

I hope to convince you, however, that part of what makes this area so fascinating is its challenging complexity. From the fact that naturalism faces significant objections we simply cannot conclude that it is not correct. No serious response to basic metaethical issues can avoid objection completely. In fact, if anything, ethical naturalism has shown new vitality in recent years.

Moreover, the fundamental questions of metaethics must have *some* answers, even if we don't know what they are. So some theory—either one we shall consider or some other, perhaps as yet unarticulated one—must be true. And if not ethical naturalism, then which? Ultimately, there is no alternative to judiciously weighing reasons for and against different theories and seeing which theory, on balance, we think best supported. This is a daunting task, but don't let that discourage you. After all, you have the rest of your life to do it! End of sermon.

What alternatives are there to ethical naturalism? If ethical propositions are not made true by natural facts, then maybe they concern a **supernatural** realm. Perhaps, contrary to metaphysical naturalism, there are supernatural facts, and maybe ethical facts are identical with some of these. In this chapter we shall consider one such possibility—namely, that ethical facts concern the will of God.

Reductive Versus Nonreductive Supernaturalism

Like naturalist metaethics, an **ethical supernaturalism** can take either a reductive or a nonreductive form. **Reductive ethical naturalism** is the view
that ethical properties and facts are natural ones we can identify with the
vocabulary of the natural and social sciences or with other common-sense
descriptive notions. For instance, the theory that to be valuable is to be desired is a reductive naturalist theory. The meaning of the term 'desire' is established by its use in psychology and common-sense generalizations about
human behavior; it is not an explicitly ethical term. Such a theory is therefore said to "reduce" the property of being good to the (naturalistic) property of being desired in somewhat the same way that the property of being
a gene can be reduced to that of being a segment of a DNA molecule. The
terms 'good' and 'object of desire' name the same property in nature, just
as 'gene' and 'segment of a DNA molecule' do. **Nonreductive ethical naturalism,** on the other hand, holds that ethical properties and facts are different from any that are identifiable by nonethical vocabulary, but that they
are nonetheless natural properties and facts.

By analogy, a **reductive ethical supernaturalism** would also seek to argue
that ethical properties and facts can be reduced to properties and facts identifiable by using terms from some body of theory or knowledge other than
ethics. Now, however, that theory would be some sort of supernaturalist
metaphysical theory such as theology rather than a naturalistic science. In
this chapter, we shall examine a leading example of such a theory: **theological voluntarism.** According to theological voluntarism (also known as the
divine command theory), ethical properties concern relations to the will of
God.

But just as there can be a nonreductive naturalism, so also there can be a
nonreductive ethical supernaturalism. A nonreductive supernaturalist
agrees with reductive supernaturalists that ethical properties and facts exist
and that they concern a supernatural realm. But she insists that they are *sui
generis*—of their own distinctive kind and irreducible to any other supernatural property. She denies, therefore, that they can be identified through
the use of terms drawn from theology, metaphysics, or any subject other
than ethics itself. In the next chapter we shall examine the leading version
of this view, **rational intuitionism,** so called because it holds nonnatural
ethical facts to be self-evident to reason.

Theological Voluntarism

Theological voluntarism mirrors, in various ways, the structure of reductive naturalism. Not surprisingly, it has been subject to some of the same
objections. A common reductive naturalist strategy, recall, is to proceed on

the assumption that the nature of value is determined by the nature of valuation. Value is understood in terms of *being valued*. For the resulting view to be a *reductive* naturalism, however, there must be some way of identifying valuation that does not require us already to know what value is. As we have seen, the reductive naturalist might try to meet this demand by holding that, for example, valuation is identical with desire.

As we saw, a view of this sort is open to several objections: (a) our desires conflict, (b) not everything we desire is good, and (c) there are good things we don't desire. On the other hand, perhaps these objections arise, not because they make goodness depend on desire, but because they make it depend on *our* desires. We are but finite beings, limited by our capacities, idiosyncrasies, and perspectives. Suppose, however, that someone were to advance the thesis that to be good is to be desired *by God*.

Assuming that God exists and that His desires don't conflict, a view of this sort can easily answer objection (a). But then so might any view that identifies goodness with being desired by some specific individual. Theological voluntarism has the added advantage that it can explain why we take value to transcend what any human being happens to desire. Value surpasses human desire because it is determined by a transcendent, supernatural desire—by God's desire. This observation responds to objections (b) and (c).

In addition, theological voluntarism can account for Harman's contrast between the world-corrected empirical observation and the genesis of ethical conviction. If ethical properties and facts are supernatural, it should be no surprise that ethical convictions cannot be explained by causal interaction with nature.

Probably theological voluntarism's greatest perceived strength, however, has been its ability to explain the distinctive character of *morality*. Morality presents itself in our experience as a kind of *law* by which we are inescapably obligated or bound. If it is wrong to do something, that doesn't just mean that it is morally undesirable or bad. What is wrong is what one *ought* not do and is *accountable* for not doing. Unexcused wrongdoing incurs guilt. But morality evidently also differs from the laws of any worldly jurisdiction, whether the formal codes of a nation-state or the mores of a society, since for any such actual laws, we can always ask whether morality requires us to follow them and sometimes think that it does not. Under a regime of apartheid, for example, morality may require one to ignore or flout immorally oppressive laws.

How can it be that morality both is a kind of law and can differ from any actual human law? The theological voluntarist has an answer to this question. Morality is a law differing from any earthly law because it has a supernatural source: It is established not by any mundane legislature or judiciary but by the will of God. The ethical property of being wrong, then, is

identical with the supernatural property of being contrary to God's commanded will.

It follows from theological voluntarism that if there is no God, or if God
exists but has no determinate will with regard to human affairs, then there
is no right or wrong. As Ivan from Dostoyevsky's *The Brothers Karamazov*
declares, if God doesn't exist, then "everything is permitted." Actually, if
morality depends on God's will and there is no God, then it is also false to
say that anything is *allowed* by morality. Of any action it is false to say that
it is morally required, prohibited, *or* permitted.

What Theological Voluntarism Is Not

To focus on these ideas, we will find it helpful to make two assumptions:
(a) God exists and commands us to do some things and not to do others,
and (b) we ought to do what God commands. Making these assumptions
will allow us to concentrate on theological voluntarism—that is, on
whether morality consists in God's will—and not confuse that issue with
the distinct questions of whether (a) and (b) are true. Theological voluntarism is a *metaethical* theory, whereas (a) is a thesis of metaphysics and
(b) is a thesis of normative ethics. It is especially important to distinguish
theological voluntarism from (b), since various reasons someone might
have for believing (b) are actually inconsistent with theological voluntarism. Or so I shall now argue.

God as Ethically Omniscient.   Suppose, for example, that someone thinks
she should obey God's commands because God knows what is right and
wrong and would only command us to do what He knows is right and not
to do what He knows is wrong. If someone thinks she should follow God's
commands for this reason, she will be logically committed to denying theological voluntarism, since she can hardly think that God's ethical knowledge, which she takes to give authority to His commands, is simply knowledge of His own commands. That would amount to ethical knowledge only
if these are commands she ought to obey. But, on the current hypothesis,
she ought to obey God's commands only if they are grounded in ethical
knowledge. To break out of this circle, it must be supposed that the knowledge that gives authority to God's commands is of ethical facts that are
themselves independent of His commands. And this rationale is precisely
what theological voluntarism denies. Hence, anyone who thinks she should
obey God's commands for this reason must deny theological voluntarism.

As an analogy, suppose we are wondering who was the Republican candidate for vice-president in 1964, when Barry Goldwater ran against Lyn-
don Johnson for president. And imagine we ask Tom, whom we regard as
an authority on such matters. Tom tells us that the Republican candidate

was William Miller. Suppose we regard Tom's general political knowledge and trustworthiness as sufficiently good reasons to believe what he says. We therefore treat Tom as an authority and think we should believe that William Miller was the Republican candidate because Tom says he was. But we will not, of course, think that Tom somehow makes it a fact that Miller ran in 1964. On the contrary, whether Miller ran in 1964 is completely independent of anything about Tom. It would have been true even if Tom had never lived. Here we credit Tom with *epistemic authority,* not with an authority that can somehow "enact" facts.

Similarly, we may think we should follow a doctor's orders because we regard her as well-informed and trustworthy about what medical measures are likeliest to work. But here again, the kind of authority we attribute to the doctor is epistemic. The doctor does not make it true that the measures she recommends are good ones just by saying they are. So, by analogy, if the reason a person has for thinking she should obey God's command is that God is an **epistemic** authority about ethics, then she is committed to denying theological voluntarism.

God as Ideal Judge or Adviser. Suppose, however, that someone thinks we should follow God's commands, not because He is omniscient about ethics, but because He is an ideal judge or adviser. What makes God an ideal adviser, this person thinks, is (a) that He is omniscient about us and our situation (He knows all natural facts) and (b) that He is omnibenevolent (He cares equally about the welfare of all). Here the idea is not that there is a realm of independent ethical facts that God knows flawlessly. Rather, *what makes it true* that we should do something is that a being who is perfectly knowledgeable and benevolent would want or advise us to do it. We should do what God commands us to do, then, because we should do whatever *an ideal judge would advise* or want us to do, and God is an ideal judge.

Now, this view may look like theological voluntarism, but, in fact, the two are inconsistent with each other. This view is actually a version of the **ideal judgment theory,** which we glimpsed in Chapter 3 and shall explore further in Chapter 6. One way of seeing the distinction is to note that, according to theological voluntarism, God must exist in order for there to be any moral facts. If what is morally obligatory is what God wills (in fact), then if there is no God, there is no moral obligation. But if someone thinks we should follow God's commands because we should do whatever an ideal judge *would* want us to do and God is an ideal judge, then it follows from this rationale that there could be moral facts even if neither God nor, for that matter, any ideal adviser actually exists. All that would be necessary is that there be a truth about what an ideal adviser would want *were* one to exist. And that could be true even if there are no ideal advisers.

As an analogy, consider the economist's ideal of a perfectly free competitive market. Even if no actual markets came close to satisfying this ideal, that wouldn't mean that there are no facts about what would happen under ideally competitive conditions. Likewise, there might be facts about what a (suitably defined) ideal adviser would want human agents to do even if no ideal adviser exists.

Theological voluntarism denies what the ideal judgment theory affirms. The latter holds that there can be moral facts only if God exists, since moral facts are facts about what He actually commands. Accordingly, someone who thinks we should obey God's commands because He is an ideal adviser must deny theological voluntarism.

Gratitude Toward God.   Or suppose someone thinks she should obey God out of gratitude for His having created and sustained our lives and everything valuable in them. This differs in an important way from the first two rationales, which entailed that if God commands us to do something, then there are good reasons for so acting that are quite independent of His actual will. If, however, we think we ought to do as someone asks out of gratitude, then only by coincidence will we think that we ought so to act whether or not he asks us to. In this case, it will seem closer to being true that God makes it the case that we ought to do something by commanding us to do it.

Nevertheless, a person who thinks we should obey God's commands out of gratitude is committed to holding that there is at least one moral fact that God does not make true by His command—namely, that it is wrong not to show gratitude. If the reason we ought to follow God's commands *at all* is that we ought to show Him gratitude, then this latter obligation cannot depend on His command. Even if He were to command us to show gratitude, it would be the case that we ought to follow this command only if it were independently true that it is wrong not to show gratitude. So here again, someone who thinks she should obey God's commands for this reason will be committed to denying theological voluntarism. There is, she must think, at least one moral fact that is completely independent of God's command. Nor, therefore, can she think that its being wrong to steal, kill, and so on (as God commands) consists in nothing but the fact that God commands us not to do these things. Without the background duty of gratitude, *none* of God's commands would have moral force.

What's more, although there is no inconsistency in holding that the ethical fact that gratitude is a fitting response to benevolence is independent of God's will, with all others deriving from His command, this seems a pretty unstable position. How could there be just the one independent ethical fact and no others? If there are any ethical facts independent of God, why couldn't there be more? Allowing the existence of one seems already to have let the horses out of the barn.

God as Superior. Similarly, someone might think we should obey God's commands because He is our superior in a structure of authority, in somewhat the same way a sergeant is a superior to a private in the army. When a sergeant issues an order to a private, it then becomes true, other things being equal, that the private should execute that specific order. Suppose the sergeant orders the private to do ten pushups. It is then true that the private should do ten pushups, and it wouldn't have been true but for the sergeant's order. There is thus a sense in which the sergeant's order makes it the case that the private should do ten pushups. By the same token, God's commands that we not steal, lie, and kill make it wrong for us to do these things. Without His commands, these would not be wrong.

Now, in the military case it should be clear that the sergeant can make it true that the private should do ten pushups by so ordering him only if a structure of authority is already in place. That is, only if it is already true that privates must obey sergeants' orders can sergeants obligate privates to do specific things by issuing specific orders. If this were not true, then a sergeant could "order" the private as much as she liked without the private having any new duties as a consequence.

The same point holds with respect to God's commands. Unless it is true that we ought to do what God commands in general, quite independent of whether He commands us to do what He commands, God's specific commands cannot generate specific duties. So, according to this rationale for following God's commands, there must be at least one moral fact that God does not create by command—namely, that we ought to obey His commands. And if this is so, then being morally obligated cannot be the very same thing as being commanded by God. Even if it would not be wrong, say, to kill but for the fact that God commands us not to, its being wrong cannot be the very same thing as God's commanding us not to. It follows that if one accepts this rationale for obeying God, one must deny theological voluntarism. And again, although there is nothing incoherent in the position that there is only one moral fact that is independent of God's will— namely, that we should obey His will—this is apt to seem an unstable position. If there is this one moral fact, then why aren't there also others?

Critics of the divine command theory have frequently pointed out that if all ethical facts depend on God's will, then it is impossible to think that we should obey God because of His goodness, since that would require us to think that God's goodness is independent of His command. However, it is possible to argue that although this ethical fact—the moral goodness of divine love—is independent of God's will, nonetheless all facts about moral obligation, about moral right and wrong, derive from God. On this view, it is because we are commanded, for example, to keep our promises and to help others in need that it is *wrong* not to do these things. Right and wrong derive from the commands of a loving God.

A Reductive Account of God's Authority

All the preceding rationales for obeying God entail that ethical facts cannot be reduced to facts about God's commands. What gives rise to this general phenomenon is our acceptance that obeying God requires some further justification, even one coming from an ultimate moral fact that we ought to do what God commands. Once we accept such a justification, we are then in the position of holding that God's commands derive normative force from this underlying justification and are unable to generate it all by themselves. To maintain *consistently* that ethics can be reduced to facts about God's commands, we would have to hold that facts about justification just *are* facts about divine command. There can be no further reason for obeying God, since a reason to do something itself just *is* something about God's commands.

Problems for Theological Voluntarism

Such a view faces a number of problems even apart from the metaphysical issues concerning the existence of God or a supernatural realm. For one thing, it seems implausible to disconnect moral qualities from the natures of things that have them. If it is wrong to torture innocents, for example, then must that not be because of what torture and its consequences are like? According to theological voluntarism, however, the wrongness of torture derives entirely from a fact quite external to the nature of torture and its effects—namely, that God proscribes it. It won't help, moreover, to say that God's omnibenevolence and omniscience determine that He would proscribe anything of that nature. For if these facts are what give God's proscriptions ethical weight, then we have an ethical truth that is independent of the fact of God's command—namely, that we should do whatever a being of this nature (an ideal adviser) would command.

The major problem facing theological voluntarism is one that faces any reductive theory, whether naturalist or supernaturalist—namely, **normativity.** How can facts about how things *are,* whether naturally *or* supernaturally, constitute the truth about how things *ought to be* or what we *ought to do?* Any force that the open-question argument has against reductive naturalism would seem to transfer also to this form of reductive supernaturalism. Two people might be in perfect agreement about all the properties (natural and supernatural) that can be referred to with nonethical terms in a given case, yet disagree about, or sensibly question, what ethical properties to attribute. For example, two people might agree entirely about the facts involved in God's commanding Abraham to kill Isaac, yet disagree about, or regard as an open question, whether Abraham should obey this command. But if that is so, and if what is at issue between them is the ethical question of what Abraham should do, it is hard to see how this ethical issue can be reduced to the metaphysical question of what God commands, since they agree about that. The general lesson here is that the same problem of normativity that confronts naturalist theories will confront supernaturalist theories as well.

Suggested Reading

Adams, Robert M. "A Modified Divine Command of Ethical Wrongdoing." In *Religion and Morality: A Collection of Essays*. Gene Outka, ed. Garden City, N.Y.: Anchor Press, 1973.

Cudworth, Ralph. *A Treatise Concerning Eternal and Immutable Morality* (1731). Cambridge: Cambridge University Press, 1996. See especially Book I, Chapters 2–3.

Plato, *Euthyphro*. (Available in various editions.)

Quinn, Philip L. *Divine Commands and Moral Requirements*. Oxford: Clarendon Press, 1978.

5

RATIONAL
INTUITIONISM

Attempts to reduce ethics to theology or some other form of supernatural metaphysics face a fundamental objection of the same sort that confronts reductive ethical naturalism. Both seem to change the subject. Whether God commands something and whether we ought to do it seem to be two different questions. Perhaps we ought to do what God commands even, perhaps, because He commands it. From neither proposition does it follow, however, that being what we ought to do is the same thing as being what God commands. It seems conceivable that two people could fully agree that God commands something, and fully agree also about all theological propositions that either thinks relevant, and still intelligibly disagree about whether the command should be followed. It seems conceivable, for instance, that two people might disagree about whether Abraham, commanded by God to kill Isaac, should do so. In such a situation there would appear to be an *ethical* issue still outstanding between the two that is distinct from any question of theology.

As we have seen, this line of thought can be pressed against reductive ethical naturalism as well. Ethics and ethical questions seem no more reducible to psychology, sociology, or sociobiology than to theology. Although the same line of thought is a formidable objection against both reductive ethical naturalism *and* supernaturalism, we are currently in no position to conclude that it is decisive. Ethical questions *seem* different from either theological or scientific ones, but these appearances may themselves be deceiving. Maybe they result from our own confusions. Perhaps we may discover that what we would have to believe in order to sustain the view of ethics or ethical thought and discourse implicit in the open-question argument is itself something that, on reflection, we cannot or should not believe. Any conclusions at this point would indeed be premature.

Irreducibility and Objective Purport

Suppose that ethics really is irreducible, however, and that ethical questions cannot be resolved into terms from some other subject or discipline, whether naturalistic or metaphysical. We still face the metaethical dilemma we first encountered in Chapter 2. Either ethical propositions can be literally true or they cannot. If we maintain that literal truth is possible in ethics, we face the challenge of saying what can make an ethical proposition true: What could an (irreducible) ethical fact be? On the other hand, if we hold that ethical propositions cannot literally be true, we must explain why we think, talk, and feel as *if* they can. We must reconcile our metaphysics with the **phenomenology** of ethical thought and experience. Perhaps we should not credit our moral experience at face value; but, if we do not, we still need to explain why things appear as they do and how we will proceed in the light of whatever disillusioning analysis we settle on.

Suppose we take seriously what we've called the **objective purport** of ethical thought and experience. Unlike tastes and preferences, ethical convictions strike us as being about something objective. When we find ourselves with a strong ethical conviction—say, that the violent torture and slaughter of vulnerable innocents for tactical military advantage is wrong—it can seem as though we have a view of a truth that is *independent of anything about us*. It's as if we are seeing something—the fact of its being wrong—that would be "there" whether we could see it or not, whether we believed it or not, or whether our emotions were touched by it or not.

Ethical Perception?

In this way, ethical conviction can seem to involve something like a perception of an independent, objective realm of ethical fact. Consider, by analogy, ordinary sense perception of the relative size of physical objects. We can tell by inspection that flounders are larger than fleas. And it seems to us, and continues to do so after reflection, that whether this fact holds depends on nothing about us. Flounders would be larger than fleas even if things looked differently to us, even if we somehow thought fleas were larger, and so on. In cases of this kind, we have the notion that things stand a certain way in the world, independent of us, and that we can perceive (at least some of) these things: We can see that flounders are larger than fleas.

Now, if ethics is irreducible to terms of the empirical sciences or other informal naturalistic descriptive theories, then there can be nothing like ethical sense experience. What we call the senses just are natural faculties for receiving experiences through causal interaction with other parts of nature. They are the very basis of all empirical investigation. Still, there might be something like ethical perception. When we credit people with wisdom and ethical insight, we do seem to attribute to them the ability to see and appreciate what matters or what their moral obligations are (though, of course, not with their eyes). Also, when we come to appreciate an ethical truth for ourselves—say, that friendship matters more than flattery—this "experience" can also seem a kind of insight that we've been brought to see. It presents itself as a kind of perception—not of how things stand in nature but, rather, of how they stand ethically.

The Nature of Rational Intuitionism

Rational intuitionism is the philosophical position that results from taking this analogy seriously. Whether advanced in ancient Greece by Plato (427?–347 B.C.E.) in reaction to the sophists' identification of value with pleasure and interest, or in the seventeenth and eighteenth centuries in response to the theological voluntarism of Jean Calvin (1509–1564) or the secular voluntarism of Thomas Hobbes (1588–1679), or in the late nineteenth and early twentieth centuries by philosophers such as G. E. Moore in reply to attempts to reduce ethics to evolutionary biology, psychology, or economics, rational intuitionism has insisted on the irreducibility of ethics. In the words of Bishop Butler, which Moore made the slogan for his *Principia Ethica:* "Everything is what it is and not another thing." Properties and propositions of naturalist empirical science or supernaturalist theology are one thing; and those of ethics, another.

For the intuitionists, ethical convictions are made true or false by how they correspond to an objective order of ethical facts. Its being true that torturing and slaughtering vulnerable innocents for tactical advantage is wrong, for example, is independent of anything about us. It would be wrong even if we thought or felt otherwise.

Necessity and Rational Perception

Rational intuitionists are also struck by the apparent **necessity** of ethical truths—an aspect that marks an important contrast with truths concerning how things (happen to) stand in nature. As things are, flounders are larger than fleas. This is a **contingent** truth; things might have been different. Perhaps in radically different evolutionary circumstances, fleas might have developed a competitive advantage by a substantial increase in size; and flounders, by a significant decrease. Or maybe, if the laws of nature had been substantially different, flounders might have been smaller than fleas for some other reason. But nothing of this sort seems possible with respect to such ethical propositions as that it is wrong to torture and slaughter innocents for tactical advantage. We simply cannot imagine, rational intuitionists insist, any change in how things happen to be in nature that could alter this ethical truth. Of course, immunities to various forms of torture could have been possible. But in such changed circumstances these would no longer be torture. Nothing could have changed the fact that tactical torture is wrong. Fundamental ethical truths, they argue, are necessary truths. They could not have been otherwise.

Perhaps ethical truths are more like mathematical truths in this regard. That 5 added to 7 yields 12 is true regardless of how things stand in nature. For this reason, knowledge of mathematical truths seems to be **a priori,** or independent of experience. Human beings cannot, of course, develop their rational capacities without experience, but mathematical knowledge is not based on experience in any obvious way. Nothing beyond rational thought and insight is needed. Empirical tests are beside the point.

Rational intuitionists hold that basic ethical facts are also necessary truths that can be known *a priori* through rational insight or intuition. Although it is only by experience that we learn, for example, what the violent torture and slaughter of innocents for tactical advantage actually involves, the judgment that any conduct like that must have the ethical property of being wrong is not itself a judgment of experience but, rather, one that concerns the (necessary) relation of properties that we can grasp directly through reflection and contemplation.

Like mathematical insight, ethical insight may not be equally distributed. Some people may be more perceptive about ethics than others. And some may have what amounts to ethical blindness, in some cases at least. Rational intuitionism claims that what is involved is the same in both cases—a purely rational insight or intuition into an independent order of necessary fact.

Problems for Rational Intuitionism

Intuitionism results from taking the phenomenology of ethical thought and "experience" at face value. Ethical conviction presents itself *as of* an objective order of ethical fact because that is what it actually is. Intuitionists provide no further account of such an order, but this refusal is principled since they hold that any such account would inevitably change the subject. Nothing but ethical facts themselves can illuminate their nature. To suppose otherwise, they insist, is to try to reduce ethics to something else.

Still, the feeling can persist that this position amounts to whistling in the dark. On the metaphysical side, it appears to amount to the brute assertion of a realm of properties and facts that could be eliminated from our picture of reality without a further ripple. Consider, for example, what things would be like without such fundamental natural properties as shape or mass. Change these aspects of reality, and you change others. Without mass, for instance, there can be no gravitational force; or without shape, nothing like displacement. But without value or normativity, it seems all (other) things could remain as they are (except, of course, insofar as they depend on an awareness of this order).

Many philosophers—especially, of course, metaphysical naturalists—have found the idea that there could be such a realm of metaphysically *sui generis* properties and facts deeply mysterious and puzzling. (Moore himself maintained that ethical properties do not so much exist as subsist.) And although they have had to respect intuitionists' refusal to provide any further account as principled, their doing so has not lessened their doubts.

Epistemologically, rational intuitionism asks us to believe in a kind of perception—direct rational intuition—that, unlike ordinary perception, cannot be explained as a natural causal interaction with its object. When I look and see that the flounder on my plate is larger than the flea on my cat, this is the result of a causal process that originates with real features in the world—the relative sizes of flounder and flea (and, of course, the other conditions of vision). But if ethical facts have the *a priori*, necessary character the intuitionists suppose, then they cannot originate any such process. Since ordinary perception is a contingent causal process, the intuitionists' analogy with perception breaks down at precisely this point.

Finally, as Hume argued against the intuitionists of the early eighteenth century, rational intuitionism appears to have no explanation of the relation between normativity or normative conviction, on the one hand, and motivation or the **will**, on the other. Above all else, intuitionism insists on the irreducibility of ethics. However, I have suggested that ethics' apparent irreducibility seems best grounded in its **normativity**—that is, in the fact that ethical properties and facts appropriately *regulate* action and feeling, since they concern what we *should* do and feel. Many philosophers, not least many rational intuitionists, have thought, however, that there is a necessary relation of some sort between thinking one *should* do something and being moved to do it—or a necessary relation between its actually being the case that one should do something and its being true that one would be so moved if one deliberated properly. These philosophers have thought, in other words, that there is a necessary connection between genuinely normative conviction or normative fact, on the one hand, and the will, on the other. (This position is called **internalism**.) Of course, they grant that it is entirely possible for a person to say to herself that she ought to do something, or to think she thinks she ought to do it, without being moved. And they grant that it is possible, as well, for her to believe that others, or society at large, will judge that she ought to do something without this moving her. What they deny is that the person can *herself* believe she should do something, or that it can be the case that she should do it, without her being moved, or being capable of being moved, in any way to do it.

But whereas rational intuitionists have been among the most vocal supporters of internalism, there seems nothing in their theory to explain why there should be a necessary connection between ethical conviction and motivation. For them, the faculty of ethical perception is no different from that of mathematical insight; both involve pure intellect. How, then, would such perception, or the conviction arising from it, necessarily give rise to some change in the will?

When it comes to the phenomenology of moral experience, no position seems more attractive than intuitionism, since it accords with our sense that ethics is objective, necessary, and open to view. However, when we step back from an ethically engaged perspective and try to think philosophically about what ethics and ethical judgment can be, we—along with many philosophers—may find intuitionism simply incredible.

Suggested Reading

McNaughton, David. *Moral Vision: An Introduction to Ethics*. Oxford: Blackwell Publishers, 1988. (Although this work does not really advance rational intuitionism, it puts forward some intuitionist themes.)

Moore, G. E. *Principia Ethica*, rev. ed. Thomas Baldwin, ed. Cambridge: Cambridge University Press, 1993. See especially Chapter 6.

Ross, W. D. *The Right and the Good*. Oxford: Clarendon Press, 1967.

Sidgwick, Henry. *The Methods of Ethics*, 7th ed. Indianapolis, Ind.: Hackett Publishing Company, 1981. See especially Book III, Chapters 13–14.

6

THE IDEAL
JUDGMENT THEORY

Rational intuitionism posits a realm of irreducible, observer-independent, and not-natural ethical properties and facts that can be known through a purely intellectual perception. Although it expresses certain core features of ethical thought, it also faces serious metaphysical and epistemological problems. Our ethical convictions may present themselves *as of* objective, irreducible ethical facts. But when we try to think through what the existence of such a realm might involve, or what it would be for such a realm to be accessible to a rational "intuition," we may well end up in puzzlement. As with the other positions we have considered, this is hardly a conclusive objection to intuitionism. It does suggest, however, that we should see what alternatives there are.

Hume's Challenge, Again

We would do well at this point to recall Hume's challenge to examine "in all lights" something we think has some ethical property in order to identify the "matter of fact" in which that ethical property consists. By "matter of fact" Hume means some natural feature of the thing we are contemplating, including both **intrinsic** features (those that make it what it is) and whatever **extrinsic** features (those concerning its relations to other things) we take as grounds for the ethical property we attribute to it. His example, recall, is a deliberate killing to which we apply the ethical property of being vicious. Hume claims that no matter what natural feature of "the object" (the killing) we fix on, the ethical property (its viciousness) will "entirely escap[e]" us. The most we can find there are features of the killing we take as reasons why it is vicious—that it involves the deliberate causing of death, and so on. But these are different from the *ethical* property of viciousness, or the property we take these features to have of being reasons why it is vicious (hence, of being vicious-*making*).

This is a version of the same irreducibility claim about ethics and ethical properties that we have encountered throughout the preceding chapters. We should note, however, that Hume restricts it to natural features of what he calls *the object*. He goes on to say that the only place we can find the killing's viciousness is *in ourselves* as ethical observers, in the response of disapproval. This is a natural property all right, but not a feature of the object we take as a reason or ground for our disapproval. We may wonder, however, how this suggestion can help, since disapproval is a response to the killing *as vicious*. Disapproval *includes* the attribution of viciousness and so can hardly be that ethical property itself. In disapproving of the killing, we judge *it* (the killing) to be vicious. And this is different from judging of ourselves that we have this response.

It is a strength of rational intuitionism that it can explain this **objective purport** of ethical response and conviction: its presenting itself *as of* objective (ethical) features. In addition, it can explain the thought lying behind Hume's challenge. If ethical properties are irreducible, observer-independent, and not-natural, then the challenge to identify which of the object's natural features they are identical with cannot possibly be met. And intuitionism can also explain why a "supernatural" version of Hume's challenge would yield similar results. If ethical properties are irreducible to such supernatural features as being commanded by God, then they cannot be identical with any of those features either. Still, rational intuitionism is problematic enough on metaphysical and epistemological grounds that we should ask whether there isn't some alternative that lacks these problems and that can also explain both the insight behind Hume's challenge and objective purport.

The **ideal judgment theory** aims to do just this. It agrees with Hume's insight that ethical properties cannot be identified with any features of an object of ethical judgment. When we make an ethical judgment, we attribute an ethical property to something on the basis of features we take it to have. So, for example, when I judge my colleague's teaching to be admirable, I see features of her teaching—such as its drawing forth of her students' best efforts—as reasons for this judgment. But these features of what I evaluate (the object) are not identical to the property I attribute on the basis of my evaluation (admirableness).

What, then, is the nature of this further ethical property? Rational intuitionists claim it to be *sui generis* and fully independent of any features of the observer or the process of ethical judgment. The other extreme is the **subjectivism** suggested by Hume's remarks immediately following his challenge—namely, that the property I attribute is none other than that of being favorably regarded by me. A reaction one might reasonably have to these two proposals is that both are extreme. Subjectivism seems to make ethical properties too subjective, since in judging my colleague's teaching to be admirable I judge not that I admire it but that it is worthy of my admiration.

At the other extreme, intuitionism may make ethical properties seem more objective than they actually could be.

Three Models of Ethical Judgment

For someone who has this reaction, the ideal judgment theory can seem an attractive compromise. Suppose we think of ethical judgment as a process that takes features of the evaluated or judged object as inputs and yields ethical judgments (attributions of ethical properties) as outputs. When we evaluate something ethically we consider it in various ways and, on the basis of that consideration, render a judgment. Consider, now, three different ways of conceiving of that process.

Subjectivism.   According to subjectivism ethical properties are features of an observer's judgment or response. In judging a killing to be vicious, the ethical property I attribute is that of being regarded in whatever way I have come to regard it. As a model of ethical judgment, this makes the output too independent of the input or the evaluative process. When I attribute viciousness to a killing, what I assert is not simply that I happen to feel outrage, but that this response would be *justified* by a careful review and correct assessment of what such a killing amounts to (that is, of the input). Subjectivism lacks any contrast between what my evaluative response is in fact and the object's being such as to *warrant* it.

Rational Intuitionism.   For intuitionism, on the other hand, ethical judgment is a matter of trying to bring an object's ethical properties into view so that they can be grasped by a kind of perception. Since ethical properties cannot be had *barely*, but only in virtue of other ethical-*making* (good- or bad-making, right- or wrong-making) features, ethical perception must proceed via some apprehension of a thing's other properties (the inputs). Thus the perception that a killing is vicious must involve a grasp of the features that make it so, for example, that it is the deliberate taking of a life without cause. Still, the output of ethical judgment, according to intuitionism, is the apparent perception of a further ethical property, which, while necessarily connected to the object's other (input) features is, nonetheless, distinct from them. The problem, again, is what this necessarily connected further property and its perception could be like, and what the nature of its connection to the inputs is.

Unlike the subjectivist model, intuitionism distinguishes between a judge's *de facto* response and an ethical property she attributes to the object—namely, that such a response is warranted. This is the difference between the "appearance" of an ethical property—someone seeing something *as* having that property—and its actually having it. The process of ethical

judgment is thus "in order" when it works so as to bring this property actually into view—when the judge's ethical perception is veridical. And that
is determined by whether appearance matches reality—a metaphysically independent, not-natural order of ethical fact.

The Ideal Judgment Theory. From an intuitionist perspective, the standards for ethical judgment are all determined *externally,* by whatever leads
to a correct view of the ethical facts. The ethical facts are, if you like, the independent variables, determining what procedures of ethical judgment are
ideal or reliable. Just as the "right" way of looking at a difficult-to-see opti-
cal phenomenon is whatever way brings it into view, so the intuitionist
holds that the correct forms of ethical deliberation and reflection are whatever ways enable one to glimpse ethical properties and facts. As we have
discovered, however, extending the analogy of vision to the ethical case
brings formidable metaphysical and epistemological problems.

The ideal judgment theory turns the intuitionist picture on its head. They
hold that an ideal of ethical judgment is actually the independent variable,
and that ethical truth is constituted by whatever deliverances (outputs)
would emerge from that. They must argue, therefore, that standards of
judgment can be derived *internally,* as flowing from the very idea of ethical
judgment itself.

Aspects of Ideal Judgment

Informedness. It is striking that people can agree to a significant extent on
what qualities make for excellence in an ethical judge, or in a process of
ethical deliberation, even when they are deeply divided on what ethical
judgments that judge or process should render or issue in. It is uncontroversial, for example, that whether a judgment is to be trusted depends, to some
extent, on how informed the person making it is about the matter being
judged (the object or inputs). When we are evaluating a teaching style, for
example, it seems clear that we should seek to discover any facts about that
style that might conceivably be relevant—for instance, its effects on students, on the climate for learning in the classroom, and so on. And we are
likely to place more or less confidence in our resulting evaluative judgments
to the extent that they are based on knowledge of these facts.

Some such knowledge will be knowledge *of facts*—for example, those
concerning the effects on students' skills and abilities. But it is also uncontroversial that good ethical judgments are informed as well by a kind of
nonpropositional, *experientially based knowledge* of how people's (or
other sentient being's) lives are affected as *they experience it,* of what "it is
like" from their various perspectives as conscious beings. Thus we shall
also want to know how teaching styles are experienced by students, what

the intellectual interactions they foster are like, and so on. And, again, other things being equal, we are likely to give greater credit to judgments that are better informed by such experientially based knowledge.

Dispassionateness. Ethical judgments can thus be more or less well informed. But, however well informed, such judgments can also be distorted by various irrelevant influences. For instance, in evaluating my colleague's way of teaching, I may be influenced by envy of her success, by anger, by a friendly desire that the evaluation turn out well, by a self-interested desire that I rather than she receive a teaching award that is at stake, and so on. Trying to encompass such distorting influences, we might say that ethical judgments are creditable to the extent that they are **dispassionate.** What this means is not that ethical judgments should be disengaged and cold (they can't be and still be informed in the right way by acquaintance with relevant experience) but, rather, that they should be uninfluenced by emotions directed at something other than the object under evaluation. If I envy my colleague's teaching skills, for instance, this is less a reaction to her teaching than a wish pertaining to our relative merits. Or if I desire that the evaluation turn out well, this is directed not so much at her teaching as at the evaluation of it.

Impartiality. Finally, it is often held that an ethical judgment must be impartial, in the sense that if some weight is given to the interests and concerns of some people, the same weight must be given to the same or similar interests of others, unless there is some relevant difference. Consideration of one's own interests, or those of one's group or species, is warranted only if the same consideration is given to all similar interests and concerns.

Let us say that an ideal ethical judgment is one that is perfectly informed, dispassionate, and impartial. We may think of these conditions as constraints on a procedure of judgment that takes features of an evaluated object as inputs and generates ethical judgments (evaluations) as outputs. Suppose, moreover, that these conditions of **ideal judgment** so constrain the process that they uniquely determine outputs. This would mean, in effect, that there is a fact of the matter about what judgment any being would render on some matter, were she to make an ideal judgment—that is, one that is perfectly informed, dispassionate, and impartial. According to the ideal judgment theory, if this were the case, then that ethical judgment would be true. The fact making it true would be that this is how a process of ideal ethical judgment would turn out.

Problems for the Ideal Judgment Theory

Perhaps the most obvious problem for the ideal judgment theory is that procedural constraints of ideal consideration may not uniquely determine output judgments. For example, we might imagine two different persons from quite different cultures—say, one from a culture of machismo that includes a code of masculine honor among its dominant values and the other from a culture that prizes harmonious relationships and turning the other cheek. When it comes to the question of how to respond to an insult, we can imagine both making conflicting judgments even when these are not influenced by any sort of self- or group-interest (in particular) or disturbing emotion or passion, and are as well-informed as they can be. If so, then there would be no fact of the matter about what judgment on the matter *an* ideal judge would render. Under conditions of ideal ethical judgment, a person from the first culture would render one judgment and a person from the second would render another. Perhaps the most that an ideal judgment theory could then say is that *relative to one cultural context of ethical judgment,* the first judgment is true, whereas relative to the other cultural context, the second is true.

But maybe this is not right. Perhaps in such cases at least one of their respective cultural values can be maintained only as **ideology**—that is, only through ignorance (perhaps even wilful ignorance) of real social conditions, including those that sustain the cultural values themselves. Maybe there is a truth about what any *human* being, say, would judge the appropriate response to an insult to be were he or she to make that judgment under genuinely ideal conditions.

This may still seem unlikely. And even if it is true, the result may have been purchased at the cost of making ethical truth depend on **contingencies** of *human* nature in ways that it may be difficult to believe fundamental ethical facts possibly can be. Can the wrongness of torture and lying really depend on anything about how *human* beings in particular happen to respond when they contemplate these under conditions of ideal judgment? As it happens, human beings can be moved by **sympathy,** by an emotionally engaged concern for the welfare of another. Because this is so, it can be argued that ideal human ethical judgment disapproves of lying and torture because they are typically against the welfare of all, impartially conceived. But is sympathy necessary (or even sufficient) to an appreciation of the wrongness of lying and torture? Mightn't these be seen to be wrong by virtue of violating a principle of **reciprocity**—of doing to others as one would not have them do to oneself—quite independent of any capacity to be concerned about the plights of others for their own sake?

Another Version of the Ideal Judgment Theory?
Ideal Practical Judgment or Agency Theory

The versions of the ideal judgment theory I have been describing are sometimes called *ideal observer* or *impartial spectator* theories. They consider the perspective of ethical thought and reflection to be that of a spectator who is disinterestedly contemplating the moral scene, as one might in reading a novel, or that of a judge assessing the merits of a case in which she is not involved. A very different approach is to consider ethical judgment from a **practical perspective,** from the point of view of an **agent** *deliberating* about what to do. We shall examine the leading example of this approach in our exploration of Kant's ethics in Chapter 15.

Kant attempts to combat the contingency inherent in ideal observer theories by arguing that any free agent is committed to universal norms of conduct by the logic of the deliberative standpoint—that is, just by virtue of what it is to deliberate freely about what to do. His theory is thus an **ideal** *practical* **judgment theory** (or **ideal agent theory**).

Both ideal agent theories and ideal observer theories are faced with daunting challenges, but of very different kinds. Empiricist ideal observer theories face the challenge that their proffered ideals do not determine a set of nonrelative ethical facts. Such theories may have to accept some form of ethical relativism, therefore—perhaps at the level of different cultures, perhaps at the level of the species. The latter relativity may not seem very troubling for practical purposes, but it will nonetheless be inconsistent with the sort of necessity that highly general ethical convictions seem to present themselves as having. Kant's agent's ideal judgment theory is designed with this challenge in mind, arguing that there are norms to which any agent is committed by the forms of deliberative practical thought. In this way, its ambitions are greater than empiricist ideal judgment theories. The worry faced by Kantianism is that its ambitions are vaulting, that no theory could deliver what it promises.

Suggested Reading

Firth, Roderick. "Ethical Absolutism and the Ideal Observer." *Philosophy and Phenomenological Research* 12 (1952): 317–345.

Hume, David. *A Treatise of Human Nature* (1740). Second edition edited by L. A. Selby-Bigge, with text revised and variant readings by P. H. Nidditch. Oxford: Clarendon Press, 1978. See especially pp. 470–476, 574–587.

Rawls, John. "Outline of a Decision Procedure for Ethics." *The Philosophical Review* 60 (1951): 177–197.

Smith, Adam. *The Theory of Moral Sentiments* (1759). D. D. Raphael and A. L. Macfie, eds. Indianapolis, Ind.: Liberty Classics, 1982. See especially Part 1.

7

THE ERROR THEORY AND ETHICAL RELATIVISM

The approaches we've considered in the past four chapters all attempt to account in some way or other for the **objective purport** of ethical thought and feeling. Since these approaches all face significant problems, we must consider the possibility that although deeply held ethical beliefs seem to be true to those who hold them, this appearance is an illusion. The metaethical theory that takes this possibility most seriously is **nihilism,** or the **error theory.** According to the error theory, all ethical beliefs are false.

The Error Theory

Recall the simple picture of ethical judgment I discussed in the last chapter along with Hume's claim that ethical judgment attributes a property to an object that is distinct from its natural features. The error theory agrees with this Humean picture; but it adds that, since no such ethical properties exist, ethical judgments are always false.

Error theorists believe that when we make ethical judgments we inevitably *project* an ethical property onto the world. In thinking about what deliberate killing involves, for example, we have a response—say, outrage or condemnation. The response is in us, but we have a tendency to *objectify* or *reify* it by taking it to be of an ethical property in the world (the outrageousness or contemptibleness of the killing). We treat our response as the recognition of some further property that is independent of it and that our response registers (as with the visual experience of shape).

The error theory appears to have quite radical implications. How can we believe that all ethical judgments are false and still seriously engage in ethical discourse and practice? Those who call themselves **nihilists** (like some existentialists) are prepared to accept that we cannot. They believe that ethical thought is undermined by the fact that nothing is as it seems to a person making an ethical judgment. Some error theorists have resisted this conclusion, however, arguing that their theory is a *second-order*, metaethical theory that need not conflict with *first-order* ethical thought and belief. Although they affirm, metaethically, that there is no such thing as value or obligation, they believe that they can still advance substantive normative ethical views.

But is it really possible to separate metaethics and normative ethics in this way? To put it simply, how can we coherently believe both that deliberate killing is vicious and that it is false that deliberate killing is vicious? We need not question whether it is *possible* to hold these two beliefs together, only whether it can be rational to do so.

The worry might be put this way. Unlike noncognitivism (see Chapter 8), the error theory does not deny that ethical convictions are genuine *beliefs*. In fact, to be an *error* theory, it must accept this thesis. It is of the very nature of belief, however, to be regulated by truth. That is what distinguishes belief as a state of mind from other attitudes we can have toward propositions, such as supposition, pretense, or desire. I can quite rationally suppose something true I know to be false—so as to consider its implications, for example—or pretend that it's true, or desire that it be true. I cannot, however, rationally believe what I know to be false (although I may try to, for pragmatic reasons). It seems to follow, therefore, that one cannot rationally believe the error theory and continue to hold ethical convictions as well. Of course, one might continue to have the illusory responses that one thinks ethical thought and conviction mistakenly objectify, just as a straight stick can continue to *look* bent in a pond even to a person who knows this appearance is mistaken. But one can no more continue rationally to *believe* that anything has value or disvalue, or is right or wrong, and believe also that these beliefs are false, than one can coherently think that the bentness of the stick is only an illusion and continue to believe that the stick is really bent.

None of this proves that the error theory is mistaken, of course. The point is that unless it is, ethical thought and practice as we know them will seem seriously misguided. If we believe the error theory, we can no longer rationally hold beliefs about value and disvalue, good and evil, right and wrong (other than the belief that there are no such things), or engage in practices, such as holding one another morally accountable, that apparently presuppose these beliefs.

Ethical Relativism

Perhaps, however, ethical thought and conviction can aspire to a kind of validity that is something short of the full objectivity it purports to have (and that, according to the error theory, it cannot have). Maybe ethical propositions can have a validity that is *relative* somehow *to the context of judgment.* Let us call the thesis that asserts this possibility **ethical relativism.** Ethical relativism holds that it is possible for apparently conflicting ethical judgments to both be correct, because they are made in different contexts (say, from the perspectives of different cultures, or by people holding different fundamental principles). As an example, imagine, again, a person from a culture that dominantly values machismo and another person from a culture that dominantly values harmonious, inclusive relations. Suppose both accept their respective cultures' dominant values and that when they consider, against that background, what someone should do when insulted by another, they disagree. Can they both be correct? Ethical relativism says that they can.

In order to avoid comparing apples with oranges, we must be sure that both persons are considering the same situation. So we need to ask, In what social context does the insult occur? Are we to imagine our two judges considering what a person should do in response to an insult delivered in the machismo culture? Or in response to an insult delivered in the anti-machismo culture? Detail is important here; otherwise, the judgments may be about different objects. In the absence of any fancy theories about relative validity or truth, it may simply be that what it is (*nonrelatively*) right or wrong for a person to do depends on features of that situation, including what values are generally accepted in the culture in which it occurs, whether the person about whom the judgment is being made accepts them, and so on. We must distinguish, therefore, between the *context of the (evaluated) object* and the *context of judgment.* Ethical relativism asserts that two different ethical judgments about the same *objectual context* can be equally valid because they are made from different *judgment contexts.* So we must imagine our two judges, in their respective contexts of judgment, considering the same objectual context—say, what someone should do if insulted in the machismo culture.

We must be careful also to distinguish this *ethical* question from the different, anthropological issue of what the machismo culture's norms dictate about the situation, or the psychological question of what relevant norms the judge herself holds. The question we are asking our judges to consider is what a person *should* do in the situation in which the prevailing norms dictate a certain response—say, challenging the insult and defending one's honor. For our ethical question, the anthropological and psychological facts are assumed to be part of the objectual context. Let us imagine, then, that the judge whose judgment is also made from within the machismo culture endorses the defensive response that the machismo norms dictate. He judges that the person should respond to the insult in kind. And imagine that the anti-machismo judge renders the opposite judgment—namely, that despite the fact that the insult occurs within a machismo culture, it should not be met (even by someone in that culture) with a counterattack, because a less defensive response both is better in itself and may help to bring about a less defensive culture.

Ethical relativism asserts that these two different judgments (about the same situation) can be equally true or valid, since both are equally valid in relation to their respective contexts of judgment. What, however, does such an assertion really come to?

I find that there are many people who believe and say that they are ethical relativists in somewhat the same sense I have been discussing. But it frequently turns out under questioning that what they believe is not ethical relativism but something else they have not yet distinguished from it. In the next section we shall consider various things that ethical relativism is not, but with which it is often confused.

This brings us to the interesting question of why so many people believe and say they are relativists. One reason is simply that it is easy to confuse relativism with various other things. But more telling, I think, is the possibility that people assert relativism as a strategy of polite avoidance. When ethical thought and discussion become difficult, and habits and customs of reasonable disagreement are under pressure (as is arguably the case in our society at the current moment), agreeing that differing parties are both correct (relative to their respective contexts of judgment) can seem a convenient way of avoiding conflict.

What Ethical Relativism Is Not

Situational Relativism.   Let us now consolidate the two distinctions we've just made. Ethical relativism differs, first, from any view according to which the ethical property something has depends on features of *that thing* (features of the objectual context). Even the view that what a person should do is wholly determined by the dominant norms of the culture in which she (the agent) finds herself is different from ethical relativism in our current sense. Assuming there always is a determinate answer to the question "What is required by the dominant norms of the culture in which this situation occurs?" (a big assumption!), then, for any situation, such a view would also determine a nonrelative fact of the matter about what a person should do *in that situation,* an ethical fact that is completely independent of any features of the context of *judgment.* And if two people disagree about what someone should do in that situation, such a view would likewise determine which of these two people, if either, is correct. Moreover, this would be so completely independent of anything about the standpoints from which their respective judgments are made.

Cultural Relativism.   Second, ethical relativism differs from any hypotheses concerning actual differences in ethical belief between or within cultures. It may be that whether ethical relativism is true becomes an interesting question only if there are, in fact, fundamental differences in ethical belief that cannot be removed when all nonethical disagreement is eliminated. Still, whether there are such fundamental differences is a question distinct from whether such differing ethical views could be equally true or valid. The former is an empirical question of psychology, sociology, or anthropology; the latter, a philosophical question of metaethics.

Toleration. Ethical relativism also differs from principles of cultural or individual tolerance according to which it is wrong to interfere with, express disapproval of, or even silently judge other cultures or persons. These latter are principles of normative ethics, telling us what we should or should not do. They neither conflict with nor entail any metaethical claims about the truth or validity of ethical convictions, either one's own or those of others. "Judge not lest ye be judged" is an injunction to concern oneself with one's own conduct and character rather than others', to think about the log in one's own eye rather than the speck in another's. It asserts nothing about the truth or validity of ethical convictions. In fact, to accept this injunction is apparently to be committed to its (nonrelative) truth.

Freedom of Thought. Similarly, ethical relativism neither is the same as nor follows from any view about freedom of thought—for example, the view that all people have a right to hold whatever ethical beliefs they choose. Freedom of thought also dictates that all people be free to believe whatever theories of mathematics, physics, or biology they choose. But it would not follow from this that conflicting views about mathematics, or about the existence and properties of black holes, or about the origins of biological species can be equally correct.

Equal Epistemic Justification. Finally, ethical relativism differs from the thesis that different people can be equally justified in holding conflicting ethical convictions. When someone has a conviction or belief, there is *what the person believes,* on the one hand, and *her believing it,* on the other. For example, if I hold that playing jazz music is an intrinsically valuable activity, there is what I believe or accept—that jazz is valuable—and the fact of my believing it. That two persons might be equally justified in believing conflicting propositions is a fact about the epistemic justification of their states of mind. It has no tendency to show that their differing beliefs (i.e., what each believes) might be equally correct.

It is a commonplace that, owing to differences in available evidence, two people can be equally justified in holding conflicting beliefs, even though only one of their beliefs is correct. Given the evidence available to her, Joan might justifiably think that William Scranton was the Republican vice-presidential candidate in 1964, while, given his evidence, Tom might reasonably think it was William Miller. Although they are both equally justified in holding their respective beliefs, only one of their beliefs is correct. What Tom believes is true; what Joan believes is not.

Ethical relativism of any interesting sort cannot simply be the view that people can be equally justified in holding conflicting ethical convictions. That would be true even if ethics admitted of the same truth and objectivity that ordinary empirical claims do. (Of course, someone might be a relativist about these latter claims also, but that's a different matter.) From the fact that two people can be equally justified in holding differing ethical convictions, nothing follows concerning whether the convictions they respectively hold (the propositions they accept) can somehow be equally valid or true.

Somewhat similarly, people sometimes say such things as that everyone's ethical beliefs are equally *true for* (or *relative to*) *them* but, when pressed to clarify their meaning, reply by saying that everyone (equally) *thinks* his or her respective ethical beliefs are true. True enough, but the latter observation has no tendency to show that *what* each thinks can be equally correct. On the contrary, if each is committed to the truth of his or her own beliefs, each must be committed also to the falsity of all beliefs that genuinely conflict with them.

Could Ethical Relativism Be True?

I've defined ethical relativism as the view that differing ethical judgments can be equally true or valid in relation to their respective contexts of judgment. But doesn't this blur the very distinction I've just been making? On the face of it, the claim that the validity of a judgment might somehow depend on the context of judgment seems to make validity depend not on features of *what is judged* (the proposition asserted) but, rather, on aspects of the judging or believing itself. And isn't it incoherent to suppose that the truth or validity of what is judged might somehow depend on its relation to the context in which it is judged or accepted? Wouldn't that be like thinking that the truth of the proposition that William Miller was the 1964 Republican candidate for vice-president might somehow depend on the context in which that proposition was asserted? But which context would that be? Returning to the ethical case, if the same ethical judgment can be made in different contexts, how do we even correlate a judgment (what is judged) with *its* context of judgment?

It would seem that the only way this puzzle can be solved is if ethical judgment itself somehow concerns (is about) the context in which the judgment is made. For example, subjectivism maintains that ethical judgments attribute to some object the property of being regarded in some way or other (by me or us). If this is so, then when I say that playing jazz is a worthy human activity, and you say it isn't but playing classical music is, what we are really doing is saying of jazz that we have our respective attitudes toward it. We are not really judging jazz, taken in itself, but reporting our respective attitudes towards it (or the contexts of our respective judgments, if you like). And so we don't really disagree in the sense of believing contradictory propositions. It is simultaneously true that I have my attitude toward jazz and that you have yours.

If something like this were what ethical relativism finally comes to, three observations would seem apt. First, ethical propositions will end up admitting of literal truth or falsity after all. Their truth will be relative to the context of judgment only in the sense that they are propositions *about* the context of judgment, so they will be true if, and only if, certain things are (nonrelatively) true about that context.

Second, understood this way, ethical relativism reduces ethical propositions to psychological propositions about the ethical judge or to sociological or anthropological propositions about the context of ethical judgment. But as we have seen, these latter propositions may lack any distinctively ethical content. Ethical judgments appear to concern, not the attitudes people or cultures actually have, but the attitudes they *should have* or what is *worthy* of some attitude or other.

Finally, if ethical judgments really concern the context of judgment, then they cannot genuinely conflict. Returning to our example from Chapter 2: If one person judges that torturing and slaughtering innocents for tactical advantage is morally heinous and another person judges it to be morally justified, there seems to be a genuine issue between them about which both cannot be correct. But if what ethical judgments really attribute is the property of some particular context of judgment, then these judgments no longer compete with each other. It will simply be true that the one person, in her context, has one attitude and that the other, in his, has another. These attitudes *differ*, but they can genuinely conflict only if what each person respectively judges can be separated from the context in which she or he judges it. Otherwise, we are threatened with losing any contrast between ethical belief and conviction, on the one hand, and mere preference or taste, on the other.

Ethical relativism confronts a dilemma, therefore. If we understand it in the way I've just been suggesting—as the genus of which subjectivism is a species—then it faces the same powerful objections that afflict subjectivism, both those that are common to all reductive metaethical theories and those directed at subjectivism in particular. If, however, we take ethical relativism to assert that, although ethical judgment is not about the context of judgment (context does not enter into what is judged), the validity or truth of an ethical judgment (what is judged) nonetheless is somehow relative to the context of judgment, it is no longer clear what ethical relativism is saying.

Suggested Reading

Harman, Gilbert. "Moral Relativism Defended." *The Philosophical Review* 84 (1975): 3–22.

Harman, Gilbert, and Judith Jarvis Thomson. *Moral Relativism and Moral Objectivity*. Oxford: Blackwell Publishers, 1996.

Lyons, David. "Ethical Relativism and the Problem of Incoherence." *Ethics* 86 (1976): 107–121.

Mackie, J. L. *Ethics: Inventing Right and Wrong*. Harmondsworth, Middlesex: Penguin, 1977.

Williams, Bernard. "The Truth in Relativism." In *Moral Luck*. Bernard Williams, ed. Cambridge: Cambridge University Press, 1981.

8

NONCOGNITIVISM

To this point we have taken it largely for granted that if no ethical facts exist, then all ethical convictions must be false, as the error theory asserts. In doing so, we have been implicitly making assumptions in the philosophies of language and mind about the nature and content of ethical conviction. We have been tacitly supposing that ethical convictions are like ordinary beliefs—specifically, that, like beliefs, they are true just in case reality has the features they represent it as having and false otherwise. The thesis that ethical convictions admit of truth and falsity in this way is called **cognitivism.** Cognitivists believe that claims made with ethical language, and the states of mind we call ethical convictions or beliefs, have **propositional** or **cognitive content,** that these contents admit of literal truth or falsity, and that ethical claims or convictions are correct or incorrect if, and only if, the propositions they assert are true or false, respectively.

Suppose you have a conviction that you would express in these terms: "It is morally heinous to torture and slaughter innocents for terroristic purposes." According to cognitivism, your conviction has a genuine propositional content—namely, that such torture and slaughter is heinous. And just as any belief is correct if, and only if, the believed proposition is true, so, likewise, will your ethical conviction be correct just in case its content proposition is true.

Noncognitivism denies cognitivism and, thus, that ethical claims and convictions have genuine propositional (cognitive) content and admit of truth or falsity. It agrees with the error theory that no ethical facts exist of the sort that could make ethical claims true, but it denies that any ethical claims are strictly false either. Ethical claims are not "apt" for truth or falsity. They assert nothing propositional. So unlike ordinary beliefs and assertions, they are not made false by there being no facts to make the propositions they assert true.

As a crude analogy, suppose a child greets a plate of spinach with the exclamation "Yeccchhh!" In so doing, she expresses a distaste for spinach but asserts no proposition. Of course, she could have said something like "I don't like spinach." That assertion would have been true. But in saying "yeccchhh," she did not say about herself that she dislikes spinach so much as *express* her dislike. And although "I don't like spinach" has propositional content, the reaction it attributes does not. A disgusted reaction to spinach itself is neither true nor false. Since "yeccchhh!" expresses this state of mind, it expresses a state of mind without propositional content. And so it also lacks such content itself.

Simply put, noncognitivism holds that ethical claims and convictions are respectively like "yeccchhh!" and the state of mind it expresses. Ethical claims express mental states without propositional contents and, hence, without truth values. Even if no ethical facts exist, therefore, ethical thought and practice will not be impugned, since, if noncognitivism is right, ethical discourse asserts no such facts.

Varieties of Noncognitivism

Emotivism.   One form of noncognitivism, **emotivism,** holds that ethical judgments express the feelings or attitudes of the person who makes the judgments. Judgments such as "It is wrong to invade another person's privacy by reading his computer files" express the judge's negative feeling or attitude rather than any propositional belief. And like the yeccchhh-response, the expressed feelings have no truth values. They are responses to a contemplated situation, not (purported) representations of one. It is as if the person making the judgment were to say, "People reading other people's computer files: tsk tsk." The "tsk tsk" adds no propositional content, and so the full utterance cannot express some distinctively ethical proposition (or belief in any proposition) that could be true or false. Its function is expressive rather than descriptive or representative.

One advantage emotivism has over subjectivism is that it can go some way toward explaining the manner in which ethical judgments can genuinely conflict. If one person says that reading other people's computer files is wrong and another person says it is not wrong, they appear to make conflicting judgments. According to subjectivism, however, there is no conflict. Subjectivism entails that the first person is really just saying that she is against computer prying and that the other is saying that he is not. But these two judgments may both be true. Thus neither person is saying anything with which the other disagrees. Emotivism maintains, on the other hand, that in making these ethical judgments, the two *express* conflicting attitudes. They do not say of themselves that they have these attitudes. And because these attitudes conflict, so do the judgments that express them.

Moreover, like other forms of noncognitivism, emotivism can explain the intimate connection that many philosophers think exists between ethical judgment and *motivation*. In particular, it entails a form of **internalism,** such that if a person judges that she ought to do something, then, necessarily, she will have some motivation to do it. To internalists, ethical judgment seems essentially *practical*. It seems not just a contingent fact that thinking something right or wrong is related to being for or against it in a way that can move one to action. Emotivism can explain why this is so, since it holds that thinking something right or wrong just *is* being for or against it in a way that is not motivationally neutral. Of course, if the adherents of **externalism** are right, if there is no *necessary* connection between ethical judgment and motives or practical reasons, then there is nothing to be explained.

Prescriptivism.   Some noncognitivists argue that the connection between ethical judgment and the will is even closer than emotivism supposes it to be. **Prescriptivism** maintains that what ethical judgments express is not a feeling or attitude but, rather, a state of the judge's will that is more like an *intention* or a prescription. In particular, someone who sincerely declares "Computer prying is wrong" expresses not her reaction to computer prying so much as her *will* that it not be done, including a resolve not to do it herself. Her state of mind might as well be expressed with the universal imperative "Let no one snoop in other people's computer files!"

Norm Expressivism.   A problem with both emotivism and prescriptivism is that it seems quite possible for someone to make an ethical judgment but to lack the feelings or intentions that, according to these theories, ethical judgments express. In particular, it seems possible for someone to distinguish between the reaction he actually has to something and the reaction he *should* have—that is, the reaction he thinks the thing he is contemplating *warrants*. And similarly for prescriptions and intentions.

Suppose you are emotionally overloaded at the end of a long day when you read about the terrorist slaughter. Under those conditions, you react not with outrage but with a barely stifled yawn. Does this commit you to thinking that the slaughter was boring rather than outrageous? It would seem that it doesn't. You might think that the slaughter warrants a very different reaction than the one it actually evinces in you in your current state.

Of course, that one *should* have a certain reaction is an ethical judgment. So if noncognitivism is true, this judgment must lack cognitive content and express some noncognitive state of mind also. But if the possibilities that emotivism and prescriptivism (feelings and intentions) are ruled out, the question arises: What state might this judgment express? **Norm expressivism** holds that the mental state it expresses is that of accepting a norm. When a person accepts a norm, she is in a distinctive state of mind that expresses itself in a variety of ways, including tendencies to conform to the norm and to avow it in thought and discussion. In particular, the person who judges that the slaughter is heinous expresses her acceptance of a norm that warrants outrage as a response to such acts. And she can make this judgment even if she is not in fact outraged, because what her judgment expresses is not outrage but her acceptance of a norm that warrants it.

The Sources of Noncognitivism

Noncognitivism results from applying certain lines of thought in the philosophies of language and mind to the case of ethical discourse and psychology. Some early-twentieth-century noncognitivists held a radically empiricist theory of meaning—the **verifiability criterion** of meaningfulness—according to which a sentence or utterance must be capable of being empirically verified in order for it to assert a meaningful proposition. Called **logical positivists**, these philosophers agreed with Moore's critique of naturalism. But because they thought all meaningful terms must refer to empirically verifiable aspects of nature, the moral they drew from Moore's critique was that ethical terms are not used to assert any propositions at all. Very few philosophers still accept the verifiability criterion. Even propositions of scientific theory go well beyond what can be observed, since, for one thing, they make assertions about all cases of a certain kind, including unobserved cases.

Much more lies behind noncognitivism than just positivism, however. Without holding anything like the verifiability criterion, one may still think that different fragments of our language and mentality have different *functions,* and that whereas the function of much discourse and mental life is to represent or describe reality, that of ethical discourse and mentality is not. Consider, for example, the difference between a *report* about the addictive properties of nicotine and an order that cigarettes be classified as a drug and regulated in various ways. The report and the order have different **directions of fit** to the world. The report aims to represent the way things are, and, if things are not as it represents them, then something is mistaken in *it*. It is **world-corrected**. The order, however, aims not to represent the world but to inform its change. If the world fails to fit the order, the error will be in the world, not in the order. It is **world-correcting**. The function of a report is to fit the world, but that of an order is for the world to fit it.

This is also true of states of mind that can be expressed with such language. The *belief* that nicotine is addictive represents reality in a certain way and is committed to the truth of that representation. Beliefs have propositional content and, hence, the same direction of fit as the statements (e.g., "Nicotine is addictive") that express them. By contrast, an *intention*—say, to outlaw the sale of nicotine until it is shown to be safe—is a state of mind with a direction of fit that is more like that of an order than that of a belief. If the world fails to match the intention, the mistake will be in the world.

According to noncognitivism, the function and direction of fit of ethical discourse and mentality are akin to those of orders or intentions rather than beliefs. Partly, noncognitivism may be proposing an anthropological or sociobiological hypothesis. For example, it might be argued that normative discourse and states of mind, such as accepting a norm, evolved not as a way of representing reality in our cognitive system but, rather, as a way of facilitating human cooperation and coordination.

Care is needed here, however, since, depending on how "reality" is understood, a cognitivist can agree with the foregoing argument, at least up to a point. Ethical claims and states of mind might have prescriptive functions and still have genuine propositional content. Moreover, ethical language has all the earmarks of propositional, "fact-stating" discourse. There is a difference between ordering or requesting someone to do something, on the one hand, and saying that it would be good for her to do it, or that she ought to, on the other. The latter certainly *seems* to involve saying something that might be true or false. After all, we say such things as "I know it's true that I should get more exercise, but I can't seem to find the time." And we also reason from ethical claims in the same way as from genuine propositions: "If I should eat more nutritious food, then I'd better lay off the glazed donuts."

What is perhaps the most powerful argument for noncognitivism, however, is a version of Moore's "open-question argument." It seems possible to imagine two people who agree about all matters of fact that either thinks relevant to some ethical issue but who nonetheless disagree in their ethical judgments. What, then, can be at issue between these two, if it cannot be settled by agreement on any fact that either thinks relevant? Noncognitivism can explain this phenomenon, since it holds that what is at issue in ethical disagreement is no matter of fact at all but, rather, something noncognitive. Ethical disagreement can persist despite perfect factual agreement, since conflicting ethical judgments express, not different beliefs, but conflicting noncognitive states of mind. If such radical ethical disagreement is possible, therefore, then this phenomenon may be evidence for noncognitivism.

Problems for Noncognitivism and Possible Responses

The greatest obstacle noncognitivism faces is that it is so obviously at odds with the surface appearances of ethical discourse and thought. Ethical claims are made in apparently fact-stating propositional discourse, in contrast with orders and requests. We attribute truth and falsity to ethical convictions and claims. And we also reason from them counterfactually in ways that we cannot when dealing with noncognitive fragments of language such as the imperatives we use to express orders. It makes perfect sense to think: "If we shouldn't outlaw the sale of nicotine, then perhaps we should strengthen the controls on advertising it." But how could one reason from the contradictory of an order (such as the order to outlaw nicotine's sale) if orders don't express any proposition that can be contradicted?

To reply to these objections, the noncognitivist must attempt to argue that talk of truth or inference can make sense *within* (noncognitive) ethical discourse even if, strictly speaking, it is mistaken when applied to ethical claims or convictions when we think *about* them philosophically from the outside. For example, saying that an ethical claim is true might be a stronger way of making that same ethical claim. A prescriptivist might understand the "assertion" that it is true that torturing innocents is wrong as simply another way of issuing the universal imperative: "Do not torture innocents!" Or, again, a norm expressivist might understand conditional, counterfactual ethical thinking as drawing out the implications of norms that one does not accept, but might. In thinking through what should be done if we shouldn't outlaw the sale of nicotine, someone might be asking herself what would follow from a norm that prohibits outlawing its sale (a norm she may not herself accept) when that norm is taken together with the facts of the case and other norms she does accept.

In making arguments of this sort, the noncognitivist must hold that normative ethical thought is entirely separable from metaethical reflection. Asked whether it is true that we should not torture innocents, the noncognitivist will reply that the question is ambiguous, inasmuch as it falls between normative and metaethical interpretations. The categories of truth and inference have, she believes, an appropriate noncognitive use within normative ethical thought, although they do not when we step back from our normative ethical thinking and attempt to apply it to our ethical thoughts from the outside.

In addition to the surface logical structure of ethical language, inter- and intrapersonal ethical discourse has the appearance of a *rational* activity. Argument about matters of value and obligation involves the giving of *reasons* for ethical claims. We distinguish, moreover, between rational and nonrational ways of changing other people's minds on ethical matters. According to noncognitivism, however, ethical argument is the expression of noncognitive attitudes in an attempt to induce similar attitudes in others. But this account seems to reduce the giving of reasons to exerting a kind of persuasive force and, hence, to eliminate any basis for the contrast between rational and nonrational methods of changing minds.

In response to these objections, the noncognitivist points out that people's attitudes on any given issue partly depend on their *non*ethical beliefs about that issue. As in our example from Chapter 1, two people may make conflicting ethical claims about a proposed law that would permit doctor-assisted suicide because they disagree about the empirical, nonethical issue of whether vulnerable people would be likelier to be taken advantage of were such a law to exist. The person who favors the law might therefore argue that the law would be a good thing, or at least not a bad thing, by giving the other person reasons for thinking that the consequences she fears would not actually occur.

Of course, the person who favors such legislation thinks not merely that what he gives are reasons for *believing* that certain things will or will not occur, but also that they are reasons for his *ethical claim*—for favoring, or at least not opposing, the law. Since the whole point of noncognitivism is to distinguish between beliefs (where evidence apparently justifies by its very nature), on the one hand, and ethical claims and attitudes (where there are no given reasons), on the other, how can it ground claims about reasons for ethical judgments in reasons for beliefs? And how, moreover, can noncognitivism distinguish between rational and irrational ways of changing people's minds about these matters?

The noncognitivist responds to these objections by pointing out that questions about normative reasons and rationality are themselves ultimately ethical issues. The judgment that a certain way of attempting to change someone's mind is nonrational and manipulative is itself an ethical judgment. Someone making it thus does not assert any proposition that could have a truth value but, rather, expresses her (noncognitive) opposition to such persuasive techniques. Similarly, in judging that some fact is a normative reason for doing or feeling something, one expresses no literal belief (beyond those on the basis of which one makes the judgment) but, rather, some attitude, feeling, or other noncognitive mental state that favors doing or feeling something when that fact obtains. For example, if you judge that the fact that the slaughter caused suffering to innocents is a reason to feel outrage, that expresses your endorsement of this response under these conditions.

Expressive or directive accounts of ethical language seem most at home when ethical convictions are already formed. But what about ethical *inquiry*? How can noncognitivism explain the phenomenon of trying to decide which ethical convictions to hold? If you are wondering whether to vote for a law permitting doctor-assisted suicide, for example, your ethical thoughts can hardly express attitudes or feelings you've already formed, since you are still wondering what attitude to have on the issue. From the perspective of your uncertainty, it will most likely seem to you that you are trying to decide which ethical claim is *true*.

Here again, the noncognitivist must attempt to explain how such inquiry can take place *within* normative ethical thinking, while maintaining that when we step back from our normative thoughts, we must recognize that, strictly speaking, there is no ethical truth to inquire into. For instance, a norm expressivist may point out that even someone who accepts various norms will inevitably confront novel situations, if only in thought. In wondering what should be done in such a situation, he may only be considering the implications for this situation of norms he already accepts. Or perhaps he holds norms that give conflicting directions for a given situation. Here he may be trying to discover which solution is most coherent within the overall set of norms he accepts.

But what about cases where no such solution is dictated? Surely someone could be facing these circumstances and still wonder what should be done. In fact, it seems that one could even be in a situation where one's general norms and attitudes do dictate a unique solution and still wonder whether this solution is correct. One could wonder whether one should continue to hold these norms and attitudes. How can noncognitivism account for inquiry that *transcends* one's currently accepted norms or current attitudes?

Noncognitivism has various possible responses, but all share an insistence that ethical inquiry, even of this radical sort, occurs entirely within (noncognitive) ethical thought and discourse, and hence that it is entirely separate from and thereby consistent with the metaethical position that there are no truths in ethics. For example, the noncognitivist can say that what seems like inquiry to us is really a kind of internalized interpersonal discourse in which we alternately adopt various familiar ethical "voices" and speak to ourselves in a kind of "self-talk," hoping by this internal conversation to settle on a stable attitude. Or the norm expressivist can say that although we think about what norms to accept no less than about the implications of norms we already accept, thinking of the former kind nonetheless inevitably takes place against the background of other "higher-order" norms—norms for accepting norms—that we already accept. And the acceptance of higher-order norms is no less noncognitive than is the acceptance of lower-order ones.

What lies behind noncognitivism's sharp separation between normative ethics and metaethics is the thesis that (normative) ethical claims express mental states that lack cognitive content. For this to be so, however, we must be able to identify the mental states that ethical claims express in some way other than through the ethical convictions with which they are associated, along with their apparent contents. It is far from clear that this can be done, however.

Some emotions and attitudes seem to require the existence of certain beliefs by their very nature. In order for someone to be in the state of fear, for example, he must think there is some possible danger in the offing. Something like this belief seems to be part of what makes certain feelings (experienced in the pit of the stomach or as palpitations of the heart) feelings of fear as opposed to anticipation or something else. It might be argued along these lines that ethical feelings have constituent beliefs also. What makes something a feeling of guilt, for example? Can a person feel guilt (as opposed to, say, apprehensiveness about being punished) if he lacks any thought or belief about the (possible) wrongness of something he's done? Or consider the state of accepting a norm. Can we really understand what it is to be in this state without an associated normative belief?

Such questions create something of a dilemma for noncognitivism. The more uncontroversially noncognitive a mental state is, the less plausible a noncognitivist position that asserts that ethical claims and convictions express that mental state is apt to seem. What convinces us that the child's spinach-response "yecccchhh!" does not have a truth value is likely to convince us as well that it cannot express any ethical conviction. Similarly, to the extent that there seems to be a clear intuitive difference between directing someone to do something and saying it is something she ought to do, so also is prescriptivism likely to seem implausible. On the other side, to the extent that it is plausible that a given mental state (approval, for example, or perhaps the acceptance of a norm) is expressed by ethical claims, it may begin to seem questionable that the mental state is genuinely noncognitive. And once this is questioned, it must seem doubtful as well that metaethics and normative ethics can be separated as sharply as the noncognitivist says they must be.

Suggested Reading

Ayer, J. *Language, Truth, and Logic.* New York: Dover Publications, 1952. See especially Chapter 6.

Gibbard, Allan. *Wise Choices, Apt Feelings.* Cambridge, Mass.: Harvard University Press, 1990.

Hare, R. M. *The Language of Morals.* Oxford: Clarendon Press, 1991.

Stevenson, Charles. *Ethics and Language.* New Haven, Conn.: Yale University Press, 1965.

9

INTERLUDE

Throughout Part 2, we have considered metaethics in abstraction from normative ethics. We have proceeded as though what value and obligation are can be determined without knowing what has value or what we morally ought to do. And we have ignored whether different metaethical positions might have different normative implications.

This is common practice. Metaethics and normative ethics are frequently presented as if they were entirely separate and independent, as according to some metaethical positions (e.g., noncognitivism) they must be. But although no metaethical position strictly entails any normative position, and vice versa, a glance at the history of ethical thought reveals various natural affinities.

For example, an important division within normative ethics is that between **consequentialism** and **deontology**. Consequentialist theories hold that what it is right to do depends always on the goodness of consequences, whereas deontological theories hold that there are right- and wrong-making considerations other than good and bad effects. For instance, a deontological theory might say that torturing innocents would be wrong even if its consequences turned out to be beneficial in the long run.

Numerous clarifications and qualifications are necessary, of course. The values that the consequentialist thinks determine the rightness or wrongness of acts must, on pain of circularity, be nonmoral values that don't already depend on which acts are right. And although a consequentialist may be an act-consequentialist, and hold that what is right depends always on which act would do the most good, she might deny this and remain a consequentialist nonetheless. Or she might be a rule-consequentialist and believe that the rightness of acts is determined by which rules would have the best consequences (and which acts those rules would require). Or, finally, she might be a kind of character-consequentialist and maintain that which act is right is determined by which character traits would promote the most good (and which acts these traits would lead to).

Consequentialism and deontology are distinctive approaches to normative ethics. They pronounce on what is good and right (and on what features are good- and right-making) rather than on the metaethical questions
of what, if anything, goodness and rightness are themselves. This difference
notwithstanding, the history of ethics reveals fascinating affinities between
these divergent normative approaches and related metaethical positions.
Nothing so neat as a one-to-one correspondence emerges, but there are
some striking trends.

For example, philosophers who are metaethical naturalists have almost
always been consequentialists, although not all consequentialists have been
naturalists. (G. E. Moore is a good example of a consequentialist who was
not a naturalist.) As we saw in Chapter 3, a naturalist may find it easier to
defend a naturalistic basis for nonmoral forms of value (the desirable or the
estimable) than such a basis for norms determining right and wrong. Thus
many naturalists are led to argue that morality must somehow be reducible
to nonmoral value—for example, in instrumental terms that would support
consequentialism.

Deontologists, on the other hand, require a metaethical account of
moral obligation that explains how the right can diverge from the beneficial, and the wrong from the harmful. Some deontologists have been theological voluntarists, basing their deontology on the nonconsequentialist
character of God's commands.[1] Some have been rational intuitionists, arguing that, for example, the wrongness of torture is both a priori and necessary. And some have followed Kant in maintaining that principles of
right and wrong are grounded in the structure of a free rational agent's
deliberations.

These associations are far from accidental. Similarly, when we look
within the thought of the great ethical philosophers, such as Aristotle,
Kant, Mill, or Nietzsche, we find a dynamic interaction between their normative and metaethical theories. These thinkers each had a characteristic
philosophical ethics—a distinctive approach that integrated their metaethical and normative thought. They did not treat metaethics and normative
ethics as altogether separate and independent. On the contrary, they
grounded their views about what has value in some philosophical understanding of what value itself is.

Parts 3 and 4 will be devoted to examples of philosophical ethics that are
both historically prominent and currently influential. By and large, we will
be examining the thought of individual thinkers rather than abstract positions. In this way, we will be able to appreciate philosophical ethics as a living human activity, as an attempt to make some integrated sense of the fundamental ethical and philosophical questions that face us as human beings.
As I tried to convince you in Chapter 1, philosophical ethics is just a more
disciplined and systematic version of a virtually ineliminable aspect of a

thoughtful human life. It is something to which, I believe, you are yourself committed.

Part 3 presents three philosophical theories of morality. When distinguished from ethics more generally, the idea of morality is associated with the notion of universal norms or laws that obligate all (human) moral agents, and whose requirements sometimes conflict with the agent's interest (or would conflict, but for the existence of the norm). Because this idea has been especially prominent in the modern period (beginning roughly in the seventeenth century), it is sometimes called the modern conception of morality. Actually, of course, it has a long history in the religious traditions of Judeo-Christianity and Islam, at least. What is distinctively modern is the project of giving the idea of morality a secular philosophical foundation, one that is consistent with the metaphysical outlook of modern science.

The background for this idea was the widespread rejection, with the rise of modern science in the seventeenth century, of an Aristotelian teleological metaphysics of nature, according to which every natural being has an inherent end or "final cause" that fits it for participation in a harmonious order of nature. As against the view that a fundamental congruence of interests is metaphysically guaranteed, ethical philosophy from the seventeenth century on often proceeded on the assumption that human interests can conflict, sometimes quite importantly, and that everyone is worse off if unbridled self-interest (however enlightened) is the sole guiding human aim. According to the modern conception, then, morality is a system of self-interest-restraining norms whose collective observance is mutually advantageous.

Thomas Hobbes, Immanuel Kant, and John Stuart Mill were all philosophical moralists. In different ways and with varying revisions and emphases, they all attempted to define and defend the modern idea of morality, beginning with Hobbes in the middle of the seventeenth century and continuing with Kant in the eighteenth century and Mill in the nineteenth. Virtually every major theory of morality represented in the philosophical debate of our own time derives from one or more of these three.

Not all contemporary philosophical ethics are theories of morality, however. A notable feature of the current scene is the rise of various critiques of the kind of moral theory we find in Hobbes, Mill, and Kant, as well as of the modern conception of morality itself. Part 4 presents three examples of philosophical ethics that are not theories of morality: the philosophical ethics of Friedrich Nietzsche and that of Aristotle, and the contemporary "ethics of care." Nietzsche's *Genealogy of Morals* (1887) is a radical critique of morality. In particular, Nietzsche argued that morality is an ideology: a set of ideas that is maintained only through willed ignorance of their real causes. The categories of moral good and evil, he further asserted, are a kind of shackle that the weak use to control the strong because they resent the natural superiority of the strong. Nietzsche's contemporary followers do not always accept this explanation of morality's existence, but they agree with him that it is an unhealthy idea and that a more satisfactory philosophical ethics would have to go beyond the categories of moral good and evil.

Contemporary ethics has another fertile source in Aristotle. By modeling ethics on virtue and character, rather than on universal principles or norms, Aristotle posed a significant alternative to modern theories of morality. For him, the central ethical question was: What are worthy ways of living, and what makes for a flourishing human life? not: What are my moral duties?

Finally, a number of recent thinkers, many of them feminist philosophers, have argued for a view that places relationships between particular individuals at the center of our understanding of ethics. According to what Carol Gilligan calls the "ethics of care," ethical questions are fundamentally particularistic rather than universal.[2] They ask: What am I to do for Jane? What is my responsibility to her? not: What should a person do in a situation like this?

Throughout Parts 3 and 4, then, we will be dealing with a variety of philosophical ethics—namely, with attempts to find satisfying answers to the normative questions that unavoidably confront us within ethical thought and that can fit with our most satisfying responses to the philosophical, metaethical questions we face when we step back and critically reflect on ethics and ethical thought. This is the project that has engaged philosophical ethicists since at least Plato and Aristotle, and that confronts anyone who takes both ethical and philosophical questions seriously.

Part Three

PHILOSOPHICAL MORALISTS

10

HOBBES I

Thomas Hobbes (1588–1679) is best known for the **social contract theory,** the idea that political legitimacy derives from a mutual contract or promise. A **state of nature** (without political authority), Hobbes famously argued in *Leviathan* (1651), is riddled with "continual fear, and danger of violent death; and the life of man [is] solitary, poor, nasty, brutish, and short" (L.XIII.9).[1] To escape this condition, citizens must promise to obey a sovereign. Their doing so establishes the sovereign's authority and the citizens' obligation to obey.

The conclusion of Hobbes's argument is a claim of political theory—namely, that political obligation rests on individual consent. But implicit in his argument is a conception of morality and its **normativity** that has powerfully influenced moral philosophers ever since. Political obligation depends, for Hobbes, on the moral obligation to keep "covenants." But what grounds this moral obligation? What makes it a moral "law of nature," as Hobbes said, "that men perform their covenants made?" (L.XIV.1). To answer this question, Hobbes had to construct a philosophical ethics, including a metaethics that could plausibly ground the obligation to keep promises.

Hobbes's Context

To see the problem as Hobbes faced it, we need to understand something of his historical context. Let's begin with a philosophical outlook that had been common in the 400-year period before Hobbes wrote *Leviathan*, but that, in the middle of the seventeenth century, Hobbes and many of his contemporaries found they could no longer accept.

Begin with the idea of an artifact that is constructed for a certain purpose—say, a knife. A knife is made to serve a purpose or goal: to cut by hand. It can be made from any of various materials: wood, metal, plastic, and so on. It can be made from anything that is suitable for the knife's end or function. What makes something a knife is not its material but its defining function. And this end or function is *normative* for the knife. Just by virtue of what it is to be knife—what knives are *for*—something will be a good knife, perform well, be as it should be, and so on, only if it cuts well.

Suppose now that every *natural* kind of thing were like knives in having a defining end. In other words, suppose that included in the "essence" or nature of everything (that which makes it what it is) is what the thing is *to do* or *be*. It is not enough to suppose that nature and its parts are created, or even that they are created for certain purposes. We must imagine that natural kinds of things are like knives in being *essentially for* certain purposes. So imagine that it is essential to what makes something an acorn, for example, that it *is to* function in a certain way—say, to grow up into a flourishing oak.

Call a thing's defining end its *good*. Of every natural kind, it will then be true that its good is normative for it. A thing of that kind will do or be as it *should* do or be just in case it realizes the good for things of that kind. Its good is thus a kind of "law" for it. Suppose also that the defining end or function of each natural thing fits with that of every other to form a harmonious order. Call the entire set of ends—that is, the "laws" that say what each living being is to do in coordination with everything else—the "eternal law." Next, suppose that some of these beings, human beings, can discover their end or law and, consequently, that they can act in knowledge of it. Call those parts of the eternal law that concern such beings "natural law." Then natural law will uniquely be such that it can be obeyed or flouted, and only human beings will be subject to the law in this way. Finally, suppose that all such phenomena are the result of divine creation.

These are the essentials of the **classical natural law theory** as it was proposed by St. Thomas Aquinas (1224–1274) and widely accepted for centuries after. Morality is a natural law that all human beings are subject to by virtue of their nature. Both the content and the normativity of natural law are inherent in human nature, since obeying it is what we are *for*.

Aquinas's theory was a synthesis of Aristotle's teleological metaphysics and a Judeo-Christian conception of morality as God's law. It was not, however, a theological voluntarist conception. In fact, there were intense debates between Aquinas and his followers, on the one hand, and more voluntarist natural lawyers, on the other. They all agreed that morality is divinely ordained, but they disagreed about what gives this divine law its authority or normative force. For the voluntarists, the moral obligation to abide by natural law derives entirely from God's commanding it. But for Aquinas and his followers, we should obey natural law because it is essential to what we are that we are *to* follow it. Just as what a knife is for is cutting, so what we are for is the virtuous activity dictated by natural law (morality).

Let's return now to Hobbes. Recall that the problem we left Hobbes with was how to account for the obligation to keep promises, which he held to underlie the obligation to obey the laws of the state. Like the classical natural lawyers, Hobbes connected morality and its normativity to what he called a natural law. But what gives the law "that men perform their covenants made" its normative force? What makes it the case that people *should* keep their covenants? What does any "ought" or normative "law" consist in? This was the problem Hobbes faced.

Now, according to the classical theory, a natural law should be followed because it codifies an end that is inherent in the nature of those subject to it. A knife's doing as it ought just is its cutting well. So, likewise, for us. Our doing as we ought just is our excelling at what we are for—namely, the virtuous activities called for by natural law. It follows that if natural law dictates keeping promises, then we ought to keep our promises.

There were two reasons Hobbes could not accept this picture. One had to do with its teleological metaphysics. By the middle of the seventeenth century, Aristotelian science and the epistemological and metaphysical framework required to sustain it were being increasingly abandoned in favor of the methods and worldview of the emerging modern science of Galileo and Huygens (and, later, Boyle and Newton). Stressing empirical experimentation, the new science explained phenomena by appealing not to inherent goals or purposes but, rather, to underlying physical mechanisms. The natural laws it was discovering were entirely descriptive rather than normative. For example, the motion of bodies came to be explained by universal generalizations or "laws" about how bodies invariably behave and the mechanisms and forces that cause them to do so, rather than by anything about their "ends" or purposes.

Hobbes believed that the teleological picture was not simply false but unintelligible. For words to be other than empty signs or sounds, he thought, they must ultimately refer to what we can know to be real through sense experience (L.IV.14–18). This category includes material things, their physical properties, and events in bodies that involve conscious thought and experience. Hobbes had special scorn for the "insignificant speech" he found in "all the universities of Christendom, grounded upon certain texts of Aristotle," like Aquinas's theory of natural law (L.I.5).

Second, Hobbes rejected classical natural law's contention that the goods of all are harmoniously ordered and that a coincidence between natural law and self-interest is metaphysically guaranteed. On the contrary, Hobbes thought, what gives morality and political society its point is that people's interests frequently conflict and, consequently, that if each simply pursues his self-interest, the collective result would be a war of "all against all."

Hobbes sought an account of the moral obligation to keep promises that did not depend on teleological metaphysics (and the assumption that self-interest necessarily coincides with the collective interest) and that could be defended consistently with the worldview of the emerging empirical sciences. Thus he was a (metaphysical) **empirical naturalist,** one of the first, indeed, to view ethics itself as an empirical science. Ethics, he told us, is the science that theorizes "consequences from the passions of men" (L. IX.3). And so Hobbes confronted head-on the very problem that, as we saw in Chapter 3, any naturalist must face: how to account for normativity in a naturalistic framework—how to place value and oughtness in a world of facts.

Desire, Deliberation, and Value

In the 1630s, more than a decade before he wrote *Leviathan,* Hobbes became fascinated with scientific experiments concerning optics and with Galileo's theory of color. Galileo's theory was that, literally speaking, there are no colors in the world—at least, not as we experience them to be. There is such a thing as color experience, of course, and this experience has **objective purport.** We experience objects *as colored,* as having color properties that "really and truly exist" in the objects. But unlike shape and size, which are real properties of objects, the color properties we experience objects as having do not really exist. So far as "objective existence" goes, color words are "mere names for something which reside exclusively in our sensitive body."[2]

Look at a ripe tomato. It seems to be red, and its seeming to you to be red is your having an experience *as of* something really red. The redness seems a real property of the tomato, not any property of you or of the conditions in which you are viewing it. But, Galileo said, there is no such property. All there is in nature are the physical properties of the tomato that cause you to have certain sensations, the sensations that are as of something with the property red.

What does any of this have to do with ethics? By the time he wrote *Leviathan,* Hobbes had arrived at a theory of value that he modeled on the Galilean theory of color. He had come to believe that value judgment and experience involve a **projection** that is similar to what Galileo thought was involved in the case of color. The key to understanding value judgment, Hobbes believed, was to see its role in deliberation, desire, and action. Just as colors lack the objective existence we experience them as having, so also are there no values really existing in the world, although there inevitably seem to be whenever we have desires and are moved by them.

Hobbes had a mechanical picture of human action. As a materialist, he believed that everything that exists is but "matter in motion." Human behavior is no exception. It is bodily motion that is caused by other bodily motions. Hobbes was a determinist, but he didn't think that determinism entailed a lack of freedom. He didn't believe in free *will,* but then he thought that that idea was unintelligible anyway, a bit of "insignificant speech." It is people who are free, not wills. And people are free just in case no obstacles exist to their doing what they will (L.XXI).

Hobbes's theory of action is as follows. All actions result from desires or aversions. A desire is (literally) a motion in the body of the person who has it toward the desire's object. An aversion is the same motion "fromward" (L.VI.2). It's a hot day, and you want an iced tea. You have a desire for the tea, which is a motion in you (an inclination) toward drinking some tea. Suppose you are moved to get some tea, and you start to drink it. If, as you are drinking it, you maintain the same attitude toward the tea, you will like it. In Hobbes's terms, you will "love" it. If, however, it is not as you expected, you may "hate" it and be averse to continuing to drink it. You may experience some motion away from it.

Love and desire are the same psychological state, Hobbes said. We call this state desire when we take its object to be absent, and love when we take it to be present. And similarly for aversion and hate. You wanted the tea (before you had it), and now you love it (having it). Or now you hate it (having it) and are averse to continuing to drink it (in the next moment, which is not now present).

So desires and aversions are psychological (in reality, material) forces that move us toward and away from actions. Of course, things are not always so simple as a desire straightway giving rise to action. But that is just because we are simultaneously subject to different desires, which in turn is what leads us to deliberate about what to do. In fact, for Hobbes, the succession of desires and aversions is all that deliberation is. Deliberation is but desires and aversions "aris[ing] alternately" until something is done. And the agent's will is simply "the last appetite or aversion" (L.VI.49,53).

But how can this be? In Chapter 1, I said that deliberation necessarily involves value or normative judgments. The question an agent attempts to settle in deliberation is "What should I do?" ("What do I have most reason to do?"). How can a succession of desires amount to thinking about and determining reasons and values?

The key to understanding Hobbes's solution to this problem is to appreciate the analogy he makes between color experience and "value experience" (my term, not Hobbes's). All that is really going on when we undergo color experience are certain material motions in us that are caused by certain motions in the matter of the object and the medium. However, this is not all that *seems* to go on. When the motion takes place in us, we experience an "appearance" that is *as of* some color property in the object.

This appearance, we might say, has both a subject and an object. Its *object* is the color property that it appears to be of—say, the redness of the tomato. And Hobbes believed that its subject, what there really is that "makes an appearance," is a bodily motion.

Like the bodily motions that give rise to color appearances, so also do the motions of desire/love and aversion/hate give rise to their distinctive experiential states. And for ethics, Hobbes believed, it is these appearances that make all the difference. Hobbes called them "delight" and "trouble of mind," respectively (L.VI.9). When you desire iced tea on a hot day, you experience "delight" when you consider that possibility. Or when you contemplate passing the rest of the afternoon without the relief of a cool drink, you experience a "troubled mind."

The motions of desire/love and aversion/hate are the subjects of the appearances "delight" and "troubled mind," respectively. But what are their objects? What are these appearances *as of*? Here is Hobbes's answer: "Delight is the appearance, or sense, of *good;* and molestation or displeasure, the appearance, or sense, of *evil*" (L.VI.10; emphasis added). Desire and aversion, for Hobbes, are what get us thinking about ethics in the first place. To desire something is to see it as good, and to be averse to it is to see it as bad.

The foregoing explains why Hobbes said that "whatsoever is the object of any man's appetite or desire, that is it which he for his part calleth good: and the object of his hate and aversion, evil" (L.VI.7). You have a desire for iced tea. This is a motion in you, but it gives rise to an "appearance" that is as of a property in an object—namely, the value of drinking iced tea. You see that possibility as good. Or, alternatively, you have an aversion to the prospect of passing a thirsty afternoon, and that gives rise to an "appearance" *as of* the "evil" of that alternative.

But as with color appearances, Hobbes believed that there are in fact no properties in "the nature of the objects themselves" answering to our appearances of good and evil. All there are in the object are the material motions that, when they interact with our material nature, give rise to the motions toward and fromward in us that we call desire and aversion. Neither is it the case that we desire certain things *because* we think them good, or are averse to others *because* we think them bad. On the contrary, we see things as good and bad because of our desires and aversions. The experience of value is a projected effect of desire.

This argument calls to mind the **error theory** of ethical judgments. Ethical judgments purport to claim something objective, but, since there actually are no ethical properties answering to what ethical appearances seem to be of, they are always false. But other statements made by Hobbes point toward some version of noncognitivism rather than toward the error theory. "The language of desire and aversion," he wrote, "is *imperative, as do this, forbear that*" (L.VI.55). If we follow out the implications of this remark, we may conclude that the judgments one makes in desire or aversion—that something is good or bad, respectively—have no cognitive content and, hence, cannot be strictly either true *or* false. In the end, it makes little sense to ask whether Hobbes was really a noncognitivist or an error theorist. These distinctions were simply not available in Hobbes's time, and there is no reason to assume that Hobbes clearly saw the differences between these two metaethical alternatives.

If Hobbes was an error theorist, moreover, he certainly didn't think that his metaethics posed any obstacle to substantive normative ethical thought or that it dissolved the ethical problems we face. The reason is that Hobbes believed we face value questions as *deliberating agents*. What matters for ethics is the way things seem from the **agent's perspective**. That all our ethical judgments are, strictly speaking, mistaken no more undermines normative ethics than does the strict falsity of color judgments undermine art criticism and interior design.

Laws of Nature and Normativity

Hobbes defined a "law of nature" as "a precept or general rule, found out by reason, by which a man is forbidden to do that, which is destructive of his life, or taketh away the means of preserving the same; and to omit that, by which he thinketh it may be best preserved" (L.XIV.3). He then went on to list and explain some nineteen examples (including one requiring the keeping of covenants), adding in conclusion that these can all be summed up in the golden rule: "Do not that to another, which thou wouldest not have done to thyself" (L.XV.35). Finally, he commented that these "dictates of reason" are only "improperly" called laws. In actuality, they are "theorems concerning what conduceth to the conservation and defence" of a person (L.XV.41).

This distinction raises two large questions. One we shall deal with in the next chapter: How can Hobbes have thought that rules of morality, such as the golden rule and the requirement to keep promises, amount to "theorems" about what will promote self-preservation and self-interest? After all, didn't Hobbes reject the classical natural law theory's metaphysical identification of morality with self-interest? Didn't he think that conflicts of interests are what make political regimes, and forms of practical reasoning, in which individuals are not guided simply by their own interest, necessary in the first place? Indeed, he did. But as we shall see in the next chapter, he also thought that morality and politics are ultimately grounded in self-interest, nonetheless.

A prior problem arises, however, about how Hobbes could think that even propositions about what will promote self-preservation and self-interest amount to *normative* laws. A theorem about what conduces to our conservation and defense is still just a statement of fact, a true representation of how things happen to stand in the world. What, then, can give it authority or normative force? How can it amount to, or entail, a "dictate" by which one is "forbidden" to fail to do it?

Take a very simple case. Suppose you know that unless you take a particular medicine, you will die. In knowing this, you know a fact about the world. But how do you get from that fact to anything normative? What entitles you to conclude that you should take the medicine? Note that I am not asking you to doubt that you should take the medicine. I am sure we both think that if taking the medicine is necessary to continue a life you want to lead, you should take it. But isn't that because we both think that it would be good for you to continue to live? Or, perhaps, because we think that you have some reason to preserve your life? We appear to need some such normative premise to add to the premise that unless you take the medicine you will die in order to conclude that you should take the medicine. And where do we get that premise?

Now, Hobbes thought that everyone *already* accepts and, moreover, *can't help accepting* the additional normative premise that their continued living is good. It is simply an inescapable feature of the human condition, he thought, that everyone desires continued life and fears death, especially violent death. This feature is hard-wired into our material makeup. Moreover, as we have seen, Hobbes also thought that we are hard-wired to see what we desire as good and what we are averse to as bad. In inescapably desiring to preserve ourselves, therefore, we can't help but see our continued living as good. And in being averse to (violent) death, we unavoidably see that as bad.

This reasoning gives us the premise to add to what would otherwise be simply a fact about what is necessary in order for our lives to continue. We then have the following practical argument:

1. My continued living is good.
   (Or: I should continue to live.
   Or: Continue living!)
2. I will continue to live only if I X.
   Therefore,
3. Xing is good.
   (Or: I should X.
   Or: X!)

What gives laws of nature their normative force is that they all concern necessary means to an end we can't avoid having *together* with the fact that *in* having that end we cannot, as deliberating agents, avoid seeing it as good, as something we should accomplish.

It is important to appreciate the difference between this idea and another one with which it is easily (and frequently) confused. Hobbes is not saying that we should follow the laws of nature because, if we do so, it will get us something we want, even something we inescapably want. Compare the previous argument with this one:

1'. I desire to continue to live.

(Or: I desire, and can't help desiring, to continue to live.
Or: My end is to continue to live.)
2'. I will get what I desire (continuing to live), only if I X.
Therefore,
3'. 'Xing is good.
(Or: I should X.)

This argument faces the same problem we confronted when we asked what gives normative force to propositions about the things that promote self-preservation. Unlike (1), but like (2) and (2'), (1') is simply a statement about how things happen to stand in the world. To get from (1') and (2') to (3), we need to assume some further normative premise, such as that it is good to get what one desires, or that one should seek means to one's ends. But where would we get that premise?

And should Hobbes have thought that it is good to get what one desires? That all depends. Hobbes was committed to thinking that *in wanting* something one will see what would satisfy one's desire as good. But from this fact it does not follow that one will see desire-satisfaction as good. That is, one need not see, say, self-preservation as good *on account of* its satisfying one's desire. After all, we sometimes wish we didn't have the desires we do. Wishing this can give rise to another, **second-order desire** that our first-order desire not be satisfied. And just as in having the first-order desire, we will see its object as good; so, likewise, in having the second-order not to satisfy our first-order desire, we will see its (the second-order desire's) object as good also. We will see satisfying our first-order desire as bad.

A good example are habits or addictions we regret having. Suppose I have an annoying habit of cracking my knuckles every fifteen minutes or so. I may find myself beset with a desire for a good knuckle-cracking while at the same time desiring that I not satisfy that desire. In having the first desire, I see cracking my knuckles as good; in having the second, I see my not satisfying my desire to crack them as good. Not only am I not committed to thinking it good that my desires be satisfied, here I think that satisfying my desire would be bad.

So, although Hobbes relied on the fact that human beings desire self-preservation, it is not that he thought that that fact provides a reason *itself* for us to do what is necessary to preserve ourselves. The fact that one wants something is not a premise we appeal to in deliberative practical reasoning. (Or, more cautiously stated, if it is, that is because we then have another, second-order desire: the desire to satisfy our first-order desires, or to satisfy this first-order desire, or some such.) That we desire something (whether as a first-order or a second-order matter) is simply a fact about ourselves that can be fully registered from an observer's standpoint without any particular normative ethical import.

Hobbes's position was that *in having* desires we have normative ethical thoughts. We see alternatives as good. And if the desire is inescapable, as Hobbes believed the human desire for self-preservation to be, then we cannot help but see its object as good. This is what gives natural laws normative force for human beings. We are led to conclude that we should do as they say once we see their connection to self-preservation, because we unavoidably see self-preservation, and what is necessary for it, as good.

Hobbes's arguments in *Leviathan* are thus addressed to human agents who deliberate from the perspective provided by their desires and aversions, not from the fact that they have these desires. Ultimately, then, Hobbes's claims about political obligation and its basis in the moral obligation to keep promises are meant to inform the deliberations of his readers and all who hear of his arguments (like you). It is because he thought he could rely on the fact that you, like any human being, can't help desiring to stay alive, and therefore must see your continued living as good, that he thought that if he could convince you that certain policies and actions are necessary for your peaceful survival, he could also convince you that you *should* undertake those policies and actions.

11

HOBBES II

In Chapter 10, we saw how Hobbes attempted to solve the problem of normativity that confronts any **metaphysical naturalist:** What place is there for value in a world of fact? Unlike that of the **ethical naturalist,** Hobbes's solution was not to identify value with aspects of nature that are empirically discoverable. It is only as agents having desires that we attribute value. Strictly speaking, then, the value we attribute does not consist in anything we might discover about what we attribute it to (nor in anything about our desires).

But if empirical investigation cannot ground the fundamental values that drive ethical thought and discourse, that doesn't mean that ethics is not in large measure an empirical subject. On the contrary, Hobbes believed that the most interesting and controversial ethical questions concern not fundamental values but empirical issues about how these are best achieved.

The value of a peaceful life, free of the fear of violent death, is a matter of consensus. No one needs to be convinced that his own peace and safety are valuable. What people disagree about are the means of realizing this good. If empirical investigation can establish that certain universal policies and actions are necessary to achieve peaceful living, however, this will enable human agents to draw the ethical conclusion that they should pursue these policies and actions.

The Problem of Collective Action

But what do strategies that might promote self-preservation have to do with morality? Why think that the moral obligation to keep promises and to abide by the golden rule somehow consist in anything about promoting this end?

We can begin to see the point of these questions *and* how Hobbes proposed to deal with them by considering Hobbes's analysis of the state of nature. By the logic of the argument to this point, every agent is logically committed to judging that she should do what is necessary to preserve her own life. But whereas this makes apparent good sense for each, it is also true that if every agent follows this strategy, and maximizes the chances of her own individual survival, the collective result will be worse for each, a "war of all against all." In Hobbes's view, individuals in a state of nature are faced with what contemporary theorists call a **collective action problem.** If each does what is best for herself, the collective result is worse for all.

A simple version of a collective action problem is the game theory situation known as "prisoner's dilemma." Suppose that two individuals are jailed on suspicion of robbery and that the district attorney approaches each with the following proposition:

> I don't have enough evidence to convict you or your partner of robbery, but I can convict you both of breaking and entering, which carries a sentence of one year. However, if you will confess to robbery and give evidence against your partner, then, if (s)he doesn't confess, you will go free without penalty. If (s)he also confesses, you will both get five years. And if you do not confess, and your partner does, then you will get twenty years and she will go free.

In addition, suppose that no communication is possible between the two prisoners, that each cares only about doing the least time, and, in particular, that neither cares about what happens to the other except insofar as it affects his or her own sentence. What should each do?

The structure of this situation can be illustrated with the following table, which displays the alternative choices C (confess) and NC (not confess) of prisoner A along the left side and of prisoner B along the top. Each pair of choices (one by A, one by B) determines an outcome (a,b), where a is the rank of A's outcome in A's preferential ordering and b is the rank of B's outcome in B's preferential ordering. Thus $(1,4)$ is A's best and B's worst outcome, $(4,1)$ is the reverse, $(2,2)$ is both A's and B's second-best outcome, and $(3,3)$ is next to worst for both.

		B	
		C	NC
	C	(3,3)	(1,4)
A			
	NC	(4,1)	(2,2)

What should A do? Suppose that what B does will not be affected by what A does. B will either confess or not, regardless. If that is so, then it seems A should confess, since *whatever* B does, A will do better if he confesses. If B confesses, then A will get his third- as opposed to his fourth-best outcome by confessing. And if B doesn't confess, then A will get his first- as opposed to his second-best outcome by confessing. So A should confess. A will do better by confessing, whatever B does.

But B's situation is exactly analogous to A's, so any reasons for A to confess apply equally to B. So if A would do best to confess, then so would B. Now you can see why this is called a collective action *problem*. A's and B's actions, each of which is likeliest to achieve the best outcome taken individually, when taken together yield an outcome that is worse for each. If both prisoners do what would be best for him or her, given the actions of the other, they will both confess. But that yields an outcome (3,3) that is worse for both than another outcome they could have achieved. In other words, if both do not confess, the result would be (2,2) rather than (3,3).

Roughly speaking, Hobbes believed that a state of nature is a situation in which people face prisoner's dilemmas with many others in choosing between aggressive and nonaggressive conduct. What makes a situation a prisoner's dilemma, in general, is a certain structure of conflicting interests—for example, that each person's most preferred outcome is the other's least preferred. Hobbes believed that there are various seeds of such conflict in the state of nature. For one thing, there is competition over the goods of nature necessary to ensure that a person in uncertain circumstances has the power to continue to satisfy his desires into the future. For another, some of the things people desire, like status and prestige, necessarily cannot be shared. There is no way, for instance, to expand the stock of "recognition" jointly to satisfy two people, each of whom wants more recognition than the other. For these and other reasons, Hobbes believed that it is near enough true that the result of one person's "invad[ing] for gain" when another does not is that the victor gets his favorite result and the loser suffers her worst. This situation yields the same (1,4), (4,1) pattern as that seen in the southwest and northeast corners of the prisoner's dilemma table. Additionally, if each holds his or her fire, the result is (2,2), a peaceful compromise, and if each invades, the result is (3,3), a "war of all against all." These are analogous to the situations in which both prisoners confess and both don't confess, respectively—as depicted in the southeast and northwest corners of the prisoner's dilemma table. If, consequently, we set C = aggress and NC = not aggress, we can generate a table for a two-person "state of nature game" from that for the prisoner's dilemma.

Assuming once more that the choices of each person are independent of those of the other (we won't worry that this scenario is unrealistic), we again have the same collective action problem. For each, aggression is the action that is individually best, since each thereby does better, whatever the other does. If the other aggresses, then one avoids being vanquished, albeit at the cost of continued war. And if the other is not aggressive, then one can get the spoils of victory rather than acquiescing in compromise. Apparently, therefore, aggression is individually best for each. But as in the prisoner's dilemma, if both do what is individually best, the collective result is worse for both. The two land themselves in a "war of all against all," which is worse for both than the peaceful compromise that would have resulted from joint nonaggression.

What If Everyone Did That?

There are various reasons why one might want to take issue with the use of prisoner's dilemma as an analysis of a state of nature (or even as an interpretation of Hobbes). But our interest is less in Hobbes's political philosophy than in his underlying view of morality, so we can largely ignore these reasons. What will matter for us is Hobbes's employment of the moral obligation to keep promises and the way he attempts to ground the moral 'ought' in the practical reasoning of a deliberating agent.

Before that, however, we would do well to notice that many questions of morality, especially those concerning fairness, are centered in problems of collective action. Take, for example, the state of nature as we've described it. Isn't it natural to think something like the following: If everyone would be better off if we all just restrained our aggressiveness, then why isn't it simply wrong to be aggressive? Perhaps it is, but might that not also depend on whether others are restraining themselves? Or, at least, on whether they are willing to do so? If others are not, then there is no role that one can play in securing collective benefit by restraining oneself. In this case, fairness to others apparently does not require self-restraint, since fairness requires only that one do one's *share*. Any obligation to act is conditional on the comparable good-faith efforts of others.

But what if others do their share? In that case, fairness does require doing one's share as well. It is unfair to take advantage of the sacrifices of others for mutual advantage and not do one's share. As we will see, Hobbes was in basic agreement with this idea, but he was not willing to take for granted that we ought to be fair. He believed that some explanation is needed of why this is so, an explanation that could be convincing from the perspective of a deliberating agent.

But again, notice how deeply this idea and the associated notion of a collective action problem runs throughout our common life and thought about morality. People are frequently prepared to accept sacrifices and burdens themselves because they know that only if everyone does so can many outcomes they highly value be achieved: a clean environment, uncluttered and safe streets, civil and honest conversation, and so on, not to mention the basic trust that provides the glue for social life. They know that if everyone simply pursued his or her own interests without concern for how things would be "if everyone did that," the world would be a much poorer place than it is. And they take this fact as giving them reason—a moral reason—not to act this way themselves.

Care is needed to see the precise point here. The idea is not just that people are prepared to sacrifice their other interests when they have weightier interests in such things as a clean environment and a peaceful society that would be furthered by their own action. When this is the situation, we don't have a collective action problem so much as a problem of balancing short-term versus long-term or narrower versus broader concerns within an agent's self-interest and furthering values about which the agent actually cares more over the longer term, even if that calls for sacrificing some of her other more pressing present interests. Collective action problems occur when collective harm results from individuals' unrestricted pursuit of even their broader and longer-term interests. Fairness may require that they restrain themselves in such situations, even if their doing so on these occasions is not necessary to promote the larger interests that are furthered by the cooperative collective scheme.

Consider the example of petty income-tax fraud (such as not declaring tips from a summer job waiting tables). For many people, it may be in their interest to make fraudulent claims on their tax returns, so long as these do not exceed a certain magnitude. The chances of being caught may be sufficiently low, the possible penalties sufficiently insignificant, and the harms to others and to mutual trust sufficiently uncertain that fraud of this order may be best from the individual's self-interested point of view, *even when* the person's interests in public welfare, mutual trust, and so on, are figured in. In certain cases, the difference made by such petty fraud may not be large enough to offset the losses to the individual of forgoing it. Yet it may nonetheless be true that if everyone were to commit tax fraud in precisely this kind of case, the collective result would be substantially worse for all.

When this is true—when, that is, a person would want to avoid the results of collective fraud—and when others forgo fraud on the condition that their doing so will be reciprocated, fairness requires doing so oneself as well. And it does so no less in the case where "doing one's share" involves some sacrifice, even a sacrifice reckoned on a full accounting of the interests one has in the valuable ends that fair cooperative schemes promote.

Fairness, Natural Law, and Political Authority

The idea of fairness—that it is wrong to take advantage of others' sacrifices for mutual benefit when one is not prepared to sacrifice oneself—is very close to the version of the golden rule with which Hobbes summarized the "laws of nature": "Do not that to another, which thou wouldest not have done to thyself." What this means is not that one shouldn't act toward others in ways that may *cause* them to treat one as one "wouldest not have." Rather, it means that one should not act toward others in ways one would not *have* them act toward one, whether or not it will cause them to act in those ways. However, Hobbes also said that this summary of the laws (and the laws it summarizes) obligate to action only on the condition that others actually follow them as well. The person who follows these laws when others do not "make[s] himself a prey to others, and procure[s] his own ruin, contrary to the ground of all laws of nature" (L.XV.36).

This is why, Hobbes believed, there can be no general moral obligation of fairness to restrain aggression in a state of nature. Without a political authority with sovereign power, people simply lack the security of knowing that others will restrain themselves. And without this security they lack any reason of fairness to engage in self-restraint themselves. Only when a political authority exists with sufficient power to compel those who are not fair-minded will those who are prepared to restrain themselves so long as others do have adequate reason to do so.

But how can political authority be established? What can make it the case that people ought to obey the sovereign? The considerations in the last paragraph might lead one to think that this problem can be solved easily enough by the sovereign's having power to compel obedience. But thinking that only pushes the problem back a step. What can make it the case that such sovereign power exists? That also depends on the willingness of others to obey the sovereign, if only those who enforce his penalties—for example, his police.

Hobbes proposed that a sovereign can acquire the requisite power and authority through a mutual covenant in which all effectively promise not to oppose him and authorize him to act on their behalf. This means, then, that *both* the (political) obligation to obey the sovereign and the moral obligations involved in all the laws of nature summarized in the golden rule depend upon the obligation to keep covenants. People are obligated to obey the sovereign only because they have promised to do so and because they are obligated to keep their promises. Additionally, they are obligated by fairness to follow the other laws of nature, and to not act toward others as they would not have others act toward them, only on the condition that others will act similarly. And others will act similarly only if sovereign authority exists. Finally, since that will be so only if people are obligated to keep their promises, it follows that the obligations summarized in the golden rule will be binding only if there is an obligation to keep covenants.

Why Should We Keep Promises?
Hobbes's Reply to the Fool

But what grounds the obligation to keep promises? What makes it the case that "men should keep their covenants made?" Here we must link up Hobbes's account of normativity and value judgment, sketched in Chapter 10, with the question of whether to keep promises. And an obvious problem arises. The former account proceeds in terms of an agent's reasoning from ends to means—most prominently, from the end of self-preservation. But there is no guarantee that keeping any particular covenant will be necessary for self-preservation. On the contrary, the agent's own ends (specifically, self-preservation) may conflict with keeping any particular covenant. How, then, could Hobbes consistently think that we should keep a covenant even when we appear to lack adequate reason to do so that can be based in self-interest?

In *Leviathan*, Hobbes put this precise challenge in the mouth of a character he calls "the fool," who says "in his heart, there is no such thing as justice" (L.XV.4). Justice, for Hobbes, is a matter of keeping covenants (L.XV.2). So in denying the existence of justice, the fool is denying any obligation to keep covenants. The fool's positive position is that a person should do only what will promote her preservation and interest, and, accordingly, that "to make, or not make; keep, or not keep covenants, was not against reason, when it conduced to one's benefit" (L.XV.4).

When we recall Hobbes's account of normativity and normative judgment as grounded in an agent's practical reasoning from ends to means, we may well wonder why the fool's position is not Hobbes's own. All human agents judge their ends to be good. So when someone views some action or policy as necessary to some end, she naturally sees the action or policy as one she should pursue. It seems to follow that anyone would also naturally regard any reason she has to make or keep a promise as being conditional on whether making or keeping the promise will "conduce to" her livelihood or benefit, just as the fool says.

But Hobbes rejected this position, and it is important to see why. To understand his reasoning, we must first appreciate the unique and pervasive role that covenants play in the state of nature, as Hobbes saw it. We already know part of the story. It is only through a mutual covenant establishing a sovereign that individuals can escape from a state of perpetual war. But Hobbes also believed that the general need for covenants in the state of nature is significantly more pervasive than this *and* that it would have to be in order for a mutual covenant establishing political sovereignty even to be possible.

No person can expect to survive in a state of nature by going it alone. People are too equal in power. No individual is completely invulnerable to the power of others, so no person can expect to keep himself in even relative safety through his own devices. As Hobbes put it, "There is no man who can hope by his own strength, or wit, to defend himself from destruction, without the help of confederates; where every one expects the same defence by the confederation, that any one else does" (L.XV.5). But such confederacies can come into existence only through covenants. Each member must agree to do his share in defending other members in exchange for their help in defending him. Covenants are therefore necessary not only to the lasting escape from a state of war through the establishing of a sovereign, but also to whatever temporary defense and security a person can secure through membership in an association united for mutual defense while in the state of nature. And since covenants are necessary even for temporary safety, it follows that preserving one's ability to make covenants is absolutely crucial to self-preservation.

Now, any covenant for mutual defense depends upon the participants being able to expect that those with whom they contract will keep it or, at least, on their having no expectation that they won't or no reasonable doubt that they will. Until a sovereign is established who can enforce them, mutual promises become void on "any reasonable suspicion" that one party will not keep her part of the bargain (L.XIV.18). In order for a covenant to be possible, therefore, the potential participants must have no justified doubts about the willingness of the others to do what they have promised to do. This means that the reputation of trustworthiness is among the most precious resources that any individual can have in the state of nature. And it means as well that individuals have substantial incentives to discover whether others actually are trustworthy.

To be of value, covenants for mutual defense must last for some time. On any given occasion, therefore, the question of whether to keep such a covenant will be significantly affected by the facts that one will want continued acceptance as a member and that others' doing so may substantially depend on whether one keeps the covenant on this occasion. In this critically important kind of case, then, we have an example of what game theorists call an "iterated" rather than a "one-shot" prisoner's dilemma. An iterated prisoner's dilemma is not a collective action problem of the same kind as the one-shot version. When a prisoner's dilemma is repeated indefinitely between the same two individuals, as is likely with mutual defense associations, each will do better collectively *and* individually by cooperating rather than competing. Here the outcomes are actually different from those in the one-shot version, since even if each individual's present choices are independent of others', others' future choices will not be independent of the individuals' present choices. Each has a substantial incentive to keep his or her promises on this occasion, to ensure that the mutually beneficial arrangement will continue.

For these kinds of reasons, we might expect Hobbes to argue that breaking covenants can never be to a person's overall benefit. There may appear to be cases when this would be beneficial, but only when we erroneously discount further effects on reputation and others' willingness to enter into covenants with us in the future. Taking full account of the risks *and* costs of reduced trust shows that such benefit can never really be realized.

This reply would meet the fool's challenge on its own terms. It would grant its premise, yet deny its conclusion. But Hobbes did not make this reply, and we can see why he avoided it. However precious trust and reputation may be, it seems implausible to suppose that keeping covenants is always in a person's interest. Surely there are *some* circumstances in which breaking a covenant would do insufficient harm to outweigh the benefits, even when all costs are fully accounted for. And maybe such circumstances are not even all that infrequent. After all, not every covenant will go on indefinitely with the same individuals. And even in cases where they do, compliance can't always be monitored.

In any event, Hobbes did not deny the fool's premise that breaking covenants may sometimes actually be in a person's interest. What he denies is that it is ever *wise* to break a covenant, even in a state of nature, unless the contract has been voided by reasonable suspicion of the other's defaulting. Hobbes's reason was that even if there are cases where breaking a covenant might be beneficial, one can never *know* for sure that one is in such a situation, and the risks and costs are such that the wisest *policy* is always to keep a covenant rather than taking a chance.

There are two important points here. One is that the wisdom of a choice does not depend on its *actual* outcome. If someone successfully plays Russian roulette to win a bet of twenty dollars, the fact that he ends up better off does not mean that his action was "reasonably or wisely done" (L.XV.5). At the very least, it matters which act the person would reasonably believe likeliest to have the best outcome on the evidence available to him.

But there are some cases where it may not even make sense to act on one's most reasonable estimate of the best outcome. The quality of one's evidence may be poor, or even pretty good, but not good enough to warrant taking a chance. To see this, consider from your *current* perspective what you would want yourself to do in a hypothetical situation in which someone offers you ten thousand dollars to play Russian roulette. Suppose that you will be permitted to decide whether to pull the trigger or not after having rotated the chamber, and suppose also that you will then be very confident that you can recognize whether the bullet is in the chamber that has come up. (For example, suppose that you will be permitted to see it put in a chamber with a recognizable mark.) In this hypothetical situation, you twirl the chamber and believe that the chances are only one in a million that the chamber with the bullet has come up and, therefore, that if you merely put the gun to your head and pull the trigger, you have a .99999 chance of being ten thousand dollars richer and only a .000001 chance of losing your life. As decision theorists will point out, under these circumstances the "expected value" of pulling the trigger is positive unless you value your life at ten billion dollars or more. Would this commit you to thinking, from your current perspective, that it is reasonable or wise for you to pull the trigger in the hypothetical situation? Would you want yourself to? Many people would not. Even if you are prepared to take risks of the same magnitude when you have no reasonable alternative to doing so, you may believe that, here, the risk just isn't worth taking.

This is the second point: Hobbes believed that breaking a covenant is like playing Russian roulette in that it is something that just doesn't make sense to do even if it is likeliest to have the best outcome in an individual case. The *policy* or *rule* of always keeping covenants is a better means, *in general*, to any human agent's self-interest and self-preservation than is the policy of determining whether to keep covenants on a case-by-case basis according to whether doing so is likeliest in that instance to have the best outcome.

The policy of always keeping covenants was Hobbes's final answer to the fool, thereby connecting up his normative thesis that a person should not break contracts with his account of normative judgment. By virtue of inescapably desiring self-preservation, any human agent regards his interests and continued living as good. For a variety of reasons, the *general* rule or policy of always keeping covenants is a more effective means to these ends than is determining whether to do as one has promised on a case-by-case basis. By appreciating this, therefore, any human agent has reason to agree that she should follow the general policy or rule of keeping her covenants. And if she should follow this general policy or rule, Hobbes apparently assumed, then she should follow it even on those occasions when she thinks, even reasonably, that she would do better by breaking her covenants.

Summary: Hobbes's Theory of Morality and Moral Obligation

For Hobbes, morality is a set of rules, the general following of which solves collective action problems. That is why he said that the laws of nature (morality) can be summed up in the idea that we should not do to others what we would not have them do to us. For morality to be in "force," however, there must be something that can guarantee that others are prepared to do their fair share in the cooperative (moral) solution to problems of collective action. Hobbes believed that, ultimately, it requires a sovereign with the authority and power to compel those who are not fair-minded to give those who *are* adequate reason to do their share.

When, however, there is some reasonable confidence that others are doing their share in the collective solution, then one should oneself. But why? Ultimately, Hobbes agreed with the fool that the mere fact that a rule is collectively beneficial is not a justification in itself for one to follow it. Rather, to convince a deliberating agent, any justification must be relevant to what *the agent* values him- or herself. And this, Hobbes agrees with the fool, ultimately requires reference to what will promote the *agent's own* preservation or interest.

For Hobbes, what brings these two ends together—the individual agent's good and the collective good—is *mutual agreement*. We cannot survive without the cooperation of others, and we cannot have that without being prepared to cooperate with them. In the end, then, morality is a system of *reciprocity*, in which all are prepared to do their share so long as others are. But even here there is a difference between the sort of reciprocity that morality (the golden rule) requires and the sort that must exist for morality to really be binding on agents, in Hobbes's view. Morality dictates that we should not do what we would not have others do, regardless of whether this will cause them to show such restraint. To put it differently, morality says that fairness is intrinsically valuable or required, and not just because it causes others to be fair.

Now Hobbes agreed that, in the final analysis, it makes sense to *regard* moral claims this way. However, he also thought that our doing so is ultimately justified by the fact that any person's (individually) so regarding them serves his or her interests. We might reconcile these two points by saying that, for Hobbes, morality consists in rules that, if *everyone* follows, *everyone* benefits from; but what makes it the case that any particular agent *should* follow moral rules is that *his* following them serves *his* own interests.

The foregoing exemplifies one thing that is meant by **externalism** in ethics: What makes it the case that a moral requirement is normatively binding, something an agent really ought to follow, is external to what grounds the moral requirement in the first place. For Hobbes, moral rules are based on *collective* interest, but what makes them normatively binding is the *agent's own* interest.

Conclusion and Remaining Issues

This conception of morality is a philosophically powerful and influential one. Its great virtue is that it aims to show how morality can be *normative* for human agents (in normal circumstances) in a way that is consistent with metaphysical naturalism. Without problematic metaphysical or epistemological assumptions, Hobbes was able to go a long way toward showing that there are universal rules or "laws" by which people should live.

Should we accept Hobbes's theories? In closing, let me mention two potential obstacles to doing so. One problem is internal to Hobbes's own project. Suppose we grant that a person will do better, in general, by following the rule or policy of keeping covenants, and by following the other moral rules when there is established political authority. Why does such a rationale show that, on any particular occasion, an agent should do what this general rule or policy dictates?

Look at it from your perspective as a deliberating human agent. You value self-preservation. And your doing so gives you a reason to follow the general policy. But here is a case where the general policy seems to give the wrong answer. It is clear to you, on this occasion, that you will do significantly better by all you value if you depart from the best general policy. Since the general policy is sensible to follow only because it promotes what you value, and since, on this occasion, what you value is clearly better promoted by departing from it, why doesn't it make sense to depart from it? This problem is hardly crippling, as the Russian roulette example shows. But it can seem troubling nonetheless.

The other problem is external to Hobbes's line of thought—namely, whether ultimately basing morality on self-interest captures the way in which, as we ordinarily think, *normativity* is *intrinsic* to morality. For an externalist like Hobbes, what makes something a dictate of *morality* is one thing and what makes it normatively binding on us (something we ought to follow) is another. When we view things from within the perspective of moral thought, however, does it really seem that the only reason we should do what morality requires is that, ultimately, it will pay us? On the contrary, does it not seem that something's being wrong is *itself* reason enough? Does it not seem, in other words, that internalism rather than externalism is true?

To return to our original example from Chapter 1: When you are outraged by the torture of innocents, do you really think that the reason people ought not to torture is that ultimately *they* will be worse off if they do? To be sure, Hobbes thought he could explain the sense we may have that this is not so, since it is for our benefit so to regard these rules in general. But isn't it a worry that this interpretation involves a kind of divided thinking? What we think from within the moral perspective seems directly at odds with the externalist justification Hobbes provides.

Suggested Reading

Darwall, Stephen. *The British Moralists and the Internal 'Ought': 1640–1740*, Chapter 3. Cambridge: Cambridge University Press, 1995.

Gauthier, David. *The Logic of Leviathan*. Oxford: Clarendon Press, 1979.

_____. "Thomas Hobbes: Moral Theorist." *Journal of Philosophy* 76 (1979): 547–559.

Hampton, Jean. *Hobbes and the Social Contract Tradition*. Cambridge: Cambridge University Press, 1986.

Hobbes, Thomas. *Leviathan* (1651). Edwin Curley, ed. Indianapolis, Ind.: Hackett Publishing Company, 1994.

Kavka, Gregory S. *Hobbesian Moral and Political Theory*. Princeton, N.J.: Princeton University Press, 1986.

Sorrell, Tom, ed. *The Cambridge Companion to Hobbes*. Cambridge: Cambridge University Press, 1996.

12

MILL I

Prelude: Ethical Thought and Social Context

Any individual's encounter with issues of philosophical ethics inevitably takes place within a specific historical context. To present-day readers, Hobbes's extreme caution about breaking covenants, together with his dire descriptions of the human condition outside of political society and his justification of absolute sovereignty, may seem a curious mix. But when we view them from Hobbes's seventeenth-century perspective, in the midst of an English Civil War in which "the world turned upside down," they are easier to understand, if not to accept.

Two centuries passed by the time John Stuart Mill (1806–1873) wrote *Utilitarianism* (1861) in the relatively staid setting of Victorian England. As we shall see, there were specific social (and personal) preoccupations that drove his thinking also. But before we begin to see what these were, we would do well to reflect a bit on the dynamic tension between philosophical/ethical thought and its roots in a particular historical context.

Any thinker—whether Hobbes, Mill, you, or I—cannot help but think about ethical and philosophical questions from where he or she is—an individual human being in particular social and personal circumstances. But, by the same token, what we are trying to think *about* from these different perspectives—the *object* of our thoughts—is something that is apparently universal and context-invariant. When you wonder what value is, you are not asking a question about your life and circumstances in particular, or about contemporary American society, or even, perhaps, about the *human* condition. Similarly, when you ask questions regarding normative ethics, such as what can justify breaking a promise, your question transcends your own social context. You are not simply asking what your society thinks on this matter. At its most basic level, your question is not directly about *your* society at all.

Your thinking about these transcendent, universal questions is likely, of course, to reflect your distinctive social and personal perspective. But since the questions are universal, if you come to believe that your answers to them depend on idiosyncrasies of your context, you will have some reason for doubting those answers, or, at least, for doubting your reasons for holding them. An important part of thinking through fundamental questions of philosophical ethics, therefore, is getting critical distance on your ideas' sources in your own personal and social context, a point that is stressed in Nietzsche's "genealogy" of morals and in feminist critiques of the role of gender in ethical thought (see Chapters 16 and 19, respectively). The point is not that philosophical and ethical thought must somehow float free of context. That is impossible. But it can attempt, self-consciously, to correct for the effects of a particular context.

Mill's Project

This sets the stage for our exploration of Mill's project in *Utilitarianism:* to discover and defend a principled basis for moral and political *reform*. Like his predecessor, the founder of utilitarianism, Jeremy Bentham (1748–1832), Mill believed that conservative appeals to intuitive, "common-sense" judgments and feelings to justify established practices and institutions were both self-serving and philosophically suspect. All too frequently, he thought, morally objectionable practices invalidly claim support from feelings and judgments that result from those very practices. As an example, consider the treatment of women in Victorian England, about which Mill wrote eloquently in *The Subjection of Women* (1869). Social practices that subject women to domination and control by men cannot be justified by the statement that this seems only natural and appropriate, if its seeming so is a product of those same social practices.

Like Hobbes and Bentham, Mill believed that controversial ethical questions can be settled only by empirical investigation. In fact, he went farther than Hobbes, since he was an **ethical naturalist** as well as a **metaphysical naturalist**. Whereas Hobbes believed that only questions of means can be settled empirically, Mill maintained that questions of ends can also. Mill believed that all ethical facts concern aspects of nature that are open to empirical investigation. And he argued on empirical grounds that everything that is good is some form of pleasure. This assertion provided the foundation for his **utilitarianism**. All questions of morality, he argued, ultimately depend on what will create the greatest pleasure for all.

We should keep Mill's opponents in mind as we consider his ideas. Despite its universal aim, ethical and philosophical thought is no less typically addressed to particular conversants than it is located in a particular context—especially when its goal, like Mill's, is to convince others of reform.

Mill saw his philosophical opponents as uncritical **intuitionists,** whether rationalist or not, who defended moral common sense as reflecting an objective ethical reality. They believed that intuitive ethical judgments function like observations in providing evidence for ethical facts. Mill was skeptical of this position on epistemological and metaphysical grounds. And he was worried as well that those who put it forward did so to support conservative practices in which they had a vested interest.

A "Criterion of Right and Wrong"

Mill began *Utilitarianism* with a declaration. Little, he said, is "more significant of the backward state in which speculation on the most important subjects still lingers" than the lack of progress in establishing a "criterion of right and wrong" (U.I.1).[1] Even his intuitionist opponents should grant the need for universal moral principles, he argued, since even they think that ethical judgment is never simply a matter of direct perception of particulars (U.I.3).

I made this point in Chapter 1, where I expressed it metaphysically by saying that ethical properties are never had "barely." Compare the difference between judging that something is yellow and judging that something is morally wrong. If a particular action is wrong, then it must have features that make it wrong. We are not always able to say what these features are, or even what we think they are; but when we judge that something has an ethical property, we are nonetheless committed to thinking that it has some properties that are *reasons for* the ethical property, that are right- or wrong-*making,* good- or bad-making. With a property like yellowness, there is nothing like this. We don't have to assess a thing's other properties to see whether it amounts to something that is yellow or not. It's enough that it looks yellow (to normal observers in standard conditions).

However, judging some particular action to be wrong does commit one to its having wrong-making properties—properties that other particular actions could have and that would tend to make them wrong also. And this commits one to a universal principle: Any action with such-and-such properties would be wrong—at least, other things being equal. If, for example, I think it is wrong not to claim on my income tax the tips I made while waiting tables last summer, then I must think that this would also be true of any other relevantly similar action. That is why we say such things in ethical discussion as "but that's no different than. . . ."

So anyone, whether intuitionist or utilitarian, must grant the need for universal principles. Intuitionists sometimes acknowledge this need, although they rarely do more than list principles. But they should be able to do more, Mill argued. They should be able to systematize their principles.

It is no good simply to list principles, since this leaves entirely unclear what to do when principles conflict. For example, suppose that you think that it is wrong to lie, other things being equal, but also that it is wrong to cause harm. What should be done, then, in a case where not lying would cause harm? Suppose you think that in *this* case, all things considered, a person should tell the truth. Does this not commit you to some further universal principle in addition to the two universal principles that telling the truth and causing harm are, respectively, right and wrong, other things being equal? Must you not think this particular case is *of a kind* in which one should tell the truth even though it will cause harm?

Mill argued that such a case does commit you to a further universal principle. For the ethical property you attribute when you say that this action would be right, all things considered, can also not be had "barely." If, on balance, it is right to tell the truth in this particular case, that must be because it is right to do so in *this kind of case*. So you are committed to holding a further universal principle. Maybe you think that the truth should always be told, regardless of the harm. Or maybe you think that the principle has to do with the kind of truth involved and/or the kind of harm. Whatever it is, you are committed to holding some universal principle or norm that explains what, on balance, a person should do when issues of truthtelling and harm are involved in cases of this kind.

This reasoning leaves the intuitionist with an even longer list of principles. And it raises (indeed, exacerbates) an obvious problem. What explains the list? What explains what is on it and what is not? Even in science we are dissatisfied if we do not have simplifying, unifying explanations, but Mill thinks that the problem is even worse in ethics. In science, "particular truths precede general theory" (U.I.2). The ultimate arbiters of scientific theory are particular natural facts. Nature just is however complex it actually is, and the adequacy of scientific theories can be tested only in terms of our best estimate of that complexity. Although we are constantly looking for reasons why things are as they are, at some point we just have to accept that "that's the way things are" and end the search for reasons.

Mill believed that the situation is the reverse in ethics. In ethics, general theory precedes particular truths. We can glimpse why Mill might have thought so by returning to the question of why ethical properties cannot be had "barely." As we noted, a particular object may simply be yellow. Of course, there is likely to be some explanation of why it is, but the existence of this explanation is no part of the very idea that it is yellow. It is no part of the property of yellowness itself that something has this property only if there is some reason for its having it. But this is precisely what *is* true with ethical properties. Something can have an ethical property—be good or right, bad or wrong—only if there is some reason why it does. This means that the holding of some universal principle or "general theory" is built into the very having of an ethical property. To judge any particular ethical fact is, implicitly, to judge some general theory or other to be true.

Strictly speaking, intuitionists need not deny any of this, since they can say that the general theory may be very complex nonetheless. But such reasoning does seem to put pressure on the idea that moral truth, however complex it is, can adequately be portrayed by a list of principles. If it is part of the very idea of ethical properties that there must be reasons that ground them, is it plausible to believe that there could simply be a list of moral principles, with no reasons grounding them?

Recall (from Chapter 1) Locke's dictum that no "moral rule" can "be proposed, whereof a man may not justly demand a reason." Mill, of course, agreed. And he agreed also with the further controversial assumption lying behind Locke's commonplace—namely, that the only thing that can suitably ground moral rules is their serving some further *end*: "Rules of action . . . must take their whole character and color from the end to which they are subservient" (U.I.2). This is a very important assumption. Even if ethics must seek unifying explanations, it is not clear why these must be based on a unifying end. Still, Mill had this going for him: A common end would certainly provide a unifying explanation for moral rules, if one is required, as it seems to be.

Nonmoral Good and Hedonism

Mill believed that the end that gives moral rules their "character and color" is the greatest pleasure or happiness of all. And that is because he accepted three other theses:

(1) Morality, by its very nature, is concerned with what is good from the perspective of the moral community.
(2) What is good from the perspective of the moral community is the greatest amount of what is good to the individuals comprising it.
(3) What is good to any individual is that person's pleasure or happiness.

Each of these claims is important for Mill, and each is controversial. If they are granted, however, they apparently yield Mill's conclusion that morality is concerned with promoting the greatest happiness of all. From (2) and (3), in other words, we can derive that what is good from the perspective of the moral community is the greatest amount of overall happiness. And when we combine the latter with (1), we find that morality is essentially concerned with maximizing overall happiness.

For Mill, (1) functions as a metaethical premise about what morality is. (We shall consider it in the next chapter.) And (2) relates a kind of value we can call **moral goodness** (what is good from the moral point of view) with what we can call **nonmoral goodness** (what is good to individuals). Even if there were no such thing as morality, there would still be good and bad in the world, since things would still be good or bad to or for individual persons (and other sentient beings). Hence the term 'nonmoral' goodness or value.

"The utilitarian doctrine," Mill wrote, "is that happiness is desirable, and the only thing desirable, as an end; all other things being only desirable as means to that end" (U.IV.2). And happiness, as Mill understood it, is simply "pleasure and the absence of pain" (U.II.2). Only pleasure and the absence of pain are *intrinsically* desirable (desirable in themselves), therefore. And something is *extrinsically* desirable only if it will lead to one of these.

This analysis cuts across the distinction between moral and nonmoral value. We get closer to Mill's idea if we say that, from any individual's point of view, the only thing that is desirable as an end is *his or her own pleasure,* and that, from the moral point of view, only the pleasure or happiness of all is intrinsically desirable. The only intrinsic nonmoral value (for an individual) is that individual's pleasure, and the only intrinsic moral value is the pleasure of all. This means that moral value is constructed out of nonmoral value. What is good from the moral point of view is the greatest amount of nonmoral value (considering all individuals).

Hedonism is what we can call the claim that the only intrinsic nonmoral value is (the agent's own) pleasure or lack of pain. Because moral value is, for Mill, composed of (everyone's) nonmoral value, hedonism about nonmoral value ultimately yields a utilitarian theory of morality. (More about this in the next chapter.)

Hedonism is a claim of normative ethics. Only pleasure, it dictates, is intrinsically worth desiring or pursuing (something we should desire and pursue for its own sake), ignoring any question about what we are *morally* required to do. But why accept this normative view? Mill didn't think there is any way to formally prove a fundamental normative doctrine such as hedonism. But he did think it possible to point to considerations that can convince people to accept it. There is, he said, a "sort of proof [of] which the principle of utility is susceptible" (U.IV.title).

Pleasure, Desire, and Mill's "Proof"

Something is visible only if it can be seen, and the only evidence of that is that some people see it. Likewise, something is intrinsically desirable only if it can be desired for its own sake, and the only evidence we have for that is that some people so desire it (U.IV.3). Mill's use of this analogy may seem misleading, since visibility is the capability of being seen, whereas being desirable is being *worthy* of desire or being something one should desire. But this may not matter much. One ought to desire something only if one can desire it. 'Ought' implies 'can'. The point of the visibility analogy, then, may be elsewhere—namely, that we can reason from actual seeings and desirings to what people *can* see and desire.

Now, Mill thought he could show that we have no evidence that anyone ever (intrinsically) desires anything other than pleasure and, consequently, no evidence that anyone can desire anything but pleasure. So if something is intrinsically desirable only if it can be desired, it follows that only pleasure is intrinsically desirable.

What explains this tight connection, Mill believed, is that pleasure and desire, and pain and aversion, are, respectively, but different aspects of the same psychological fact. As Hobbes held about desire and love and aversion and hate, Mill held that "desiring a thing and finding it pleasant, aversion to it and thinking of it as painful," differ only by virtue of their objects being represented as possible or actual (U.IV.10). Like desire, pleasure always has some *object*—that which pleases or in which pleasure is taken. And similarly for aversion and pain. If you want a cool glass of iced tea on a hot day, then you have a positive regard for this object *as possibility*. If you get the iced tea, and if it is as you imagined it would be and you don't change, you will then have the same positive regard for it, but now *as actual*. In the first case, your regard is a desire; in the second, it is a pleasure. But in either it is the same "psychological fact." Mill concluded that "to desire anything except in proportion as the idea of it is pleasant is a physical and metaphysical impossibility" (U.IV.10).

It is thus metaphysically impossible that anything other than pleasure could be intrinsically desirable. Simply by virtue of being something that *can* be desired for its own sake, that thing will be identical with some (possible) pleasure—that is, when (and if) it is represented as actual.

I'll let you think about this argument for a moment. One way to test it would be to consider how somebody might try to disagree with it, and Mill did exactly this. He allowed that it may well be thought that people sometimes desire things that "in common language, are decidedly distinguished from happiness" (U.IV.4). And he admitted that people can intrinsically desire, for example, virtue and the absence of vice "no less really than pleasure and the absence of pain." But this doesn't mean that they are desiring something *other than* their own pleasure, Mill said, since, for such people, virtue is "part of" or an "ingredient in" their pleasure. However "common language" may distinguish between desiring virtue for its own sake and desiring pleasure, they are the same thing in fact: Virtue is no less part of what such people find intrinsically pleasing than it is part of what they intrinsically desire.

You may well be thinking that things are getting pretty blurry now, and if so, you are right. 'Pleasure' is multiply ambiguous, and Mill's argument may depend on one sense, and hedonism, at least as it is standardly interpreted, may involve another. Suppose we accept Mill's theory that pleasure always involves some object's being entertained with favorable regard (the same favorable regard that is a desire when the object is entertained as merely possible). Distinguish now among three different things: (a) the favorable regard (i.e., the psychological state of being pleased [or the psychological state of desire]), (b) the object of this favorable regard (i.e., that with which one is pleased [or which one desires]), and (c) the complex whole composed of (a) and (b) together. For example, suppose you are enjoying drinking an iced tea on a hot day. In that circumstance, then, (a) is the state of your being pleased with or enjoying your drink; (b) consists of the drinking-experiences you are pleased with or enjoying; and (c) is the whole composed of your enjoyment together with what you are enjoying.

Return now to Mill's argument that something is intrinsically desirable only if it can be desired for its own sake. The sense in which only pleasure can be desired for its own sake is (b), rather than (a) or (c). To desire something is to entertain it (as a possibility) with favorable regard. So only what can be the object of favorable regard for its own sake can be desired intrinsically. In other words, only what one can enjoy or be pleased with—pleasure in sense (b)—can be desired for its own sake. That is why Mill speaks of "parts" or "ingredients" of pleasure or happiness.

But now notice how different the claim that only pleasure and the absence of pain are intrinsically desirable is starting to look from what you might have expected. You might have thought, for example, that the claim that only pleasure is desirable entails the claim that only certain kinds of experiences or conscious states are desirable, thinking that, if anything is an *experience* or *conscious state*, pleasure certainly is. But this is not necessarily true if we mean by 'pleasure' the *object* of favorable regard—that is, (b) rather than (a) or (c).

To see this, consider the hypothetical possibility of an "experience machine" that can perfectly simulate conscious life, but with the difference that nothing that your experience seems to be of really is so. All the machine-induced experiences are virtual rather than real. Your states of consciousness are entirely identical to what they would be in real life, so you can never tell that nothing is as it seems, but, in fact, your experience is systematically illusory. It seems to you as if you are eating a delicious banana split, but actually you are not. It seems to you as if you are receiving the Nobel Peace Prize, but actually you are not. And so on.

Now ask yourself, Are you indifferent about the difference between the two following possible futures, as you *currently* contemplate them? One future would be just the continuation of your current life. Your experience would be rooted in the real world, things would often be as they seem, and so on. The other future would involve being hooked up to an experience machine that would give you the very same experiences and conscious life that you would have had if you had not been hooked up to it, but with the difference that the experiences are all illusory. We may take it for granted that, from *within* either of these alternative futures, there will be no conscious difference that will enable you to distinguish between them. But does that mean that, if you *now* face the question of which alternative future you prefer to have, you must be indifferent about the difference between them? It is hard to see how it could. I don't know about you, but it surely would not be a matter of indifference to me which occurred. I'm sure not indifferent about this distinction. I would vastly prefer to have the real future rather than the illusory one. As far as I can tell, the illusory one would be not much better than death. What about you?

Suppose you care intrinsically about having the real rather than the ersatz future; that is, suppose the fact that one would be real and the other ersatz makes a difference to you *in itself*. (If it doesn't, then you may have to think about me rather than you.) It then follows that being real rather than ersatz is an object of your intrinsic favorable regard and, hence, a pleasure in sense (b)—an "ingredient" or "part" of your happiness, as Mill put it. But its being a pleasure or part of happiness in *this* sense doesn't mean that it (the object) is an experience or state of consciousness. On the contrary, what you care about here is distinctly *not* a state of your consciousness, since whether it was real or ersatz would make no difference in your conscious life.

Suppose you carry this concern into either future, and suppose that, in either, things will seem to you to be real. Then in either you will get (a) the pleasure associated with those conscious states; that is, you will be pleased *with* the (apparent) fact that your experiences are real. But in only one future would (b) the object of this (a) pleasure (the fact that your experiences are real) actually exist. And only in that future, and not in the other, would one also have (c)—that is, the whole consisting of being pleased (a) with a really existing object of favorable regard (b).

There are other cases, moreover, where a person can apparently care about something that she will be in no position at all to be pleased with because she will not know of its existence, or even where she can be in a position to have no beliefs about it—say because *she* won't exist. For example, a parent may care greatly about the welfare of her children and take great care to make provision for them, even if she knows she will not live to see the fruits of her concern. It follows from the logic of Mill's proof that the welfare of her children after she dies is part of the parent's own happiness or pleasure; but here, obviously, it can only be in sense (b), not in either (a) or (c).

At this point, it may seem that the doctrine that Mill "proved" is hedonism in name only. The only real restriction that the proof places on the intrinsically desirable is that it be something that people can desire for its own sake, and no critics of hedonism have ever denied that. What they have denied is that the only thing that is desirable is pleasure as a conscious state, in sense (a); or even the complex composed of that conscious state together with what pleasure is taken in (c). A Stoic, who holds that virtue is the only good, or even an ascetic, who holds that pain is, will end up a hedonist, if we count as hedonism any position that says the intrinsically desirable must be a potential object of intrinsic favorable regard, in sense (b). The ascetic who intrinsically desires his own pain views that prospect with favorable regard. In sense (b), then, his pain is a part of or an ingredient in his own happiness. Of course, he need not view with favorable regard the prospect of his being pleased by his own pain (as he would be disposed to be if he views the prospect of his pain favorably).

Hedonism and the Genesis of Desire

As we shall see in the next section, the reasoning in Mill's "proof" derives from a deep strain in his value theory that actually runs counter to hedonism. It represents what amounts to an Aristotelian reaction to the simple hedonism typified by Jeremy Bentham (more on this later). But there is also a more hedonist, Benthamite strain in Mill's thought. (As you have no doubt appreciated, any actual human being may be deeply attracted to different abstract positions that are hard to reconcile.) We see this strain in some of the things Mill said about the psychological genesis of desires. In particular, he drew an analogy between the way someone may come to care intrinsically about virtue and the way people come to value money for its own sake. People initially value money only extrinsically, for the things it will buy: "There is nothing originally more desirable about money than about any heap of glittering pebbles" (U.IV.6). But through a process of psychological association they come to want money for itself. A similar process is at work with respect to the desires for power and fame and, Mill said, the desire for virtue. By a "provision of nature," things that are "originally indifferent" in themselves but "conducive to, or otherwise associated with, the satisfaction of our primitive desires, become in themselves sources of pleasure more valuable than the primitive pleasures" (U.IV.6).

I don't know about you, but I find it hard to reconcile this psychological account with the idea that virtue is, nonetheless, "desirable in itself" (U.IV.5). Even if we come to desire virtue (and money, power, and fame) for their own sake, it is difficult to see how Mill could count this as evidence of their intrinsic value if the only explanation for our doing so is that we associate them with other things that we desire intrinsically and to which they are frequently means. There is no mistake involved in thinking of virtue, power, and fame as *extrinsically* valuable, but if it is only by *association* with what they tend to cause that we count these as intrinsically valuable, there seems to be some confusion of ends with means. Of course, even if it

is only by association, virtue, money, and power can still give rise to pleasure intrinsically. One may be pleased by one's wealth or virtue intrinsically,
even if the explanation is only psychological association. And as Mill went
on to say, these pleasures may be more permanent, stable, and reliable than
the more "primitive" satisfactions they were initially valued for producing.
But what is seemingly being recommended here is not the *object* of these
pleasures for its own sake, in sense (b), but the pleasure taken in them—
that is, pleasure in sense (a).

If, accordingly, Mill really believed that the only explanation for our ever
desiring anything other than certain simple satisfactions is by conditioning
or association, this would seem a far better argument for hedonism—as it
has been traditionally interpreted, in sense (a) or sense (c)—than is his
"proof."

Desire, Higher Goods, and the Ideal Judgment Theory

As I mentioned, this hedonist element in Mill's thought is in tension with
another, more Aristotelian strain. We can better understand this tension if
we see how it reflected a struggle that took place within Mill's own life. To
begin with, we need to know something about the first philosophical utilitarian, Jeremy Bentham. Bentham held a very simple version of hedonism:
Only pleasurable states of mind are intrinsically valuable, and then only to
the extent of the pleasure's "intensity" and "duration." For Bentham, it is
only pleasure in sense (a) that is valuable. All pleasurable states of mind are
qualitatively identical. They differ only *quantitatively,* with respect to how
pleasant they feel (their intensity) and how long the feeling lasts (their duration). Pleasure is essentially the same whether it results from a job well
done, a difficult insight gained, harmony with nature or one's fellow human
being, or scratching an annoying itch. These are just different causes of the
same positive feeling. As pleasures, they differ only with respect to how
positive they feel and how long they last. And similarly for pain and negative feelings.

Bentham's **quantitative hedonism** formed the basis for his utilitarianism.
Since pleasure is the only intrinsic value in people's lives, and since everyone should "count for one and no more than one," the moral defensibility
of social practices and policies and individual conduct can depend only on
whether they advance the "greatest happiness for the greatest number." For
Bentham, utilitarianism was not just a theoretical doctrine but a principle
to inform public debate aimed at political, legal, and moral reform. Indeed,
Bentham was a leading figure in an important early-nineteenth-century
group of reformers known as the "philosophical radicals." With some success, Bentham's group argued that social practices and policies must be
evaluated by their consequences for human happiness, and that the fact

that they were rooted in "ancient custom" or "common law" was, taken in itself, no justification at all.

There are distinct echoes of this reformist critique of conservatism in Mill's *Utilitarianism*, as we have seen. This is no accident. Mill's father, James Mill (1773–1836), was a central figure in Bentham's circle of philosophical radicals, and John Stuart was Bentham's godson. The young John Stuart's childhood was steeped in Benthamite ideas. As a teenager, he had already edited some of Bentham's manuscripts for publication. During his twentieth year, however, Mill found himself in the depths of a depression. Following Benthamite principles, he later came to believe, had landed him in a state of nearly total apathy, without passion or enthusiasm for anything. The way out, he found, was by cultivating his powers of imaginative, emotional, and aesthetic experience. Especially through poetry, Mill found a kind of satisfaction that seemed to him decidedly superior to anything he had felt before.

Mill's own experience led him to reject Bentham's doctrine that pleasures differ only quantitatively and not qualitatively. Pleasures don't just have causes; they also have objects. Whenever there is pleasure there is always something enjoyed or taken pleasure in. And just as their objects differ qualitatively, so also do the associated pleasures. The enjoyment of a hot shower on a cold day differs as much from the pleasure of being gripped by the majesty of a mountain as do the two experiences that are their objects or contents. Moreover, Mill came to feel, these qualitative differences give rise to differences in value that are independent of any quantitative difference in positive feeling. Some pleasures, like the aesthetic and emotional satisfactions involved in appreciating fine poetry, are more fulfilling than others because they involve more of oneself—feelings in something more like the depths of one's being rather than at the surface of one's skin. They require the cultivation and development of sensibilities and powers of appreciation that amount to growth in oneself. By developing these capacities, we realize ourselves.

We can call Mill's value theory **qualitative hedonism,** in contrast with Bentham's quantitative hedonism. Mill consistently said that anything intrinsically good must be some form of pleasure (although, as we've seen, his arguments sometimes required him to include things that are only potential objects of pleasure). He agreed with Bentham that, other things being equal, the value of pleasure varies directly with its amount. But only "other things being equal." Mill decisively departed from Bentham in holding that some pleasures are intrinsically superior to others simply because they are the kind of pleasures they are *qualitatively*—that is, owing to the nature of their objects. Sometimes such intrinsic superiority is so marked that no quantitative difference can outweigh it. But this is not always the case.

Mill remained true to the empiricist naturalism that characterized Bentham's ethics and argued within that philosophical framework that qualitative hedonism has better empirical support than quantitative hedonism. This was his own experience, after all, and Mill believed that there are good empirical grounds to think that what he experienced is common to the human species.

We should distinguish among three different claims in Mill's defense of qualitative hedonism. First, there is the normative doctrine of higher and lower pleasures itself: Some pleasures are intrinsically superior to others. Second, there are metaethical premises that Mill relied on in defense of this normative doctrine. And third, there are empirical psychological premises that Mill combined with these metaethical premises to yield his normative conclusion.

One metaethical premise is epistemological. We know already that Mill took the fact that people actually desire something for its own sake as evidence of its intrinsic value, since it is evidence that something can be desired, and that is a necessary condition of its being something we should desire. But not all desires are equally good evidence of the value of their objects, since not all desires are equally based on knowledgeable acquaintance with their objects. Other things being equal, a desire that is based on experience and knowledge of its object is better evidence of its object's value than one that is not.

For this reason, Mill proposed the following test: "Of two pleasures, if there be one to which all or almost all who have experience of both give a decided preference, irrespective of any feeling of moral obligation to prefer it, that is the more desirable pleasure" (U.II.5). What matters are the desires of *experienced* judges, and Mill included in this category the capacity to "appreciat[e] and enjoy" both pleasures. So far this claim is only an epistemological one: Experienced desire is the best evidence of value. But what metaphysical theory of value might stand behind this epistemological doctrine? If, as Mill evidently believed, value can be empirically discovered in this way, this must be because it is itself an aspect of the natural world—as **ethical naturalism** would hold. But what aspect? Mill does not say, but it may be that he accepts some version of the **ideal judgment theory**—namely, that what it is for one thing to be more desirable than another just is for it to be the case that ideally experienced judges would agree in their preference for one over the other.

The psychological speculation that Mill combined with this empirical naturalist metaethics was the Aristotelian idea that human beings naturally grow and mature in various ways; that we have intellectual, imaginative, and emotional faculties and sensibilities that must be cultivated to develop properly; and that we naturally prefer a life in which we grow and flourish in exercising our maturing (and mature) faculties. Thus Mill's doctrine of higher and lower pleasures is an empirically based bet about what experienced people will prefer. The idea is not that people should feel ashamed or guilty about activities that are beneath them but, rather, that a life in which capacities are stunted and people do not grow and mature is a less satisfying life, one that those who have also known the experience of growth and satisfactions that call upon more developed capacities naturally disprefer to a life of growth and development. "Men lose their high aspirations," Mill wrote, "as they lose their intellectual tastes, because they have not time or opportunity for indulging them; and they addict themselves to inferior pleasures, not because they deliberately prefer them, but because they are either the only ones to which they have access or the only ones which they are any longer capable of enjoying" (U.II.7).

Mill's Value Theory: A Summary

This leaves Mill's theory of value in some tension, one that reflects a tension in his psychology. As we saw, Mill's associationism points in the direction of a form of hedonism that is very close to Bentham's. If all desires except those for "primitive pleasures" are formed by a conditioning process of associating means with ends, then the resulting desires can hardly provide evidence of their objects' *intrinsic* value. How can money be valuable in itself if we simply associate money with what it tends to cause and desire it for that reason? If, consequently, desires to exercise higher faculties are formed by association, this would seem to undermine any evidence for qualitative hedonism. On the other hand, if "higher" desires are the result of a natural pattern of growth and development, it makes greater sense to regard the resulting desires as evidence of superior values. But now another problem opens up. Why think that this superior value is based, either normatively or metaethically, on *pleasure?*

Because their views are otherwise similar on this score, a useful point of comparison with Mill here will be Aristotle (see Chapters 17 and 18). At the level of normative ethics, Aristotle held that what is intrinsically good for human beings is not pleasure but, rather, the excellent exercise of the distinctively human capacities that we naturally enjoy. The pleasure we take in these activities is, he thought, a symptom of their value, not the value itself. And metaethically, Aristotle believed that the value of these activities consists in their inclusion in a *telos* or end that it is part of human nature to aim at and realize. Even the empiricist naturalist metaethics that Mill relied on in defense of his theory of higher and lower goods seems to point in a direction different from hedonism, since it seems clear enough that some of our desires are for objects other than our own conscious states.

13

MILL II

Good To and Good For

In this chapter we turn from Mill's theory of value to his moral theory. We ended Chapter 12 by noting a tension within Mill's value theory that is rooted in conflicts within his psychology and metaethics. One line of thought leads toward hedonism, but a hedonism that is quantitative rather than qualitative, whereas another apparently leads toward value theories that are not hedonist at all. This tension reflects a real conflict in Mill's own thinking, but there may be ways of muting it when we consider how his theory of (nonmoral) value can be fit into a theory of morality.

What Mill means by something's being intrinsically (nonmorally) valuable *to* an individual is its being something he should aim at for its own sake as an *end* (independent of considerations of moral right and wrong). Hedonism seems implausible as a theory of what is intrinsically valuable to individuals in this sense. There are many things that people devote themselves sensibly to as ends other than their own pleasure. Think of the struggling artist who suffers materially so that she can pursue what she loves. Of course, she probably wouldn't be happy if she didn't, but that doesn't mean her own happiness is her end. On the contrary, her happiness itself depends on her devoting herself to her art as an end in itself.

But what if we ask not what ends make sense for a person to desire and aim at for *their* sake, but what is good *for* and benefits *her;* that is, what makes sense to aim at for *her* sake? Hedonism may be a much more plausible theory of what is good *for* a person, in the sense of her own welfare or well-being, than of what is good *to* her, in the sense of what she should aim at. It may be that a person sensibly desires many things other than her own happiness (not least, of course, the happiness of others), yet still be true that nothing can be intrinsically good for or benefit *her* without making some contribution to her happiness.

One way to see this difference is to notice that caring about someone and wishing the best for her is not the same thing as wanting just what she wants, even what she sensibly wants. Suppose your friend Sheila is in the following situation. By donating all her wealth she can realize an outcome she cares very much about—say, rebuilding a city ravaged by war to a certain degree, D. But there is a catch. Sheila also has a degenerative disease that, if not checked, will create memory loss and confusion severe enough that she will be unsure where her money has gone and unable even to hold stable beliefs about the state of rebuilding in the war-ravaged city. Happily, there is a drug that can arrest the symptoms of Sheila's disease without side effects. However, the drug is expensive, Sheila will not accept donations, and she cares so much about rebuilding the city that, even though the difference the cost of the drug would make in the rebuilding effort is relatively small (call it d), she nonetheless wants (and would continue to want on reflection) to forgo the drug and donate all she has.

Sheila ranks the outcome of the city's being rebuilt to degree D together with her advanced disease, memory loss, and uncertainty about the city's actual state (call this outcome O_1) higher than the outcome of the city's being rebuilt to degree D-d but with her knowing about the rebuilding, her knowing about her role in it, and a generally improved mental state (call this outcome O_2). You are convinced that Sheila prefers O_1 to O_2, and that her ordering of outcomes would survive informed reflection. You care about Sheila and so desire what is for her good. Does caring about her and wanting what is good for her dictate your ordering these outcomes in the same way Sheila does, even on reflection? It seems obvious that it does not. Although Sheila prefers O_1 to O_2, this in no way directs your concern for her to the same ordering. On the contrary, insofar as you care about Sheila and what is good for her, won't your ordering be the opposite of hers? Won't you prefer O_2 to O_1? Suppose that you would. Then you believe that what is for Sheila's good is not the same as what she would want on reflection.

Now, Mill said that what a person would desire if experienced and informed is what it is desirable for her to aim at as an end. And the problem, again, is that this statement seems at odds with hedonism, as Sheila's case reminds us. But the statement could be granted and some version of hedonism could still be correct as an account of what is good *for* a person, in the sense of what benefits *her* or is for her good or welfare. One alternative would be that the only intrinsic goods for a person are pleasurable conscious states—that is pleasure in sense (a). But this would mean that, as far as a person's good or welfare goes, it makes no difference whether her real life continues or is perfectly simulated by an experience machine. And that seems implausible also. Pleasurable conscious states may well be valuable for a person in themselves, but their value may also be vastly increased by whether the objects of these states really exist, rather than only seeming to. In caring for Sheila, would we not wish that she could herself enjoy the accomplishment of what she cares so much about? This is the (c) sense of pleasure that I defined in the last chapter: a whole consisting of the conscious state of being pleased (a) together with the object in which pleasure is taken (b). I propose, therefore, that we provisionally accept hedonism (in the sense of considering the combination of pleasurable states together with the existence of their objects) as the correct account of what is for a person's good or welfare.

From Value to Morality

Recall now the three propositions that I claimed function as Mill's main argument for utilitarianism:

(1) Morality, by its very nature, is concerned with what is good from the perspective of the moral community.
(2) What is good from the perspective of the moral community is the greatest amount of what is good to the individuals comprising it.
(3) What is good to any individual is that person's pleasure or happiness.

In Mill's own "proof" of the utility principle, just after he established that "each person's happiness is a good to that person" (3), he added with breathtaking swiftness, "and the general happiness [is], therefore, a good to the aggregate of all persons" (U.IV.3). Mill didn't think this proved that the general happiness is *the* criterion of morality, but he thought it showed that it is "one of the criteria." Once, however, he proved that pleasure is the *only* intrinsic good to a person, he believed he could conclude that the general happiness is the only good "to the aggregate of all persons." And this permitted him to conclude, he thought, that the general happiness provides "the criterion of morality" for which humankind has heretofore so vainly searched.

What is going on here? Even if we grant (3), which we have seen significant reason to doubt, why did Mill think he could get from that to any *moral* principle? [N.B.: Neither (1) nor (2) are explicit in Mill's "proof".] Obviously, Mill thought that he was able to take an important step when he concluded that the general happiness is "a good to the aggregate of all persons." But how are we to understand this? Especially, how are we to understand it in a way that will both follow from (3) *and* help establish that the general happiness provides a moral principle?

If the good to each person is that person's happiness, then there is a tautologous sense in which the general happiness is the good to the aggregate of all persons. As Mill understood it, the general happiness just *is* the aggregate of the goods to all persons—the good to Jones, to Cortez, to Chan, and so on. We might define "good to the aggregate of all persons" to mean "aggregate of the goods to all persons." Then it would be tautologous that the general happiness is the good to the aggregate of all persons. Thus Mill would have been permitted to conclude (trivially) that the general happiness is the good to the aggregate of all persons from the fact that an individual's happiness is uniquely good to that individual. However, this conclusion provides no help whatsoever in clarifying what the general happiness has to do with *morality*. It just states that the general happiness is the sum of the goods to all persons (i.e., the sum of their individual levels of happiness and unhappiness).

In order for a premise about what is good "to the aggregate of all persons" to play a significant role in an argument for the fundamental principle of morality, Mill apparently must have thought of the aggregate of persons as something like *the moral community*. If that were so, then what would be good to the aggregate of all persons would be good to the moral community. And if he could have assumed (1), that morality is concerned with what is good from the perspective of the moral community, then he could have concluded that *if* something is good to the aggregate of persons, then it is the end with which morality is concerned. To complete his "proof," therefore, he would need to be able to show or assume that the general happiness (the aggregate of goods to individuals) is (uniquely) good to the aggregate of individuals.

Something like this argument is a deeply appealing line of thought leading to utilitarianism. If the only thing that makes sense for an individual to aim at is his or her own happiness, then why does it not also make sense for a community aggregated of all persons to aim at the aggregate of goods to individuals—that is, the greatest aggregate happiness?

Without denying the genuine appeal of this line of thought, we should also note some real problems it faces. One springs from what is called, following John Rawls, the *moral separateness of persons*.[1] It makes perfectly good sense for an individual to balance goods and evils in her own life, since an evil to her at one moment can be compensated by a good to her at some other. The same person is being benefited and harmed, so she is compensated for her harm by the benefit. When it comes to maximizing the aggregate of goods across individuals, however, the same principle does not apply. A greater aggregate of happiness overall may be bought by purchasing benefits for some at the cost of harms to others. Although balancing benefits and harms to maximize overall benefit makes good sense *within* a life, because the same person is involved, we cannot assume that it also makes good sense to maximize overall benefit *across* lives. In other words, it may be that although maximizing individual good is an appropriate principle of *individual* choice, maximizing aggregate good is not an appropriate principle of *social* choice.

Another problem that specifically infects Mill's "proof" is, again, that it assumes that hedonism is the correct theory of what is good *to* an individual, in other words, that pleasure is the only thing it makes sense to aim at as an *end*. But this assumption is implausible, as we have seen.

Even so, some version of hedonism may be far more plausible as a theory of what is good *for* a person. And if we make the latter assumption, moreover, other traditionally appealing lines leading to utilitarianism open up. It is broadly agreed, for example, that **impartiality** is at the center of our conception of morality. Moral judgment, by its very nature, aims to be impartial. It is natural to think, therefore, that the **moral point of view** is one of *impartial, equal concern* for all persons. When we are concerned for an individual, we naturally want her good; we want things to go well for her. And if a person's good is her happiness, as we are assuming, then in being concerned for her, we must want her to be happy. So if the moral point of view is a perspective of impartial, equal concern for all, then it must entail an equal desire for the happiness of all. From this the utilitarian concludes that the moral point of view involves a desire for the greatest overall happiness, counting everyone's happiness equally. What is good from the moral point of view is the greatest amount of good for individuals—that is, the greatest overall happiness.

From Moral Good to Moral Right: Act-Utilitarianism

Suppose we grant Mill that the general happiness is the end of morality, and that outcomes can be ranked from the moral point of view by how much overall net happiness they involve. A state of affairs that involves more happiness than some other will then be better, overall, from the moral perspective. It will be morally better (or, perhaps more appropriately, morally "more fortunate").

But how could Mill argue from this statement to a principle that determines which acts are right and which are wrong? Here is what he said: "The creed which accepts as the foundation of morals 'utility' or 'the greatest happiness principle' holds that actions are right in proportion as they tend to promote happiness; wrong as they tend to produce the reverse of happiness" (U.II.2). Taken by itself, this passage might naturally be read as a statement of what is called **act-utilitarianism (AU)**: An act is right if, and only if, of those acts available to the agent in the circumstances, it would produce the greatest total net happiness. For the moment we will proceed, provisionally, as if the latter is Mill's view. Later we shall see some reasons for thinking that it may not be.

Whether it is Mill's view or not, AU can seem a sensible thing to believe if the end of morality is the general happiness. After all, if what morality is *about* is producing the greatest happiness for all, then why shouldn't this end also always determine what a person should do, what it would be morally right for him to do?

Before we begin to evaluate AU as the "criterion of right and wrong," we should note various features of it. First, although Mill was a qualitative hedonist, AU is a quantitative criterion. At this point, however, we would do better to ignore this problem. One way of doing so is to suppose that the quantitative measure of happiness that figures in AU is one that already takes account of intensity, duration, *and* quality.

Second, we have to assume that there can be a quantitative *interpersonal* measure of happiness, one that compares amounts of happiness and unhappiness across individuals. We don't have to assume that we know how to measure happiness. We just have to assume that there are facts about how much happiness or unhappiness one individual would experience in an outcome, compared to someone else. This is far from a trivial assumption, and there are some deep issues concerning it. Then again, people make rough-and-ready judgments about relative amounts of happiness all the time. In deciding to whom to give an extra ticket to a concert, for instance, you may well think something like "Joan would probably enjoy it more than Jerome." To get to the interesting ethical issues about utilitarianism, we will simply assume that there are such facts.

Third, we should note that AU holds that *whatever* effects on happiness and unhappiness an action would *actually* have—*wherever, whenever,* and to *whomever* they would occur—are all equally relevant to determining what the person should do. Let's consider each of these separately.

> *Wherever.* If my action would cause happiness or unhappiness on the other side of the globe, this has the same relevance to whether I should do it as if it were to occur right next to me.
>
> *Whenever.* If my action would cause happiness or unhappiness twenty centuries from now, that has the same relevance to whether I should do it as if it were to occur presently.
>
> *To Whomever.* The happiness and unhappiness of all persons (or sentient beings) are equally morally relevant to what I should do.

Putting these together, we can reason as follows: If two alternative actions that I could perform would cause the same amount of aggregate happiness, but with one act causing benefits to be realized presently to neighbors about whom I care greatly, and with the other act causing benefits to be realized many years from now for people far from my home about whom I care not at all (assuming that my happiness has been taken account of, like everyone else's), then there is as good a moral reason to perform the second act as to perform the first. And if the second would produce slightly more happiness, I should do it. (N.B.: We have to assume that the benefits actually *would* be realized in the future; it is not enough that I set events in motion that would realize the benefits *unless* some obstacle arises, *if* some obstacle would arise.)

Fourth, AU holds that an action is right if, and only if, it would produce the greatest total *net* happiness—that is, after we have subtracted the unhappiness from the happiness that would result.

Finally, AU holds that I should perform that act, *of the ones available,* which would produce the *greatest* total net happiness. It is not enough to make an action right that it would produce happiness, since there may be some other alternative that would produce even more. Likewise, it is not enough to make an action wrong that it would produce net unhappiness, since there may be no alternative available that would produce net happiness.

The intuitive idea behind AU can be put this way. Actions have consequences. Whenever we act, there are things that happen as a result of our actions that wouldn't have occurred otherwise. Some of these consequences are proximate, but others can be quite remote in space, time, or both. C_i, referring to an action's consequences, is what we can call the set of things that would occur if a particular action A_i were taken. Within this set C_i there will be instances of people being happy and unhappy to various degrees. Suppose that for each set of consequences C we can associate a number H_i, which is the total net happiness in C_i.

Now, in any choice situation, there are many different things an agent could do. Each of these actions A_i will have a consequence set C_i with a total net happiness equal to H_i. Since what is best from the moral point of view is the greatest total net happiness, an agent should always perform the act that would cause the greatest total net happiness. Within the set of acts (A_i) there will be one or more (say, A_j) whose consequence set C_j produces a greatest total net happiness H_j. The right thing for the agent to do, then, is to perform that act (or one of the acts that tie for the highest H).

Defending AU Against Some Objections

The philosophical line of thought leading to AU is very powerful. Who can deny that, morally speaking, one person's welfare is the same as any other person's? Of course, we all care more about some people than about others. That is only natural. But can we defend the idea that these people are really more important than others about whom we happen to care less? To be sure, they are more important *to us.* But that doesn't make them more important, period, or more important morally. Of course, some people don't just happen to be more important to us; rather, it is inherent in various morally important relationships, such as those of mutual love, friendship, and family, that they be more important to us. But then what makes these relationships important can't be that they involve people important to us. There must be some way of defending them from a standpoint in which all people are taken to matter equally. And AU argues that this standpoint is one of equal concern for the happiness of all.

If you want to feel the force of this thought, imagine that someone steps on your toe. You protest, and he says, "But you are not important to me." Won't this seem beside the point? Might you not think something like "Well, I may not be very important to you, but I am no less important than you." If, however, everyone's welfare matters equally from the moral point of view, then each person's welfare would seem also to matter equally to what we morally should do. AU can seem a natural conclusion to this line of thought.

Still, there are many reasons why AU is difficult to accept, and Mill attempted to address some of these objections. He noted, for example, the frequent complaint that "there is not time, previous to action, for calculating and weighing the effects of any line of conduct on the general happiness" (U.II.24). But this objection mistakes what AU aims to be. AU is a criterion of what makes an action the right thing to do. If the objection's assumption is correct, it will follow from AU that there is not time before acting to *know* which action is right. But how is that an objection to AU, since the latter could still tell us what we should need to know in order to know which action is right?

Consider an analogy. Suppose someone offers as a theory of **prudent** action the principle that an action is the most prudent act if it is the one, of those available, that will produce the greatest total net happiness for the agent. If the objection applies in the moral case, then an analogous objection should apply here. But it would seem that the only thing we can conclude if this objection's assumption is correct is that there is not time before acting to know which action is most prudent. Would this conclusion pose an objection to the theory of prudence? It is hard to see how it would. In both cases, it might be urged, we would be best advised to do whatever is likeliest, according to available evidence, to promote the greatest happiness. That would be the **subjectively right (or prudent)** act, whereas the act that would actually promote the most happiness would be the **objectively right (or prudent)** act.

Neither does AU necessarily say that agents should attempt to follow AU in great detail in their *deliberations,* in terms of making difficult calculations and so on. How should agents deliberate? Deliberations are also things we *do.* So AU says that agents should deliberate in whatever way will have the best consequences. And here, Mill argued, we have the benefit of centuries of accumulated wisdom concerning what sorts of actions are likely to have what sorts of effects. Much of moral common sense, concerning the keeping of promises and being fair, honest, kind, and so on, can be viewed as "rules of thumb" or "secondary principles," as Mill called them, by which people sensibly guide their deliberations in the knowledge that, generally and in the long run, their doing so will have the best consequences for human happiness.

Nonetheless, according to AU these "intermediate generalizations" have no moral validity in themselves. The fact that an action falls under some such rule of thumb has nothing to do with whether it is the right action or not. That depends entirely on the consequences of the action for human happiness.

Another objection is that AU may seem to require that we love all people equally. But that is impossible—and probably undesirable even if it were possible. Personal relationships in which we care for each other in special ways are an important source of human happiness. Mill replied to this objection by saying that it mistakes a "rule of action with the motive of it" (U.II.19). AU, then, is a rule or principle of action that says what must be true in order for an action to be morally right. And, moreover, it says that the rightness of an action depends entirely on its consequences. So which motive an action is performed from is irrelevant to whether, according to AU, it is the right thing to do. Thus AU does not tell us that we must love all people equally.

Objections to AU: Some Case Studies

No doubt the most serious source of objection to AU is that it conflicts so clearly with moral common sense about particular cases. I will briefly describe four kinds of cases where objections of these sorts frequently arise.

1. *Promises.* Common sense holds that the fact that an act would break a promise is intrinsically relevant to its moral rightness, whereas AU maintains that only an act's consequences determine whether it is right or wrong. Whether an action would break a promise is a *backward-looking* consideration, whereas, according to AU, only *forward-looking* considerations matter to what a person morally should do.

Of course, AU will indirectly recognize many backward-looking considerations that are related to promising. Usually people to whom promises have been given have increased expectations that would be frustrated by breaking a promise. Also, trust is an important social resource, and breaking a promise usually tends to undermine trust. And so on.

But these consequences may be lacking in a particular case. A promise may have been given to someone no longer alive, or to someone who is alive but has forgotten about the promise (although she still continues to have a stake in it). Or no one else may know about the promise. And so on. In such cases, there may be few, if any, bad consequences attributable to the fact that a promise would be broken. And even in cases where there are such consequences, AU holds, contrary to common sense, that the fact that a promise was made has no moral weight in itself.

2. *Other Actions Thought to Be Wrong in Themselves.* Promise-breaking is only one example of a number of kinds of acts that are thought to be wrong in themselves, at least other things being equal. Don't you think, for example, that the fact that an action would amount to betrayal or dishonesty is a serious moral reason against it, a wrong-making consideration in itself? According to AU, however, such a fact is morally irrelevant, since it does not intrinsically concern consequences for human happiness.

3. *The Moral Asymmetry of Harm and Benefit.* According to AU, a harm can be compensated by an equal benefit. Suppose that an action of yours will create a benefit for Brown, but at the cost of an exactly equal harm to Green. AU holds that there is no greater reason to avoid causing harm (to Green) than there is reason to create a benefit (for Brown). But don't you view the moral duty not to harm differently from the moral duty to benefit? Common sense seems to hold that the duty not to cause harm is stronger than the duty to benefit. The fact that causing harm to Green will cause an equal benefit to Brown is normally thought insufficient to justify the harm to Green.

4. *Distributive Justice.* Suppose that there are only two actions (A and B) you can perform, that only four people (w,x,y,z) will be affected, and that their happiness can be represented as follows:

	w	x	y	z
A	-2	2	2	2
B	1	1	1	1

According to AU, it is morally equivalent whether one does A or B, since both would produce the same total net happiness. It does not matter how happiness or unhappiness is distributed. However, common sense holds that goods can be distributed justly or unjustly. Especially if it doesn't make a difference to the total, don't you think it would be morally preferable to perform B rather than A? The benefits are spread equally in B, whereas some benefit and some lose in A.

Justice and Rules: Rule-Utilitarianism

These are only some examples of the ways in which AU can conflict with intuitive moral judgments that many people find themselves disposed to make when they consider specific cases. But what, exactly, should we make of this conflict between AU and moral common sense? Should we take it as disproving AU? Or, at least, as some evidence against AU?

At the level of normative ethics, we really have no alternative to taking our intuitive moral judgments seriously. After all, we *believe* them, so we can hardly disregard them in thinking about moral questions. But we also face philosophical questions about what value and morality could possibly be. That, again, is the challenge of philosophical ethics. So we can also hardly be satisfied with our intuitive judgments if we cannot fit them into a coherent philosophical outlook: a philosophical ethics. And at the abstract philosophical level AU has significant appeal. Additionally, the act-utilitarian may regard it as a good thing that we are disposed to make the particular intuitive judgments we are, even if they conflict with AU. She might hold that although AU is the correct theory of right and wrong, it is nonetheless beneficial for people to have and be guided by intuitive beliefs of moral common sense. If people were to try to follow AU, they would be prone to various kinds of mistakes, some self-serving, some due to ignorance, and so on. Defenders of AU, therefore, have not been at a loss for things to say in response to conflicts with common-sense morality.

But Mill took a different tack, one that ultimately involved a different philosophical conception of morality than underlies AU. To see how his thinking ran, notice, first, that there is a common theme in the cases we have considered. They all seem to involve issues of **rights** and **justice**. When, for instance, one person makes a promise to another, she gives the other a right to expect that the promised action will be performed. Similarly, people often *resent* betrayal and fraud. They see these as forms of unjust treatment. Or again, if there is a difference in "strength" between the duty not to harm and the duty to benefit, this difference might be thought to reflect the fact that we have a right that others not harm us but no general right to benefit from others' efforts (even if we have a right to certain forms of aid and help in certain kinds of circumstances).

"One of the strongest obstacles to the reception of the doctrine that utility or happiness is the criterion of right and wrong," Mill wrote, "has been drawn from the idea of justice" (U.V.1). Mill devoted Chapter V of *Utilitarianism* to meeting this challenge and to arguing for a "connection between justice and utility." It is undeniable, he granted, that the concept of justice is connected to "powerful sentiment[s]" and "apparently clear perception[s]" in our moral experience. Nothing is more frequent than the sense of injustice that arises when a person resents ill-usage by others. When a person is betrayed, defrauded, or harmed, she feels not just that a wrong has been done but that she has been wronged. Her standing and dignity as a moral person with certain basic moral rights have been impugned, and she resents this injustice. But the fact that we have this feeling, Mill argued, "does not necessarily legitimate all its promptings. The feeling of justice might be a peculiar instinct, and might yet require, like our other instincts, to be controlled and enlightened by a higher reason" (U.V.2). And although "mankind are always predisposed to believe that any subjective feeling, not otherwise accounted for, is a revelation of some objective reality," it does not follow that the "feeling of justice" reveals objective ethical facts that are irreducible to considerations of utility.

Still, there is no doubt that Mill held justice to be absolutely central to morality. Indeed, he believed that its function is to protect what is most important to people's happiness. Similarly, he considered equal rights and justice not only useful instruments in promoting human goods but also essential constituents of some of the most important human goods. Thus, Mill listed a "sense of dignity" as "so essential a part of the happiness of those in whom it is strong that nothing which conflicts with it could be otherwise than momentarily an object of desire to them" (U.II.6). The importance of reciprocal relationships of equal respect is an important theme of *The Subjection of Women* and other works.[2]

Mill began by canvassing the various things that justice has been taken to mean over the centuries. He found much inconsistency but also noted a common element: Judgments of justice are invariably related to the ideas of *law* and *sanctions*. Initially, justice simply meant "conformity to law," and rights referred only to legal rights. However, once societies were able to step back from their laws and consider them critically, they thought of morality as the relevant critical standpoint. Thus a more enlightened conception of moral justice and moral rights became possible. As Mill explained, "The sentiment of injustice came to be attached, not to all violations of law, but only to violations of such laws as ought to exist, including such as *ought* to exist but do not, and to laws themselves if supposed to be contrary to what ought to be law" (U.V.12).

The difference, then, between what is thought morally better for a person to do and what would be unjust for her not to do is that the latter is held to be appropriately penalized in some way. In many cases, the appropriate sanctions are formally codified in law. So we have laws that create penalties for various forms of violence and harm, fraud, breaking of contract, and so on. But notions of justice and rights may still apply in other cases that "neither are, nor is it desired that they should be, regulated by law" (U.V.13). Someone may resent an unjust betrayal and feel that his rights as a friend have been violated. But that doesn't mean that we should have a "friends' court" where such cases might be tried. As Mill put it, "Nobody desires that laws should interfere with the whole detail of private life" (U.V.13). But "even here," he continued, "the idea of a breach of what ought to be a law still lingers in a modified shape" (U.V.13). So we may think, for example, that the former friend should at least feel guilty for what he has done.

Justice and rights are things it makes moral sense to protect with some rule-governed, social **practice**—that is, either with laws or with more informal mechanisms such as reproach, guilt feelings, or even gossip. "A right,"

Mill said, is "something which society ought to defend me in the possession of" by such formal and informal social mechanisms (U.V.25). But this, he further argued, is as far as the idea of rights and justice can take us. What we cannot get from these ideas themselves is which rights we should protect and, hence, what moral rights we actually have—what really is just or unjust. To determine that, we need some basis for choosing between alternative laws or informal social mechanisms. And this, Mill believed, is precisely what utilitarianism gives us. Not only is it the case that the idea of justice does not conflict with utilitarianism, when these are both rightly understood, but utilitarianism also provides a moral criterion of laws without which the idea of justice would be *incomplete*. For something to be unjust, he argued, is for it to be contrary to a rule-governed, social practice (again, the laws or less formal rules) that it would promote the general happiness for society to have.

The sentiment of justice, Mill believed, partly involves the "animal desire to repel or retaliate a hurt or damage to oneself or to those with whom one sympathizes" (U.V.23). In human beings, this feeling can be regulated by an "enlarged sympathy," since it can be directed by an equal concern for the welfare of all. Only from this, Mill wrote, does "the feeling deriv[e] its morality," making it a sentiment of *justice* rather than mere revenge. "The idea of justice supposes two things—a rule of conduct and a sentiment which sanctions the rule" (U.V.23). And, for moral purposes, such a rule exists if, and only if, it would promote the general happiness for society to have it.

Finally, Mill related these ideas to the general idea of *moral wrong*. We never "call anything wrong unless we mean to imply that a person ought to be punished in some way or other for doing it—if not by law, by the opinion of his fellow creatures; if not by opinion, by the reproaches of his own conscience" (U.V.14). In short, the very idea of moral wrong is that of conduct that is appropriately punished or *blameworthy,* lacking adequate excuse. As Mill thought of it, therefore, morality is a system of *social accountability* in which individuals are held responsible for their conduct. Whether conduct is wrong, then, cannot be determined simply by looking at *its* consequences. Rather, conduct is wrong if, and only if, it is the sort of thing for which people can be appropriately blamed in formal and informal social practices of holding people accountable. And that in turn will be true if, and only if, it would promote the general happiness for people to be blamed and sanctioned for doing things like that.

The criterion of right and wrong implied by what Mill said here is quite different from act-utilitarianism. That criterion is rather a theory called **rule-utilitarianism (RU):** An act is wrong if, and only if, it is contrary to a (possible) rule, such that were society to have a practice of enforcing that rule (formally or informally), this practice would maximize overall net happiness. To see the difference between AU and RU, consider a situation that Gilbert Harman has described. Suppose someone goes to the hospital for his yearly physical. As it happens, there are five patients in the hospital, each of whom needs a different organ (heart, kidney, etc.) to survive. Suppose that with the organ each person could look forward to roughly as many years of life as the healthy person would have. And suppose that otherwise the situations of all six people are roughly comparable in terms of the impact their lives would have on other people's happiness, and so on. Suppose, finally, that a doctor is in a position to kill the healthy person and distribute his organs to the five patients in a way that no one will suspect. Assume, therefore, that this action would create the most happiness overall and, accordingly, that AU would require it. Would RU?[3]

To answer that question, we have to ask what sort of social practice governing the conduct of doctors, with what kinds of rules, would promote the greatest happiness. Consider three possibilities. In one practice, doctors are required by the rules to promote the general happiness, which would include killing patients and distributing their organs if that would best promote it. In a second, doctors are required never to kill patients for the purpose of organ distribution, even if it would have beneficial consequences in a particular instance. And in a third, doctors are neither required to kill patients to harvest their organs nor forbidden to do so. They may or may not kill patients at their own discretion when doing so would have better consequences. Now let's ask, Which social practice is likely to have the best social consequences?

In other words, if you could write the code of ethics for the American Medical Association so that society's being governed by the resulting code would maximize happiness, what rules would you write into the code? Notice, specifically, that the question is which rule, *if publicly acknowledged as governing,* would maximize happiness. Thus a rule requiring or permitting doctors to harvest healthy patients for organs, if they could do so secretly, would not itself be a secret rule. And society's having a rule permitting secret organ harvesting might, for example, undermine trust in hospitals and doctors, even if a single secret organ harvesting might not. Would you trust doctors as much as you currently do if you knew that they were permitted or required to harvest organs from healthy patients when it would produce more general happiness to do so? Suppose you would not, and you think that others would not also. If so, then must you not think that according to RU it would be wrong for a doctor to harvest organs of healthy patients, even in cases where it would maximize happiness to do so?

It is generally believed that RU is much closer to moral common sense than AU and that, in the kinds of cases just described, its dictates would conflict with AU and coincide with common sense. You should think about these cases to see if you agree. And you should also ask yourself whether, if this were so, it would mean that RU is likelier to be a correct moral theory than is AU.

RU Versus AU and the Normativity of Morality

Act-utilitarians and rule-utilitarians agree that morality has the general happiness as a defining end. But rule-utilitarians, not act-utilitarians, add that morality is also defined by its *social* character. It is central to what morality is that it be realizable in social practices of criticism and accountability. Whereas act-utilitarians view moral *action* as the best instrument to realize morality's defining end, rule-utilitarians view morality itself (as a set of socially realizable practices) as the best instrument for realizing morality's end.

But which theory should a utilitarian hold, AU or RU? She cannot hold both, since they are mutually inconsistent. Defenders of AU and of RU can agree that it is a good thing to support generally beneficial social practices and rules. What they disagree about is whether the fact that a socially beneficial rule prohibits an action makes the action wrong. The act-utilitarian believes that utility should always serve as the moral criterion—of which rules society should have, which acts one should perform, which traits of character should be inculcated, and so on. The rule-utilitarian, on the other hand, holds that although utility is the correct criterion of which rules to have, it is not the correct test of which acts are right and wrong; what determines that is which rules there should be, and what those rules would permit or prohibit.

What Mill has on his side is the deep connection between the idea of morality and that of an ideal *law*, a connection that goes back at least as far as the classical natural law theory, if not much earlier. But what can the *normativity* of the moral law consist in for Mill (or for any rule-utilitarian)? Suppose we press this issue by asking the following question: If a person is in a position where she can either promote the general happiness or follow a general-happiness-promoting rule, which should she do? We know that Mill thought it would be *wrong* for her to do the former, since promoting the general happiness would violate the best sanction-furnishing rule and this, in turn, is the only thing that can make an action wrong. But suppose we grant Mill's point and still press the question: Should she or should she not do what is wrong? The fact that 'right' and 'wrong' are *defined* in relation to ideal rules does not help answer that question. Since all utilitarians believe that the final source of moral justification is provided by morality's defining end, the general happiness, it is hard to avoid the conclusion that she should do what *those reasons* (i.e., *reasons of general happiness*) recommend. But this conclusion means that she should follow AU, not RU.

Finally, both act-utilitarians and rule-utilitarians face the question of what makes morality binding on a moral agent. In other words, what gives morality its normativity, and why should a person follow *either* AU or RU? Mill considered this question in Chapter III of *Utilitarianism*. His main object there was to show that unreformed moral common sense should not be thought a better representation of morality than utilitarianism simply by virtue of the fact that it "is the only one which presents itself to the mind with the feeling of being *in itself* obligatory" (U.III.1). Mill argued that this feeling is entirely the result of social training, and that if the society were to reform itself by teaching and inculcating more beneficial rules, then these would in time present *themselves* as intrinsically obligatory also. Moreover, Mill continued, utilitarianism can claim a basis in human psychology that the intuitionist defenders of common sense cannot. There is a "powerful natural sentiment" leading us to want to promote the general happiness—namely, "the desire to be in unity with our fellow creatures" (U.III.10). Because we naturally identify with and care about others, we have reason to desire the general happiness. This reasoning underlines the question raised at the beginning of the paragraph. If the normativity of morality derives from the natural human sympathy and desire for solidarity, why should we follow socially beneficial rules when doing so will produce less happiness?

Suggested Reading

Anderson, Elizabeth. "John Stuart Mill and Experiments in Living." *Ethics* 102 (1991): 4–26.

Bentham, Jeremy. *Introduction to the Principles of Morals and Legislation* (1789). J. H. Burns, H. L. A. Hart, and F. Rosen, eds. Oxford: Clarendon Press, 1996.

Berger, Fred R. *Happiness, Justice, and Freedom.* Berkeley: University of California Press, 1984.

Brink, David. "Mill's Deliberative Utilitarianism." *Philosophy and Public Affairs* 21 (1992): 67–103.

Donner, Wendy. *The Liberal Self: John Stuart Mill's Moral and Political Philosophy.* Ithaca, N.Y.: Cornell University Press, 1991.

Lyons, David. *Rights, Welfare, and Mill's Moral Theory.* New York: Oxford University Press, 1994.

Mill, John Stuart. *On Liberty* (1859), with *The Subjection of Women* (1869) and *Chapters on Socialism.* Stefan Collini, ed., Cambridge Texts in the History of Political Thought. Cambridge: Cambridge University Press, 1989.

_____. *Utilitarianism* (1861). George Sher, ed. Indianapolis, Ind.: Hackett Publishing Company, 1979.

Morales, Maria H. *Perfect Equality: John Stuart Mill on Well-Constituted Communities.* Lanham, Md.: Rowman & Littlefield Publishers, 1996.

Schneewind, J. B., ed. *Mill: A Collection of Critical Essays.* Garden City, N.Y.: Doubleday & Company, 1968.

Skorupski, John. *John Stuart Mill.* London: Routledge & Kegan Paul, 1989.

14

KANT I

Moral Internalism and Externalism

Hobbes and Mill are **externalists** about morality. Both believe that the reasons why an action is morally right or wrong are not *necessarily* reasons *to act* morally. In any given case, they believe, there may be conclusive reasons for acting wrongly. For Hobbes, what makes an act wrong is that it violates a rule, the collective following of which is mutually advantageous. But reasons for action derive from the agent's own advantage, either directly or indirectly (via some advantageous rule). Similarly, Mill believed that actions are wrong if they violate rules that, if established as a social practice, would produce the greatest overall happiness. But although societies can develop motives for following such rules through moral education, there is no guarantee that everyone will have such motives.

This can seem an unsatisfactory situation. Suppose you think that income tax fraud is wrong. I don't mean that you just think it is *considered* wrong. You think it really *is* wrong because, let us suppose, you think it amounts to taking unfair advantage. But now ask yourself, If tax fraud is wrong for this reason, doesn't this give you (or anyone) reason not to engage in it? You may, of course, believe there are additional reasons not to be fraudulent—for example, that fraudulence would be imprudent. But don't you think that the unfairness is reason enough in itself? If you don't, it may be because you think that others submit fraudulent returns, so why shouldn't you? But this thought sits uneasily between two possibilities. Either fraud is so rampant that you don't think anyone has a reason of fairness to avoid it, and so it isn't really wrong or, at least, isn't wrong for that reason. Or, although some engage in tax fraud, you still wouldn't want everyone (else) to, and so on reflection you think it would be wrong for them to do so. But if that is what you think, won't you also think this gives you and them a reason not to engage in it?

Since Hobbes and Mill held that the grounds of moral right and wrong differ from what gives agents reasons for acting, externalist theories like theirs must deny that the wrongness of an action guarantees reason not to do it. According to them, moral right- and wrong-making considerations are not necessarily reason-giving in their own right. Moreover, for philosophical utilitarians like Mill, morality and moral action have value only because they are *instrumental* to other, **nonmoral** values. For all utilitarians, whether act- or rule-utilitarians, the ultimate source of moral justification is nothing inherent in a moral agent's conduct but, rather, only the consequences of acts and practices.

In Immanuel Kant (1724–1804) we find a philosopher who rejects virtually every aspect of this picture. Whereas Hobbes's theory and the utilitarians hold that the value of moral actions and practices is only derivative and instrumental, Kant's ethics maintains that morality has its own intrinsic value, one that is uniquely exemplified in the will of a free moral agent. And whereas externalists believe that moral distinctions of right and wrong are grounded in principles or "criteria" that have no intrinsic normative or reason-giving authority, Kant was a **moral internalist** who argued that any agent is committed by the logic of her own free rational deliberation to morality's fundamental principle, the **Categorical Imperative (CI)**.[1]

Kant claimed that morality is **autonomous** in two senses that seem initially quite different but are intimately related for him nonetheless. First, Kant maintained that morality is an independent or autonomous subject in precisely the sense that philosophical utilitarians and Hobbes denied. Morality's principles and values derive from its intrinsic nature, not from its relation to anything external to it to which it is an instrument (as with the nonmoral value of happiness). Second, Kant believed that morality essentially concerns the will of autonomous (self-determining) moral agents. "Autonomy of the will," he wrote, "is the property the will has of being a law to itself"(G.440).[2] The moral law is *internal* to the moral agent, since, as Kant put it, the agent "makes" it herself in her own practical reasoning. (See, for example, G.431.) Don't worry if you can't yet imagine what Kant meant by this.

The Critical Philosophy: Theoretical and Practical

Kant began his philosophical life as the kind of rational intuitionist who believed that reason can directly perceive necessary, **a priori** facts—for example, that every event has a cause. When he encountered Hume's critique of this idea, however, Kant said it woke him from his "dogmatic slumbers."

We often speak and think as though we directly perceive causal connections in nature. When we watch balls on a billiard table, for example, we may say that we see the cue ball's movement *cause* the three ball to move into the side pocket. This common-sense belief involves a number of constituent notions—most notably, those of **necessity, universality,** and **natural law.** Having seen the cue ball strike the three ball in a certain way, we think that the three ball *must* move as it does, that it is a law of nature that whenever billiard balls are so struck, they will move in that way, other things being equal.

Hume argued that we can find no basis for these ideas in experience. All we experience is a series of sensations or "impressions," first of the cue ball's movement, then of the three ball's movement. We have no sensory impression of a *connection* between these. The most that we can say on the basis of sense perception is that, in the past, movements of cue balls like this have been "constantly conjoined" with movements of three balls like that.[3]

The reason we think of the movements as connected, Hume argued, is that we acquire a psychological habit of expecting what has been constantly conjoined in our past experience to continue to be so in the future. Having seen billiard balls regularly move in certain ways when struck by cue balls in other ways, we expect the former movement when we see the latter. What's more, we *project* our expectation onto our experience. The common belief that we perceive causal connections is simply the result of this projection. We seem to experience things as though there were an objective connection in nature, whereas all there really is is a subjective expectation built up from the experience of constantly conjoined natural events.

Hume's critique convinced Kant that it is impossible to derive the ideas of necessity, universality, and natural law from perception. As a corollary, Kant also agreed with Hume's hypothesis that these ideas must result from a contribution of our minds. But whereas Hume believed that this mental contribution is caused by habit, and so is nothing that can warrant the judgments of objective necessity it explains, Kant believed that judgments of objective causal necessity can be warranted, since the mental contribution from which they result is itself necessary to the very possibility of experience.

If it is to provide a basis for empirical judgment, experience cannot consist of utterly unstructured sensations (William James's "blooming, buzzing confusion"). Rather, Kant argued, experience must be structured by various "categories," including causation and its constituent ideas of universality, necessity, and natural law. We therefore have an *a priori* warrant for supposing that every event has a cause. Being structured through this supposition is a necessary condition for the possibility of experience and empirical knowledge in the first place.

"Critical philosophy" is what Kant called the general project of critically evaluating the powers of reason. His *Critique of Pure Reason* (1781) proceeds roughly along the lines just sketched to assess the powers of *theoretical reason* in coming to warranted *beliefs*. But reason is not concerned only with belief. What matters most for ethics, Kant thought, is *practical reason*: an *agent's* deliberative reasoning about what *to do*. And just as theoretical reason requires *a priori* concepts of universality and necessity, so likewise, Kant argued, are practical versions of these ideas presupposed in practical reasoning. Moreover, he insisted, these necessary practical concepts are bound up with others—most significantly, with the ideas of *freedom* and *morality*. What a critique of practical reason reveals, he claimed, is that any free agent is ultimately committed to guiding her conduct by the fundamental moral principle he called the Categorical Imperative: *Act only on principles that one can will all others to act on as well.*

Rational Agents, Reasons, and Universal Laws: A Preliminary

To get a taste of Kant's approach, we can begin with the famous passage from his *Groundwork of the Metaphysics of Morals* that I alluded to in Chapter 1: "Everything in nature works in accordance with laws. Only a rational being has the power to act *in accordance with his idea* of laws—that is, in accordance with principles—and only so has he a *will*. Since *reason* is required in order to derive actions from laws, the will is nothing but practical reason" (G.412; original emphasis). "Law" enters into this passage in two places. First, Kant mentioned natural laws, the kind that explain the movements of billiard balls. These he contrasted with laws that are *practical* principles of the *will*, which rational beings (unlike billiard balls, or even other intelligent creatures) can obey or flout, since they can choose in accord with or contrary to *their idea* of them.

As in Chapter 1, we can put Kant's point in terms of *reasons*. Whenever something happens, we suppose there must be some reason why it occurred. In fact, Kant argued, we *must* generally suppose this, since our doing so is a condition of experience. (Recall what I said earlier about conceiving of our experience as caused.) But compare reasons that explain the movements of billiard balls with reasons *for acting* that make intelligible the actions of the billiard-playing agents who strike them. Unlike the balls they set in motion, billiard players *have* reasons for doing what they do. They have what we call "*their* reasons." Suppose I strike the cue ball in a certain way, and you ask me why. One way of answering will be for me to give you *my* reason for my shot—namely, what I regarded at the time as a (normative) reason *for* taking it in the way I did. For example, I might say that if I hit the three ball at a certain angle it would go into the side pocket. This statement may help you to see my action as I did from my deliberative perspective, as a *rational* thing to do for this reason. Alternatively, of course, I might answer by giving reasons explaining my action that weren't *my* reasons. I might even try to explain what I did as a kind of mistake—"I always get suckered into trying that shot in that situation." Or I might explain my behavior as a result of habit or conditioning. (Make sure you see why these reasons for what I did couldn't possibly have been my reasons for acting.)

It is distinctive of the actions of a rational being—a rational *agent*—that they are performed for reasons that the agent believed to favor or recommend the action (whether consciously or not). What's more, Kant held, when an agent takes something as a reason for acting, doing so commits her to a universal normative principle or "practical law." When I deliberate about what shot to take, I think not about myself but about the practical situation confronting me. Of course, if I am prudent, I will take account of my strengths and weaknesses, and of my own ends in playing billiards in the first place. I will try to figure out what shot *to* take in light of these factors and the general strategic situation on the table. But even here my deliberation is not *essentially* about *me*. It is about the deliberative situation facing me: what to do in light of my abilities and goals and the position of the game on the table. It is implicitly about what anyone (like me) should do in a situation like this. And if I come to the conclusion that I should shoot the cue ball in a certain way, that there are good reasons for doing so, then I will be committed to thinking that this is a shot that would be sensible for anyone to take who is like me in whatever respects I take to be relevant to my own choice.

This is our old familiar point about ethical judgments and properties, appearing in a new guise. Ethical properties cannot be had *barely,* and *my reasons* cannot be had *barely by me.* If a consideration is a reason for me to do something in a certain situation, then it must also be a reason for anyone who is relevantly like me to act similarly in any relevantly similar situation. Which situations and actions must I think are relevantly similar? That all depends on what I take to be relevant to my own case, as we shall see in Chapter 15.

If this is right so far, it means that any agent commits herself to universal principles (practical laws) whenever she acts. But don't we sometimes do what we think we have good reason not to do? This is what philosophers call the problem of **weakness of will.** However, we need not settle that, since even if we don't always do what we think best, Kant could still insist that we always have *some* reason for acting, and that this commits us to a universal principle concerning what anyone should do in this kind of situation, *other things being equal.*

The foregoing gives us a glimpse at Kant's thesis that the concepts of *law* and *universality* enter into an agent's deliberative standpoint in a distinctive way, as part of the structure of thought from that perspective, analogous to

Kant's understanding of the way that the theoretical versions of these concepts are essential to the standpoint of empirical cognition. Thinking about what to do commits me to universal principles of practical reason (practical laws) just as experiencing an occurrence as something to be believed commits me to universal principles of theoretical reason (for example, that every event has a cause).

Kant's Project in the *Groundwork*

Kant's aim in the *Groundwork of the Metaphysics of Morals* (1785) is to defend the moral internalist proposition that moral norms are binding an any rational agent. There are actually two parts of this proposition, requiring two separate arguments. One is the claim that it is internal to the very idea of morality that morality obligates all rational agents. This is a **conceptual thesis**. It maintains that if an agent is morally required to do something, then necessarily she is rationally required to do it (i.e., there exist conclusive reasons for her doing it). Consider something you are inclined to think is a moral obligation—for example, the moral duty not to torture and terrorize innocents for strategic advantage. What **conceptual moral internalism** holds is that if this is a moral obligation, then there must exist overriding reasons for those subject to it to act accordingly. Conversely, if there are better reasons for someone to act otherwise, then she cannot have a moral obligation not to do so. Our best candidates for moral norms are thus staked upon their providing conclusive reasons for acting. According to conceptual moral internalism, if we come to believe that someone has better reasons not to abide by some candidate moral norm, then we must deny that the candidate actually is a valid moral norm to which she is subject. It is part of the very idea of a moral obligation that there are overriding reasons for following it.

The second part of Kant's moral internalism we can call **metaphysical moral internalism**, since it asserts the existence of universally binding moral norms. Arguing for this claim requires something more than an analysis of our ideas of morality and moral obligation. As we've just seen, conceptual moral internalism might be true even if nothing we believe to be a moral norm actually binds all rational agents. In that case, what we take to be moral obligations wouldn't really be. To establish metaphysical moral internalism, then, we need an argument that can show that our best candidate moral norms really are binding on all rational agents.

Kant argued for conceptual moral internalism in the Preface and Chapters I and II of the *Groundwork*, proceeding "**analytically**" from premises he hopes his readers will agree are deeply embedded in their own moral convictions (G.392) and concluding that the Categorical Imperative is morality's "supreme principle." Inherent in our deepest convictions, he argued, is the idea that morality requires acting only on principles we can will all to act on and treating rational personality always as an end in itself.

This first line of thought proceeds entirely *within* the moral perspective. But even if moral duties *present themselves* as categorically binding on any rational agent, we can step back from the moral point of view and ask, Why should I be moral? What makes it the case that moral duties actually *are* binding? And what gives morality the normativity or rational authority that it presents itself as having?

Answering these questions requires a second line of argument, one that does not take the authority of morality for granted. In Chapter III of the *Groundwork,* Kant makes such an argument, developing themes we glimpsed in the passage I quoted earlier. Free rational agents necessarily act under the idea of law. And this, Kant argued, ultimately commits them to guiding themselves by the Categorical Imperative, morality's "supreme principle."

We shall start our examination of the first line of argument in the remainder of this chapter, leaving the second for Chapter 15.

Morality: Necessity, Universality, and the *A Priori*

We can begin by considering Kant's claims that the ideas of *necessity, universality,* and *a priori* validity are presupposed in our deepest moral convictions. It is "already obvious from the common Idea of duty and from the laws of morality," Kant wrote, that fundamental moral principles are valid *a priori* and, therefore, not based on any natural contingency that is subject to empirical investigation. The idea of a law, moreover, "has to carry with it absolute necessity if it is to be valid morally." Since "the command 'Thou shall not lie' could not hold merely for men, other rational beings having no obligation to abide by it, . . . the ground of obligation must be looked for, not in the nature of man nor in the circumstances of the world in which he is placed, but solely *a priori* in the concepts of pure reason" (G.389).

That's a mouthful. To see what Kant was getting at, let's relate his example of lying to the case of tax fraud we examined earlier. Suppose you think it would be wrong to lie about your income on your tax forms. This conviction is about your own conduct, but not essentially. Although if you lie it will be *your* fraud (the one involving the tax forms you signed) that will be wrong, the property of being wrong cannot be had by your act barely. If your act is wrong, it must be by virtue of features of you and your situation that could also be instantiated by other particular situations and agents.

What Kant was saying, then, is that if you press hard enough on your conviction that it would be wrong to commit tax fraud, you will see that you must hold it to be grounded in a principle that applies to the conduct of all rational agents. We should be careful here, however. Kant was not saying that you must think that all rational beings should or do have systems of taxation similar to ours, or even that they all have the same need for information and vulnerabilities to deception that make fraud problematic for us. Rather, his idea was just this: Press as hard as you can on your conviction that it would be wrong for you to commit tax fraud and see what most deeply underlies it. In other words, figure out what the most fundamental features of your situation are that, *in your own view*, make it wrong for you to lie in this situation. For example, suppose you come to the conclusion that something like the following is what would make your act wrong. You are involved in a cooperative scheme with others for mutual benefit in which everyone is prepared to cooperate (pay taxes) only if others do also. In submitting a fraudulent form you would be taking advantage of their good will without doing your share. You would be doing what you would will that they not do.

Now ask yourself, Do you think it would be wrong for you to do this because you are an American citizen (if you are)? Or because you have a functioning kidney or are a human being? Kant believed that if you reflect sufficiently, you will ultimately agree that the features that make this wrong for you to do are simply that you are a rational agent who is reciprocally interacting with other rational agents. If you think it is wrong for you to take advantage of others' good will, then you should think that this would be no less wrong for Vulcans than for you. And if this is right, then underlying your conviction about the wrongness of your tax fraud is a universal moral principle (or law) that you are committed to believing applies to any rational being.

At this point, you may think I have rigged things by supplying you with the supposition that the reason you think lying would be wrong is because it violates the Categorical Imperative—doing what you could not will that others do. But nothing really hangs on that for my present point. Suppose you think it would be wrong because God commands you not to lie. Without going too far into theology, wouldn't that commit you to thinking that any agent to whom God's commands are addressed should not lie also? Or suppose you are a utilitarian and think that your tax fraud would be wrong because it would not promote the general happiness. Wouldn't you be committed to thinking that other rational agents should maximize overall happiness also?

If this is right, then any conviction about moral duty is ultimately grounded in a principle of duty or law to which one must believe all rational agents are subject. This gives us universality, but what about necessity and *a priori* validity? Kant believed that a similar series of reflections should convince us of these also. Suppose you think it is wrong to do what you would want others not to do to you. Do you think that this just *happens* to be wrong? Can you imagine any way the world might have been such that it would not have been wrong? If you can, then, according to Kant, you have not yet gotten to the bottom of your moral convictions.

Much of what is true is only **contingently** true. As it happens, I cannot hold my breath for more than three minutes. But with changed evolutionary circumstances affecting the functioning of human lungs, things might have been different. When we are not yet at the bottom of our moral convictions, we can conceive of changes like this. Recall the person from Chapter 1 who opposed a law permitting doctor-assisted suicide because he thought it would lead to the exploitation of vulnerable people. He might well think that, in changed social circumstances, the law would not be morally objectionable because it wouldn't cause exploitation as a consequence. But his more fundamental moral belief concerns, not the law, but the wrongness of exploitation. Are there circumstances in which that would not be wrong? If he thinks there are, then, according to Kant, he has not yet articulated to himself the most fundamental principle underlying his conviction.

If we are committed to thinking our most basic ethical convictions universal and necessary, then we must also take them to be *a priori*. The most we can learn through sense experience is how things happen to be. If fundamental moral convictions can be known at all, therefore, it would seem they have to be knowable *a priori*.

However, even if moral common sense is committed to the existence of universal, necessary, *a priori* principles of moral duty, where do these come from? What makes them true, necessarily and *a priori*? As we shall see, Kant rejected the rational intuitionist theory that there are necessary ethical facts that reason can directly perceive. His position, rather, was that universal principles of duty are grounded in the deliberative perspective of a free rational agent—that is, in an **ideal agent theory** of normative reasons.

Likewise, Kant believed that particular universal principles of moral duty (for example, concerning the wrongness of lying) are not simply given through a kind of moral perception. What is rock bottom in our moral convictions, he thought, is a view about the distinctive value of moral character and will that leads to an **ideal moral agent theory** of right and wrong.

The Good Will

Chapter I of the *Groundwork* begins with Kant's famous claim that "it is impossible to conceive anything at all in the world, or even out of it, which can be taken as good without qualification, except a *good will*" (G.393; original emphasis). Since he has told us that his claim concerns "ordinary rational knowledge of morality," we should interpret him as talking about moral value. And we should remind ourselves that he held that "the will is nothing but practical reason" (G.412). The will is our power of acting on reasons or principles. Putting these together, we can conclude that the only thing that is unqualifiedly morally good is excellence in the exercise of moral agency.

Other views to which we might be tempted, Kant argued, have implications we cannot accept. Thus "talents," such as intelligence and wit, and "temperament[s]," such as "resolution" and "constancy of purpose," though valuable in some contexts, can be utilized for evil ends. And similarly for "gifts of fortune" such as power, wealth, and well-being. Note that the issue is not whether any of these things have an intrinsic worth or merit that warrants esteem other than moral esteem. Artistic genius, for example, seems clearly to be admirable in itself. What Kant is claiming, rather, is that only a good will is an unqualified object of moral esteem.

Kant's contrast here is between features of the agent's deliberative situation as she finds it (that are not up to her) and what is up to her as an agent. Moral evaluation, Kant claimed, is of how we exercise our agency with respect to what is up to us. This, he said, is what we reserve the notion of *character* for. One person may simply be naturally warmer than another, but this is a matter of temperament rather than character, something that is not up to either of them. But how each deals with and acts in light of their respective temperaments *does* concern character. And this, Kant asserted, is what we esteem and value morally.

Notice the contrast with utilitarianism. Utilitarians view morality instrumentally in relation to human happiness, so they also see moral evaluation in relational terms. Against all forms of utilitarianism, Kant claimed that it is intrinsic to the very idea of moral evaluation that it is fundamentally of persons *as agents*. Accordingly, Kant wrote, "A good will is not good because of what it effects or accomplishes" or "because of its fitness for attaining some proposed end: it is good through its willing alone—that is, good in itself" (G.394). Since it is good in itself, it is good unqualifiedly— that is, in any context. Even were it to bring about bad consequences, that would not lessen our moral esteem for a good will in itself.

But what *is* a good will? Kant's answer rests on his view of the will as practical reason. The will is the capacity of acting for reasons and, thus, on universal normative principles. For Kant, therefore, a person of good will is an agent who governs herself by the moral law—who acts, as he also said, "from duty."

We should notice here what may seem to be a tension in Kant's view. On the one hand, Kant held that *any* action of a rational agent involves some commitment to universal practical law. On the other, Kant said that only actions manifesting the distinctive excellence of moral agency (good will) are *actually* governed by universal practical law. What, then, is the difference between the commitment to universal law that is implicit in any action and the kind that characterizes the good will?

A person of good will shows a seriousness and wholeheartedness in following the law that not every agent manifests. People sometimes show weak will, acting contrary to what they believe are better reasons. Or again, although any action involves *regarding* something as a law, the person of good will is not content with what she may happen so to regard. She is concerned to find out what the moral law really is, and to guide herself by that.

But *what* moral law? Where does *it* come from? And how does a good will know what it is? It is important to Kant's claim that, at the present point in the argument, this cannot be specified. In particular, Kant was not assuming that the person of good will guides herself by the Categorical Imperative. As we shall soon see, however, Kant's first argument for the Categorical Imperative was that it uniquely meets the conditions set by the idea of a fundamental principle by which a person of good will guides herself.

Moral Worth

Kant's thesis of the unique, unqualified goodness of the good will is reflected in a set of claims he made about the distinctive moral worth of actions that express good will (G.397–400). Actions can have genuine moral worth, he said, only if they are done *from the motive of duty*, the governing motive of a good will. It is insufficient that acts accord with duty. They can't simply be the right thing to do. For an agent's action to have moral worth, the agent must do it because it accords with duty.

Note that Kant was not saying that an action cannot be the right thing to do unless it is done from a sense of duty. On the contrary, his point is about actions as they manifest character. His claim concerns not acts (alternatives one might choose in deliberation for some motive or other) but *motivated actions,* as we might consider them after the fact. The perspective of judgments of moral worth is not the first-personal, agent's standpoint of deliberation but, rather, the third-personal perspective from which we assess persons, character, and motives. We take up the former standpoint to figure out what to do; and the second one, to evaluate what to think or feel about what someone has done, how it reflects on her character, and so on. Someone may do the right thing but for the wrong reasons. Kant's claim was that for an action to exemplify the distinctive value or worth of good moral character, the agent must do what she does because she believes her act to be morally right.

We should also understand that Kant was not saying that an action cannot have moral worth if the agent has other motives in addition to the motive of duty. What matters is whether the agent *governed* her will by the moral law in the sense that she would have done what was right even if she had lacked other motives for doing so, and that she wouldn't have done what she did if she had believed it to be wrong.

Kant's most persuasive illustration involves a contrast between doing the right thing because it is right and doing it out of self-interest. A grocer charges "inexperienced customer[s]" the same price as the street-wise, but only because this is prudent business in light of the risk of incurring a reputation for cheating (G.397). The grocer does the right thing, but his action lacks the worth it would have had if he'd charged the same price but done so because that was the right thing to do. Since his governing motive was self-interest, if, contrary to fact, his interest had conflicted with what was right, the grocer would have acted wrongly. So his action, albeit the right thing to have done, does not reflect the distinctive moral value of good character and will.

The most controversial implication of Kant's thesis is that actions can derive no moral worth from any motive other than duty—for example, from benevolence or love. One might agree with Kant's claim that the value of good will or character is intrinsic (not derived from consequences or other extrinsic features) but believe that benevolence or love are intrinsically morally good motives. It is instructive here to contrast Kant's encomium to good will in the *Groundwork* with Paul's praise of love or charity in Corinthians: "Though I speak with the tongues of men and of angels, and have not charity, I am become as sounding brass, or a tinkling cymbal. . . . And though I bestow all my goods to feed the poor, . . . and have not charity, it profiteth me nothing" (Cor. I.13). Paul praises love as intrinsically valuable—estimable quite independent of whether it leads to good consequences such as feeding the poor. And you may agree.

So why did Kant think that actions motivated by love and sympathy, "however right and amiable" they may be, nonetheless have "no genuinely moral worth?" (G.398). Kant's description of a benevolent person as one who finds "an inner pleasure in spreading happiness" may lead one to think that he would have seen this case as fundamentally no different from actions motivated by self-interest. Whereas the shopkeeper's self-interest is served by just pricing, the benevolent person's is served by helping others. But if this is Kant's argument, it is not very strong, for reasons we noted in our discussion of hedonism in Chapter 12. Sympathetic people do derive pleasure from helping others, but that is because they care about them. It's not that they care about others because helping them is a source of pleasure.

Kant has better arguments, however. Here is one. It is obvious that concern for any *particular* person or persons will not necessarily lead to doing the morally right thing in any circumstance, even in the agent's own view. For example, concern solely for Jerome's interests might lead me to slander Jerome's hated rival. Or concern solely for the interests of one group might lead me to advance them unfairly at the cost of some other's. And even an equal concern for the interests of all will invariably motivate right action only if act-utilitarianism is true. In this respect, Kant said, concern for the welfare of others is "on the same footing as other inclinations . . . which if

fortunate enough to hit on something . . . right . . . deserves praise and en-
couragement, but not esteem" (G.398).

What, exactly, is Kant's argument here? First, by "esteem," Kant clearly
must have meant a distinctively moral evaluation. This is obvious from the
fact that he conceded that benevolently motivated actions are intrinsically
"amiable." Second, his argument can't really be that the motive of duty is
more likely than other motives (including benevolence) to get agents to do
what actually is right. He has said nothing to support this claim, and there
are reasons to doubt it. Maybe the motive of duty is relatively weak and
concern for others relatively strong. Maybe people are likely to mistake
their duty, and perhaps, in some cases at least, concern for others will be
likelier to lead them to their real duty. Think, for example, of Huck Finn,
whose concern for Jim, a runaway slave, leads him to hide Jim from those
who would return him to captivity, against what Huck apparently believes
to be his moral duty.

We get closer to Kant's argument if we say that the problem with benevolence, as with any motive other than the sense of duty, is that it is only accidental that it "hit[s] on" what, *from the agent's own point of view,* is the
right thing to do. There is no necessary coincidence, in other words, between the acts these motives motivate and what the agent himself has good
reason to think morally right. (Unless, that is, the agent has reason to believe act-utilitarianism.)

But now we can factor cases into two kinds. On the one side, we have
agents who are motivated by benevolence and lack any views whatsoever
about moral right and wrong. On the other, we have agents who are motivated by benevolence and have such moral views. In a case of the first kind,
it will be hard to regard an action motivated by sympathy or benevolence
as having moral worth, since it will be hard to regard the sympathetic being
as a full-fledged moral agent. Kant granted that altruistic concern (for example, that of a young child) is "amiable" in itself. What he denied is that
it has moral worth.

In a case of the second kind, we have someone who has moral views but
is prepared to disregard them. So in this situation, even if altruistic concern *fortunately* points in the same direction as moral duty, had it not, the
person would have done what was wrong by his own lights. And how can
that have moral worth? (And what about Huck Finn? The question, again,
is not whether Huck did the right thing in hiding Jim but whether his doing so warrants moral esteem of his character. Suppose you think it does.
Would Kant have disagreed? Not necessarily, since he could have argued
that, despite appearances, what Huck *really* thought it would be right to
do is not as obvious as it may seem. It is obvious that Huck thinks that
hiding Jim will generally be *considered* wrong, but less obvious that he
thinks it really *is* wrong. On the contrary, Kant might have said, We think

Huck's hiding Jim is morally estimable because we believe that, deep down, Huck really thinks it would be wrong to turn Jim in and doesn't for that reason.)

Moral esteem therefore concerns how a person exercises the capacity for principled action that makes her a moral agent. And this suggests a second argument for Kant's controversial claim. If all rational agents are equally subject to morality, it would be odd if moral evaluation were based on features other than those a person shares with all rational agents. To be a rational moral agent, however, one does not necessarily require a capacity for sympathy. If being motivated by sympathy were sufficient to give an action moral worth, then some moral agents would be prevented by something that was in no way up to them from doing what has (that kind of) moral worth. And this seems an odd result.

A Derivation of the Categorical Imperative?

Let's accept all this for purposes of argument. Let's grant that a morally good will is governed by moral laws and that, in order for an action to have moral worth, its governing motive must be to conform to moral laws. As Kant put it, "Nothing but the *idea of the law* in itself, *which admittedly is present only in a rational being*[,]. . . can constitute that pre-eminent good which we call moral, a good which is already present in the person acting on this idea and has not to be awaited merely from the result" (G.401). But still, what makes a principle a *moral law?*

Since a good will is guided by the law, it may seem surprising that Kant defined the "concept of duty" as "includ[ing] that of a good will, exposed, however, to certain subjective limitations" (G.397). In short, there is no way of determining what principles are moral laws other than by determining what principles a good will would govern herself by. Here we have an example of an ideal moral agent theory of moral duty. It holds that something's being a moral duty consists in its being required by a principle that an ideally moral agent (a good will) would follow.

This is actually a quite natural thing to think if we rule out various alternatives that Kant rejected. First, Kant believed that fundamental principles of moral right and wrong are necessary and *a priori*, so he had to reject naturalism. And he also denied any view like theological voluntarism that makes right and wrong depend on some arbitrary act of will, since no such view can explain the necessity of moral duties. Finally, Kant rejected the rational intuitionist doctrine that there exist ethical facts that can be directly perceived or intuited by reason. How, then, are *a priori*, necessary principles of moral duty to be grounded?

Recall the general strategy of Kant's critical philosophy and of his critique of pure reason. There the problem was how to account for *a priori*, necessary truths (e.g., every event has a cause) without falling into dogmatic rationalism. Kant's solution was to argue that the supposition that events have causes is necessary for the very possibility of empirical thought and cognition. Similarly, in the moral case, Kant argued that *a priori,* necessary principles of moral duty are grounded in the structure of moral deliberations—specifically, the deliberations of a morally ideal agent or good will.

Recall also the general rationale for the **ideal judgment theory** discussed in Chapter 6. We may be more confident that we know the qualities of a good ethical judge than that we identify true particular ethical judgments, especially controversial ones. Kant's doctrine of the good will echoes this theme. What is rock bottom in our moral convictions, Kant claimed, is our belief in the moral worth of a person of moral integrity who governs herself by her moral duty as she sees it.

In general, ideal judgment theories hold that ethical facts concern what judgments an ideal judge would make. Thus the theory of nonmoral value that Mill apparently presupposed is that value consists in being valued (preferred) by an ideally informed and experienced judge. Kant's form of ideal judgment theory is an ideal agent theory (or ideal deliberative judgment theory). And his theory of moral right and wrong is an ideal moral agent theory.

According to an ideal moral agent theory, what makes something a moral law is that it would be so regarded by an ideally moral agent—it is a principle by which a person of good will would govern herself. But what constitutes such a principle? Kant put the question this way: "What kind of law can this be the thought of which, even without regard to the results expected from it, has to determine the will if this is to be called good absolutely and without qualification?" (G.402). Here is his response:

> Since I have robbed the will of every inducement that might arise for it as a consequence of obeying any particular law, nothing is left but the conformity of actions to universal law as such, and this alone must serve the will as its principle. That is to say, I ought never to act except in such a way *that I can also will that my maxim should become a universal law.* Here bare conformity to universal law as such (without having as its base any law prescribing particular actions) is what serves the will as its principle, and must so serve it if duty is not to be everywhere an empty delusion and a chimerical concept. (G.402; original emphasis)

A good will, as such, is not characterized by a desire for any consequence, like the greatest overall happiness. This condition rules out any consequentialist attempt to derive moral principles from some end that is somehow given to morality. But neither are any "law[s] prescribing particular actions" given to moral agents as, for example, rational intuitionists believe.

So the person of good will has no alternative but to base her commitment to a particular principle on whether the principle is *fit* to be a law. And she has no way of determining that, Kant appears to have assumed, other than by whether, on reflection, she would invariably *will* that it be regarded as a law by herself and all other rational agents. It is a necessary condition of her regarding any principle as a practical law, therefore, that she could will that everyone so treat it. This means that the Categorical Imperative must function for a good will as her most fundamental law. But since this is so, it follows from an ideal moral agent theory that the Categorical Imperative actually *is* the most fundamental moral principle.

To see the force of this argument, note a distinction implicit in it between what must be true in order for an agent to regard the principle of her will *as law* and what must be true in order for her to regard the principle of her will as *fit to be law*. It is easy to think that Kant's argument is a *non sequitur* if we take him to be arguing from the premise that an agent must regard her principle of acting *as law* to the conclusion that she must will that everyone follow it (and, hence, that if she cannot will this, then she cannot regard her principle as law). To see that this does not follow, suppose that an agent believes it to be a moral law that everyone should promote only his or her own interests. Clearly, it doesn't follow from the fact that an agent accepts this principle as a law that she wills that everyone follow it. In fact, willing that everyone follow it may be inconsistent with what the law requires of the agent herself.

But this is not Kant's argument. The good will wants to do what is right, but, unlike the person in our example, he cannot take "any law prescribing particular actions," like the egoistic principle just considered, as given. What he requires, therefore, is something that can serve for him as a (second-order) test of possible laws, of whether a (first-order) principle is *fit* to be a moral law. What's more, the considerations underlying an ideal (moral) agent theory require that this test concern his will. This leaves Kant with what seems the only remaining possibility—namely, that principles of moral right and wrong are grounded in whether they can be *willed as law,* whether, that is, one (anyone) can will that he be treated as law in the deliberations of all moral agents. And that is just what the Categorical Imperative says: *Act only on principles that one can will all others to act on as well.*

15

KANT II

Kant's normative theory is often cited as the paradigm of **deontological** ethics, the polar opposite of **consequentialist** theories such as utilitarianism. (See Chapter 9.) Deontological theories hold that actions can be made right or wrong by the kinds of acts they are, independent of their consequences. Since we have already seen how the Categorical Imperative (CI) springs from an ideal of agency and not from "any law[s] prescribing particular actions," we shall want to understand how deontological norms can be grounded in the CI and the philosophical considerations that underlie it. Our task is made more challenging (and intriguing) by the fact that Kant formulated the CI in seemingly different ways, insisting that these are "merely so many formulations of precisely the same law" (G.436). The reason, Mill suggested, is that Kant's ethics actually reduce to a form of rule-utilitarianism (U.I.4). If so, Kant's normative theory may not pose an alternative to consequentialism after all.

Categorical Versus Hypothetical Imperatives

To begin, we should note how the Categorical Imperative (big 'C') relates to an important distinction that Kant makes between **categorical** (small 'c') and **hypothetical imperatives** generally.

Suppose someone has resolved to improve his critical thinking skills and seeks a means to doing so. You convince him that the best means would be to take a philosophy course. Thus you have given him grounds to think something like the following: "If (or since) I want to improve my critical thinking, I should take a philosophy course." This is an example of what Kant calls a hypothetical imperative. The term is misleading, since it suggests anything that can be put in hypothetical form: "If p, then S ought to do A." But many things of that form are actually categorical imperatives—for example, "If you promised Joan you would sublet your apartment to her, then you should do so." What makes something a hypothetical imperative is, roughly, that the condition in the 'if' clause is simply that one has some end (to which the act in the 'then' clause is a good, or the only, means). "A hypothetical imperative thus says only that an action is good for some purpose or other, either *possible* or *actual*" (G.414; original emphasis).

The validity of hypothetical imperatives is entirely uncontroversial, Kant thought, because they are entailed by the very idea of a rational agent pursuing ends. To have an end just *is* to will some effect, and this already involves the idea of "myself as an acting cause" (G.417). In adopting the improvement of his critical thinking as his end, our person must already be intending to use some means or other to accomplish this. Otherwise, he hasn't really made it his end. It follows, therefore, that "whoever wills the end, wills (so far as reason has decisive influence on his actions) also the means which are indispensably necessary and in his power" (G.417). "So far as willing is concerned," Kant concluded, "this proposition is **analytic**" (G.417). Its truth is guaranteed by the meanings of terms.

It would be incoherent, therefore, for someone to have improving critical thinking as an end, believe that the *only* way to do this would be to take a philosophy course, and not intend to (worse: intend not to) take a philosophy course. The point is not that this would be impossible but that it would be *irrational*. To act rationally, the person must remove the incoherence. If he persists in his end and in the belief that he can accomplish it only by taking a philosophy course, the only remaining alternative is to take a philosophy course.

By the same token, however, he can remove the incoherence equally well by renouncing his end. Since what underlies hypothetical imperatives is simply the rational demand to avoid incoherence, practical reasoning of the following form is invalid when (1) is interpreted as a hypothetical imperative.

(1) If S's end is A, and B is the only means to A, then S should do B.
(2) S's end is A, and B is the only means to A.
Therefore,
(3) S should do B.

To see this, substitute "killing Jones in the most gruesome way" for A and "starving Jones to death" for B. And imagine a case in which, when (1) is read as a hypothetical imperative, (1) and (2) are both true. Would (3) follow? It would not. When (1) is read as a hypothetical imperative, the most that would follow would be:

(4) Either S should do B or S should not have A as his end.

Categorical imperatives differ from hypothetical imperatives in that they make 'ought' claims that go beyond the demand for practical coherence. Thus the following reasoning is valid when (1') is a categorical imperative.

(1') If p, then S should do B.
(2') p.
Therefore,
(3') S should do B.

Since one possible substitution instance for p is "S's end is A, and B is the only means to A," it follows that when the resulting proposition ("If S's end is A, and B is the only means to A, then S should do B") is read as a categorical rather than a hypothetical imperative, the resulting reasoning is valid also. Read as a categorical imperative, the proposition says that if A is S's end and B is the only means to A, then, categorically, S should do B. However, read as a hypothetical imperative, it says only that S should either do B *or* give up A as his end.

Another way of putting the point is to say that hypothetical imperatives say what there is reason to do (or what one should do) *relative* to the assumption that one has reason to have some end. For whereas it is invalid to reason from (1) and (2) to (3), the following *is* valid.

(1") If A is an end S should have, and B is a necessary means to A, then S should do B.
(2") A is an end S should have, and B is a necessary means to A.
Therefore,
(3") S should do B.

Hypothetical imperatives transfer rational support from end to means, and, likewise, they transfer lack of support from means to end. If it makes sense to pursue a given end, then it must make sense to pursue the only means to it. And if it doesn't make sense to take the only means, then it can't make sense to pursue the end. But, again, the most this tells us is that one should either take the means or give up the end. It can't tell us which. Hypothetical imperatives are impotent, therefore, to provide the sort of practical guidance one seeks in deliberation. Only categorical imperatives can give that kind of practical guidance.

The ineliminability of categorical imperatives from practical reasoning is a theme to which we shall return when we consider Kant's argument in Chapter III of the *Groundwork* that the CI is actually binding on all agents, since any free rational agent is committed to governing deliberation by it. But what is the relation between the Categorical Imperative (big 'C') and categorical imperatives (little 'c')? Kant's answer is simple: The validity of any categorical imperative is grounded in its relation to the CI.

All moral imperatives, Kant claimed, are categorical imperatives. This statement is uncontroversial. Our convictions about moral right and wrong—about what people should and should not do morally—are not about what they should and should not do in order to act coherently with their ends.

We have already seen why Kant thought that the CI is the fundamental principle of morality. A person of good will, committed to governing herself by moral laws, but with no specific given laws, has no alternative but to govern herself by the CI. Now, specific moral imperatives of duty, such as "one should not submit fraudulent tax forms," are categorical imperatives. So if the validity of any categorical imperative depends on its relation to the CI, then the validity of specific moral imperatives must also. But how, according to Kant, does the CI ground specific moral principles of duty? What kind of normative moral theory does the CI underwrite, and how does that theory relate to utilitarianism and Hobbes's theory?

The Formula of Universal Law

Kant gave two versions of his first formulation of the CI, commonly called the "universal law" formulation: *Act only on that maxim through which you can at the same time will that it should become a universal law* (G.421) and *Act as if the maxim of your action were to become through your will a universal law of nature* (G.421). We shall treat these as equivalent and as saying that an agent's acting on some maxim is morally acceptable only if the agent can will a "world" in which every rational agent regards the maxim as practical law and acts on it (as though by a law of nature).

Maxims.   By the "maxim" of an action, Kant meant the principle implicit in the agent's actual reasons for acting. Whenever an agent acts, she does so for some reason. Her maxim is the principle that specifies her reason. For example, suppose you decide to submit an honest tax form, thinking that doing otherwise would wrongly take advantage of others' good will. Then the maxim of your action, for starters, is something like this: "When one is (I am) in a position either to falsify or to accurately represent one's (my) income in paying taxes, then one (I) should do so honestly, even if it would be personally advantageous to submit a fraudulent return." This may only be a beginning, however. You may think that there are circumstances in which you shouldn't pay taxes (say, to support a thoroughly corrupt and evil regime) or, at least, in which it is not the case that you should, and that, even though those circumstances don't obtain here, they could. If so, then your maxim will be more complicated. It will include every feature of the situation that was actually relevant to your decision from your point of view—that is, any consideration that, consciously or unconsciously, played some role in your deciding to do what you did (and hence was part of *your* reason for acting).

To apply the CI, we must first figure out the (proposed) maxim of action. Imagine an agent deliberating about what to do and tentatively deciding to do something for some reason. She then applies the CI test. She asks whether she can will a world in which everyone acts on her maxim and regards it as practical law. If she cannot, then the CI tells her not to act on that maxim herself.

Contradiction in Conception?   Kant thought the cases that fail the CI test fall into two kinds. Some maxims are such that we cannot even conceive a world in which everyone acts on them. And other maxims are such that, although such a world is conceivable, one cannot will it. In cases of the first kind, there is a *contradiction in the conception* of a world in which everyone follows the maxim. In cases of the second, there is a *contradiction in the will* of someone who wills to act on the maxim *and* wills that everyone act on the maxim as well.

As an example of the first kind, Kant asked us to imagine someone who is considering making a promise (which he has no intention of keeping) to repay a loan in order to receive the loan (G.422). His proposed maxim goes something like this: "Whenever I am in a position to advance my interests by making a promise I don't intend to keep, I will do so." He now considers whether he can will that everyone act on this maxim. Kant argued that he cannot—in fact, that he cannot even conceive this possibility. It is inconceivable that everyone act on this maxim, since (assuming that circumstances are otherwise, as they are in our world) the conditions necessary for anyone to be able to act on the maxim would necessarily be absent in such a world.

The reason is that promising is possible only if there is some measure of trust that promises will be kept. Perfect trust is not necessary, of course. Witness our world. But in a world in which there were no trust, or radically reduced trust, it would be impossible to promise, in the sense of saying words like "I promise to . . . ," with the expectation that others would thereby expect one to do what one said one would. Some threshold of trust is necessary for the very possibility of promising. In our world, trust decreases as promise-breaking increases. So a world otherwise like ours, except for the fact that all agents are disposed to make false promises when they can get away with it, would also be a world of radically reduced trust. After all, if you thought everyone were so disposed, would *you* be inclined to trade something you value for a "promise" of future payment? So such a world would be one in which promising is impossible. Since a world in which everyone acts on a maxim of self-serving false promising is inconceivable, Kant claimed that the maxim fails the CI test. And since it does, the person should not act on the maxim himself.

However, this argument may prove too much. What seems to be doing the work is the idea of a **practice** that has certain background conditions, whereby departures prohibited by the practice tend to undermine the conditions on which the practice itself depends. In such a case, one cannot imagine everyone making the practice-prohibited departures, because this circumstance would remove the condition necessary for the practice, and hence for the practice-prohibited departures, to exist in the first place. But what moral force does this phenomenon have? If the practice is, like promising, one that is valuable or mutually advantageous (or which an agent is otherwise committed to willing), then the fact that everyone's acting on a maxim will undermine the practice seems to show that it would be wrong for one to do so. But what if the practice has no particular value? Or worse, what if the practice is thoroughly evil?

John Rawls once described a hypothetical practice he called "telishment," which is like punishment except that innocent people are capriciously selected for sanctions—say, as part of a reign of terror.[1] Suppose that this practice depends on credible threats by the regime to official underlings who are called upon to administer telishment. The regime warns that if they refuse to go along with the practice and telish innocents, others can be found who will. The practice has a name for disobeying a command to telish: "nullishing."[2] Only an official who has been commanded to telish can nullish. Suppose finally that, if a critical mass of officials were to nullish when commanded to telish, their doing so would undermine the practice of telishing.

Now since one can nullish only if one has been commanded to telish, if nullishing tends to undermine the practice of telishing, it also tends to undermine the possibility of nullishing. In this respect nullishing is like promise-breaking. (There are still differences, of course. *If* someone were commanded to telish under the circumstances brought about by universal nullishing, she could still nullish, although one could not promise in circumstances brought about by universal false promising. In both cases, however, universal action on the maxim removes the opportunity to act on the maxim.) But imagine a public-spirited official who has been commanded to telish and who is considering nullishing in order to help destroy the practice of telishment. If we cannot imagine a world in which everyone makes self-serving, false promises, so also are we unable to imagine a world in which everyone nullishes. But how can this show that it is morally unacceptable to nullish, especially if one's purpose is to undermine the practice of telishing and, even more, if the practice is thoroughly evil?

Clearly something has gone wrong here. What has gone wrong, I think, is that Kant was misled by certain features of his example and generalized too quickly. He would have done better to rely exclusively on the test of whether it is possible to *will* a world in which everyone acts on one's maxim. This would have given us the "morally expected" answer in both the promising and nullishing cases. As Kant himself said about a self-serving false promise, if everyone were to act on this maxim it would make not only promising, but "the very purpose of promising, itself impossible" (G.422). That matters because in making such a promise oneself, one wills this purpose (that others trust one so that one can benefit from their trust), but in willing everyone to act on the maxim, one wills in contradiction with this purpose. This is not so in the nullishing case. The official who is determined to nullish in order to help end telishing does not will anything that is in conflict with what he wills in willing that all act on his maxim. Quite the contrary.

So perhaps we should take the universal law formulation exclusively to require that one not act on a maxim one cannot *will* that all agents act on. Interpreted this way, the universal law formulation entails that it is morally unacceptable to act on a maxim of self-serving, false promising but morally acceptable to nullish.

Contradiction in Will. One of Kant's examples of a maxim that fails the contradiction in a will test concerns the duty of mutual aid (G.423). We are to imagine someone who is prepared to help others when they are in need only when doing so will benefit him. We can easily imagine a world in which everyone acts on this maxim, but Kant argued that we cannot will it. The reason is that a world in which people help others only when it benefits themselves is unlikely to benefit the agent, which, after all, is what the agent wills in acting on the maxim himself.

This puts us back in the region of the collective action problems and prisoner's dilemmas we considered in our study of Hobbes in Chapter 11. Suppose Hobbes was right in saying that collective unrestrained pursuit of self-interest leads to a worse situation for each than would result from everyone's acting on rules (maxims) requiring various restraints on self-interest. For example, it is reasonable to believe that we will all be better off if everyone recognizes, and is governed by, a principle requiring a degree of mutual aid when the cost of rendering it is below some threshold, than we would be if everyone were to act entirely self-interestedly. But if this is so, then, in applying the CI test, an egoist's will would be in conflict. In willing that *he* not help others, except when it pays, he would be willing his own benefit. But in willing that everyone act on this maxim, he would be willing his own detriment. "By . . . a law of nature sprung from his own will, he would rob himself of all hope of the help he wants for himself" (G.423). What he would most prefer, of course, is that others not act on the maxim he proposes to act on himself. But this is precisely what the universal law formulation forbids.

Impermissible Maxims Versus Wrong Acts. So far, the CI rules out only acting for certain reasons—that is, on certain *maxims*. How, then, can the CI ever ground any principles that determine right and wrong *acts*, or "imperatives of duty" as Kant called them? For example, from the fact that it is wrong to make false, *self-serving* promises it doesn't follow that it is wrong to make a false promise in a given situation period. (N.B.: I don't mean it doesn't follow that it is *always* wrong. I mean it doesn't even follow that it is wrong, regardless of one's reason, in *any* situation.) What if someone had the same attitude toward promising that our hypothetical official has toward telishing and made false promises to hasten the practice's demise? For her, acting on the maxim herself would not conflict with her willing that everyone do so also. On the contrary, the two would coincide. Or what if someone refuses to help others, not in order to line his own pockets but out of a misanthropy he directs toward everyone, himself included? Or because he thinks any reliance on others is wrong? Here again, there would be no conflict between his maxim and a will that everyone act on it.

In order to derive from the CI that certain kinds of false promising or aid refusals are wrong just because of what they amount to in their respective circumstances, it would have to be the case that *any* maxim recommending these acts in these circumstances would be morally unacceptable. But we have just seen that it is not true that every maxim recommending these acts in their respective circumstances violates the CI by virtue of a contradiction between the individual's will in acting on the maxim herself and her will in willing that all agents do so. If, consequently, there is a conflict, and if it is to hold for all agents and maxims, it will have to exist between willing that every agent make that kind of false promise or refuse aid of that kind on any maxim, on the one hand, and willing other things that one must will as a rational agent, on the other.

How might such an argument go? Suppose there were goods that agents require in order to act rationally over a life at all. For instance, rational human beings are likely to require such goods as physical and mental health, freedom from fear, and some level of material resources in order to pursue their ends rationally and effectively, more or less whatever their more specific rational ends are. They also need to live in circumstances fostering trust and mutual honesty, not just to get reliable information to accomplish the ends they have but also to have the supportive, critical engagement with others that human beings need to deliberate effectively about what ends *to* have. We can call these goods that any rational human being can be presumed to need **rational human needs** (or **rational needs**, for short). (The restriction to rational human beings is unproblematic, since it simply includes what any rational beings would need were they in the condition of human existence.) Any rational (human) being therefore wills that she have her rational needs met.

If this is so, then an argument is available from the CI regarding the wrongness of false promising and refusing mutual aid. In willing that everyone act on any maxim that would dictate making false promises or refusing help in circumstances where doing so would be advantageous, one wills a diminishing of the satisfaction of one's rational needs. Universal false promising undermines trust, and universal unrestrained self-interest undermines material and social support. But both conflict with one's will, as a rational agent, for rational needs. Therefore, one cannot rationally will that everyone make false promises or refuse mutual aid.

This is the beginning of an argument that would derive duties of sincerity and mutual aid from the CI. You should ask yourself what objections might be raised to it. For example, would this argument work for all agents? And are some agents so situated that their desire for goods necessary to meet rational needs might actually conflict with a will that everyone act on maxims requiring mutual aid and forbidding false promising? We shall return to these issues below.

The Formula of the End in Itself

Equal Dignity. One of Kant's greatest contributions to ethical thought was his articulation and defense of the thesis that all persons are entitled to *equal respect*—that every moral agent equally has a **dignity** that is "exalted above all price" (G.434). Kant can't be credited with discovering this idea. Versions of it have been advanced in the Judeo-Christian tradition, and the doctrine can be found in Seneca (4 B.C.E.–65 A.D.) But Kant certainly deserves credit for providing a highly influential philosophical account of the idea and for making it central to modern ethics.

For a vivid illustration of this idea, think about what is involved in such fundamental assaults on human dignity as rape and racist terror. What makes these forms of violence especially injurious is that they involve not just physical or other psychological harm (fear, for example) but violence to a person's sense of dignity and self-respect. One feels violated *oneself*. One's sense that one is a person to whom certain things *cannot* (i.e., must not) be done is undermined. ("Hey!" we imagine ourselves saying, "you can't do that to me!" Obviously this doesn't mean that the other person is unable to do what he did.)

But what exactly is the dignity or standing that all persons (for Kant, all moral agents) have, and what does it derive from? Rational nature, Kant said, is an end in itself (G.429). Every rational being is an end in herself with an inviolable claim never to be treated as a mere means. What gives every person equal standing is what makes her a person—her having a will with the capacity and need to act for her own reasons. This is what we must respect. As the second formulation of the CI puts it, we must do the following: *Act in such a way that you always treat humanity [rational nature], whether in your own person or in the person of any other, never simply as a means, but always at the same time as an end* (G.429).

Treating Someone as an End.   For social rational beings like us, action is almost invariably *interaction,* explicitly or implicitly. Other people figure prominently in our plans and projects. We hope or expect that they will act in certain ways and that they will accept our actions. It is common to any moral outlook, then, that we must take other people into account. The question is, How? According to utilitarianism, it is the capacity of others for pleasure and pain that constrains what we may do to them. For Kant, it is what makes them subject to morality in the first place—their being agents who act for their own reasons.

Morality, Kant believed, requires that we respect all equally as rational wills. We must act toward others in ways that *they* can somehow consent to as independent rational persons. This requirement rules out various forms of manipulation, fraud, and intimidation that attempt to influence others' conduct in ways other than through reasons that they can themselves accept. Others have the capacity to make their own reasoned choices, and we must respect this. They are not simply instruments to be used for our ends, even for an end like the greatest happiness of all.

Although we may have an intuitive grasp of what Kant had in mind in the "end in itself" formulation, many questions arise. Why did Kant think it is a formulation of the CI? What is its relation to the universal law formulation of the CI? And what *grounds* it in Kant's philosophical ethics?

Rational Nature as an Intrinsic Objective End.   Kant lays out one answer to these questions (G.427–429), which I shall sketch in this subsection, but which I don't think works very well. There are other, more promising answers implicit in the text, however, and these I shall develop presently.

Here is the answer Kant explicitly gives.

(1) Moral imperatives are categorical imperatives.
(2) Any imperative that is conditional on an end "that a rational being adopts arbitrarily" is merely hypothetical.
(3) So there can be categorical imperatives only if some end (or ends) is (are) essential to practical reason (necessarily shared by any rational agent).
(4) The only possible such end is rational nature itself. Rational nature must be its own end.
(5) That can be so only if rational nature in *any* being is an end for any rational agent.

(6) There can be categorical imperatives only if rational nature in anyone is an end in itself.

Therefore:

(7) Morality requires that we treat rational nature as an end in itself.

Steps (1) and (2) of this argument are unproblematic. And we saw reason to accept (3) when we considered how Kant might have derived specific moral duties from the universal law formulation of the CI. This led to the suggestion that Kant required a notion of needs for rational agents as such, things any rational agent can be presumed to will. If we interpret "rational nature" in (4) to refer to the well-functioning of the agent's *own* rational capacities, then we might interpret (4) as saying that any plausible theory of rational needs will include this as well.

But how do we get from (4) to (5)? From the fact that any rational agent necessarily values her own rational functioning, it does not follow that she necessarily values, or that she should value, rational functioning in *any* rational being. Consider, for example, the kind of commitment to rational functioning that is implicit in the very activity of deliberation. You cannot deliberate at all unless you care, for purposes of your deliberation, about deliberating *properly*. Otherwise, what you are doing is not really deliberating. But although deliberating commits you to valuing *your* deliberating properly (and, hence, to your rational well-functioning), it doesn't commit you to valuing *my* doing so, or to respecting me as a deliberating being. (Of course, there are various connections between these premises. Successful deliberation is almost always at least implicitly social and interactive. So if you value your own rational functioning, you will have reason to value mine. But now we have brought in an extra premise.)

If (5) were true, this would yield a powerful argument for the second formulation. But for the reasons I mentioned, it is hard to see how (5) could be true, and without it the argument is obviously invalid. Even if (5) were true and the argument sound, it would still be mysterious how the second formulation is supposed to relate to the first, universal law formulation. What could make them both formulations of the same underlying idea and based on the same philosophical foundation? We will leave this problem for the moment, however, and return to it when we consider what Kant might have meant when he said that the various formulations of the CI are "so many formulations of precisely the same law"(G.436).

Principles and Will. In respecting another as a rational agent, I must treat her with respect for her having a will and her own reasons for acting. But does this mean that I can never do what someone else does not want me to do? Can we never act contrary to others' wills?

This is a caricature of Kant's idea. His whole point is that when people act, they commit themselves to *principles*. The first formulation of the CI says that I must not do something if I cannot will the principle underlying my action as law. Similarly, we might interpret the second formulation as saying that I must act toward others only on principles that *they* can accept and will as law.

For example, a judge who sentences someone convicted of a crime in accordance with due process need not have the criminal's consent. She will not treat the criminal with less than full respect for his rational personhood if she requires a punishment he would prefer not to serve. It is enough that the criminal would will the principles underlying the sentencing process. Criminals are rarely anarchists. They typically want the benefits of a system of law even if they want not to be sentenced themselves. Or, again, two people in an athletic competition may set their wills against each other without treating each other with anything less than full respect as rational persons, since both share the principles underlying their respective actions.

The Formula of Autonomy and the Realm of Ends

This interpretation of the second formulation is borne out by the "third practical principle of the will," which Kant held to follow from the requirement to treat "every rational being as an end in himself." Kant presented this as an "idea" rather than as an imperative: "the Idea of the will of every rational being as a will which makes universal law" (G.431). Not only are all rational agents *subject* to the law, we are also equally *authors* of it. The will of each is "so subject that it must be considered as also making the law for itself." (G.431).

The foregoing leads to Kant's idea of the moral community as a "realm of ends" in which every rational agent makes, and also treats every other rational agent as making, a universal law to which all are subject. But this is possible only if the universal moral law is a *common* law. And this in turn is possible only if every rational agent would will the same universal laws in common. What can guarantee that?

The first formulation of the CI tells us that we should not act on maxims that we (*agents*) cannot will to be universal law. The second formulation says that we must respect moral *patients* (those we affect by our agency) as agents who must also be able to accept and will our principles as universal law. The (third) principle of autonomy and the realm of ends make explicit what was already implicit in the first two formulations, namely, that these tests can be satisfied simultaneously only if the principles each would will as universal law are the same principles—that is, only if there is a common set of principles that each would will everyone to act on.

Thus Kant thought it is a condition of the existence of moral laws dictating acts as right or wrong that there exists a set of common principles that every rational agent would will as universal law. However, it seems obvious that different rational agents, situated as they are in different social and historical circumstances, with different tastes and preferences, different resources and talents, and so on, would will different principles as universal law. Only one example: Someone with secure access to a stock of goods necessary to satisfy rational needs might will that everyone accept and act on a much weaker duty of mutual aid, one that required less (or no) help to the poor, than would be willed by someone who was poor. So long as their respective wills for all are substantially affected by individual differences of this sort, it seems clear that no common set of principles would result.

But according to Kant's general approach, it seems equally clear that the fact that individuals' wills would differ from *their different situated standpoints* should not affect whether a common moral law exists. If I know that the reason why I will a weaker duty of mutual aid is that I am rich, then I cannot regard the fact that I will this principle as evidence of its being the moral law. Similarly, if I know that the reason that I will a stronger duty of mutual aid is that I am poor, then, again, I cannot regard my willing of this principle as evidence that it is the moral law. If the moral law is a common law that everyone can will, then it must be because there exists a common standpoint that they can, in principle, share as rational agents, from which they would will this principle in common. As Kant put it, "If we can abstract from the personal differences between rational beings, and also from all the content of their private ends," then we can conceive a "systematic union of rational beings under common objective laws" (G.433). Accordingly, what must be true for there to be moral laws is that there be a set of principles any rational agent would will from this common standpoint, one that "abstracts from the personal differences between rational beings."

One Categorical Imperative?

The relevant question, then, is this: What principles would a person will all to act on *if* his willing were independent of any features of himself *in particular*? To answer this question, we need to know, for example, what a person would will if her choice were unaffected by any particular beliefs about herself— that is, if she were behind what John Rawls calls a "veil of ignorance" about her own tastes, social position, race, gender, and so on.[3] Yet even this isn't enough, since individual differences can affect the will even if one is unaware of them. What principles would a person will all to follow if personal differences of any kind were to make no difference?

This question, of course, cannot be answered directly. There is no way a person can simply step into such a perspective and check. At best, we can form an *idea* of the common perspective and try to triangulate it in thought, especially in interaction with others. In particular, we can try to correct for differences of gender, status, race, and so on, and accept as a constraint on public moral discourse that universal preferences that are explainable by any of these are to be discounted.

However abstract, this hypothetical perspective does not leave us without anything to think. Assuming some theory of rational needs, plausible arguments can be made for some convergence of will on principles of duty that, for example, dictate mutual aid and prohibit false promising and other forms of dishonesty, other things being equal. For instance, if any rational (human) agent wills the trust necessary for her rationally to choose and pursue ends, then she can hardly will that everyone make false promises.

If, consequently, there is really only one Categorical Imperative, it must be formulated in some such way as this: *Always act consistently with principles that, from a perspective common to all rational agents, anyone would will that all agents act on.* Each of the more specific formulations can then be understood as stressing different aspects of this underlying idea.

Deontology or Consequentialism?

At this point, you may see why Mill thought that the CI reduces to rule-utilitarianism. Although the principles of duty Kant sought to ground in the CI conflict with act-utilitarianism, they may nonetheless seem to depend on consequences in the same way that rule-utilitarianism does. To be sure, the CI procedure does make the consequences of everyone's following a principle (rule) the crucial element in determining whether it is morally acceptable or required to act on it oneself. But there are two important differences between Kant's ethics and rule-utilitarianism.

One difference is that, for the rule-utilitarian, moral rules are assessed by their impact on human *happiness,* whereas, for Kant, they are assessed by their impact on people *as agents.* The underlying normative difference here might be put something like this: The utilitarian believes that we are collectively responsible for everyone's happiness, whereas Kant's ethics holds that we are collectively responsible for the conditions necessary for all to have what they need in directing our own lives.

A deeper difference comes in the way the rule-utilitarian and Kant's ethics attempt, respectively, to justify their theories of right and wrong. The philosophical rule-utilitarian begins with the premise that promoting the general happiness is, by definition, morality's goal. Morality just is the social practice that is designed to promote this goal. But Kant denied that morality has any such goal; it is not an instrument. Rather, he said, it is the expression of the agent's own free will. What the CI procedure ultimately looks to, then, is not whether the effects of some rule further or clash with some externally given goal, but whether they are such that someone can endorse from within her own practical reasoning as a free agent.

This difference is reflected in the fact that *if* Kant were able to make out his claim that rational agents are committed to the CI in their own free practical reasoning, his ethics would avoid two objections that are often raised to rule-utilitarianism. First, if the goal of ethics is the general happiness, why should someone follow a happiness-maximizing rule even on occasions when violating it would best promote the general happiness? Kant's ethics denies that morality has any such external goal, so it avoids this objection. The second objection is the internalist critique with which I began Chapter 14. Any externalist theory of morality, like utilitarianism, cannot explain why the reasons making it wrong for someone to do something are themselves reasons for her not so to act. "OK," the critic may argue, "I see how my act will violate this thing you call morality, but why does that give me any reason not to do it?"

Kant's Internalism: An Ideal Agent Theory of Normative Reasons

This brings us, finally, to Kant's argument for **metaphysical moral internalism**, which appears in Chapter III of the *Groundwork*. By the end of Chapter II, Kant had defended the CI and its various formulations only from *within* the moral point of view. He had also laid out an **ideal moral agent theory** of morality by analyzing what is most fundamental in our moral ideas as he found them. As he put it, "We have shown by developing the concept of morality generally in vogue that autonomy of the will is unavoidably bound up with it or rather is its very basis" (G.445). But we can't take the idea of morality simply for granted. Convictions of moral duty present themselves as binding on all rational agents, but that fact doesn't ensure that they really are. Perhaps the idea of morality is a "mere phantom of the brain," having no real claim on rational agents? (G.445). To show that this is not so, Kant undertook a critique of practical reason in Chapter III.

The argument takes as fundamental a distinction between an **observer's theoretical perspective** and the **practical perspective** that an agent necessarily adopts in reasoning about what to do. When we view ourselves from the first standpoint, we see ourselves as part of a natural order, which in turn is a realm of occurrences predictable by universal causal laws of nature. From the practical perspective, however, an agent reasons not about what will happen but about what *to do*. And from this perspective, Kant argued, an agent cannot help but regard her activity through the categories of freedom and practical law that ultimately commit her to the CI.

To see the distinction Kant had in mind, consider the difference between deciding what to do this evening and predicting what you will do. When you are deliberating, you can't help but treat your future as *up to you*. As Kant put it, you "cannot act except under the Idea of freedom" (G.448). You are deciding between possible future paths, and you simply cannot deliberate without looking for normative reasons for your choice.

Notice how different this is from prediction. Although as an agent only you can *decide* what to do, in principle anyone (or no one) can predict what you will in fact do. Moreover, you may know that whatever you end up doing will be determined by prior causes without this having any effect on your deliberations. Suppose you know that a perfect predictor (say, God) knows what you will do this evening. Will that knowledge help you decide what *to* do? Suppose even that the predictor reveals his prediction to you and that you believe him. He says, "You will go to the movies." How will this fact affect your deliberation about what to do? Of course, if you were to think that this reason for believing that you *will* go the movies is also somehow a reason for you *to* go to the movies, then it could enter into your deliberations. But otherwise, it is of no help. So if the predictor is right and you will go to the movies, you will nonetheless need, as an agent, some reason *for going*. And, of course, if he is right, you will have such a reason.

It is essential to the practical standpoint, therefore, that agents regard themselves as free—in other words, that they reason as though they were free. And this requires that they seek, not reasons for beliefs about what they will do, but *reasons for doing* one thing rather than another. As we saw before, Kant believed that regarding themselves as free requires that agents act on what they regard as practical laws, as categorical imperatives. To regard anything as a reason for me to do something, I must believe that it would also be a reason for any rational agent who was relevantly like me in circumstances relevantly like mine. Hypothetical imperatives are impotent to ground such reasons, moreover, since they leave entirely unsettled whether I should take the means to my ends or adopt different ends.

So thinking with the ideas of freedom and practical law is a necessary condition for the very possibility of deliberation. But what makes something a practical law? Thus far all we are able to conclude is that we cannot deliberate without supposing there are practical laws (categorical imperatives) that are valid for all rational agents. But what actually makes these laws or imperatives valid?

We are now back in the same region of ideas that we encountered near the end of the last chapter, but with the difference that we are no longer thinking explicitly from within the moral point of view. You may recall that, in this connection, Kant had argued that a morally good will is governed by the idea of the moral law. And then he asked, What does the moral law itself derive from? His solution was an *ideal moral agent* theory. The moral law must derive somehow from what a good will can regard as law. And since there exists no moral law to be discovered external to the will (the will is **autonomous**, a "law to itself"), a good will has no alternative but to be guided by a formal, second-order principle for "authoring" or "legislating" law—namely, the CI.

At our current juncture, Kant has argued that the practical standpoint of any rational agent commits her to deliberating under the ideas of freedom and practical law. But how does a rational agent know what the practical law is? Since Kant rejected rational intuitionism, he could not believe that practical laws are given to a rational agent through any kind of perception. Rather, the will of a free rational agent is autonomous, a "law to itself," intrinsically and independent of anything externally given to it. Of any candidate rational norm, a free rational agent can reasonably ask, "Why should I follow this principle?" And, as in the moral case, she has no way of answering such a question except in terms of whether she can will the principle as law. She has no alternative to treating the Categorical Imperative as the fundamental principle of her deliberation.

This reasoning amounts to an **ideal agent theory** of normative reasons. It holds that there are no truths about normative reasons that are independent of what a free rational agent would regard as reasons. What makes something a reason for acting is that it would be treated as such in an ideal agent's deliberations. This line of thought requires a formal rather than substantive deliberative ideal. Whether a deliberative process is ideal cannot depend on whether it properly registers considerations whose status as normative reasons is independent of their issuing from the ideal process. Moreover, since the question at hand is what principles are practical laws (norms any rational agent should follow), the deliberative standpoint cannot be an *individual* agent's but, rather, must be a common standpoint available in principle to any agent. And since a free agent is committed to guiding herself by practical law, she has no alternative to guiding herself by the CI: *Always act consistently with principles that, from a perspective common to all rational agents, anyone would will that all agents act on.* It follows that a free rational agent and an agent subject to the moral law are one and the same! As Kant stated in the conclusion of his *Critique of Practical Reason*, the concepts of freedom and the moral law are "so inextricably bound together that practical freedom could be defined through the will's independence of everything except the moral law."[4]

If some argument like this can be made out, then Kant could have claimed that since free deliberation is committed to the CI, moral imperatives grounded in the CI do not simply present themselves as binding on any moral agent, they really *are*. In other words, he could have maintained not just the conceptual claim that it is intrinsic to the idea of moral requirements that they are categorical imperatives (as conceptual moral internalism would hold) but also the substantive claim that moral imperatives (grounded in the CI) really are categorical imperatives, binding on all rational agents (as metaphysical moral internalism would hold).

Final Thoughts

Kant's claims and arguments are extremely ambitious—too ambitious, many philosophers would say. Perhaps we can't help but deliberate as though we are free, but what if we aren't in fact? Shouldn't that affect the validity of any argument that takes our freedom as a premise? Or maybe we can't help but deliberate in terms of categorical imperatives, but many people are apparently able to do this without treating the CI as their supreme principle. Or perhaps no specific categorical imperatives can be taken for granted, but why suppose that we have to be able to derive valid ones from some fundamental procedural principle, such as the CI? Why isn't it enough to critically assess particular imperatives by considering them from the perspective of other categorical norms that we accept? These are only some of the many questions with which anyone attracted to Kant's approach must continue to wrestle.

If, however, you find Kant's philosophical ethics implausible, you will want to ask yourself why. Is it because of Kant's particular way of trying to establish moral internalism, or because of moral internalism itself? If the former, then the challenge will be to find some other, more convincing internalist conception of morality. If the latter, then there are two alternatives. Either an adequate philosophical conception of morality can accommodate the fact that it sometimes makes sense for people to do what is wrong (externalism), or there can be no philosophically adequate conception of morality since morality necessarily presents itself as though internalism were true (conceptual moral internalism)—although it isn't in fact (metaphysical moral externalism). The latter line of thought suggests a different kind of philosophical ethics, one springing from a philosophical *critique* of morality. And that brings us to Part 4.

Suggested Reading

Allison, Henry. *Kant's Theory of Freedom.* Cambridge: Cambridge University Press, 1991.

Baron, Marcia. *Kantian Ethics, Almost Without Apology.* Ithaca, N.Y.: Cornell University Press, 1995.

Herman, Barbara. *The Practice of Moral Judgment.* Cambridge, Mass.: Harvard University Press, 1993.

Hill, Thomas E., Jr. *Dignity and Practical Reason in Kant's Moral Theory.* Ithaca, N.Y.: Cornell University Press, 1992.

Kant, Immanuel. *Critique of Practical Reason* (1788). Lewis White Beck, trans. New York: Macmillan Publishing Company, 1985.

_____. *Groundwork of the Metaphysics of Morals* (1781). H. J. Paton, trans. New York: Harper & Row, 1964.

Korsgaard, Christine M. *Creating the Kingdom of Ends.* Cambridge: Cambridge University Press, 1996.

Rawls, John. *A Theory of Justice.* Cambridge, Mass.: Harvard University Press, 1971.

_____. "Themes in Kant's Moral Philosophy." In *Kant's Transcendental Deductions.* Eckart Förster, ed. Stanford, Calif.: Stanford University Press, 1989.

Schneewind, J. B. "Autonomy, Obligation, and Virtue: An Overview of Kant's Moral Philosophy." In *The Cambridge Companion to Kant.* Paul Guyer, ed. Cambridge: Cambridge University Press, 1992.

Part Four

PHILOSOPHICAL ETHICS WITHOUT MORALITY?

16

NIETZSCHE

Recall, again, Kant's two lines of argument for moral internalism. The argument for conceptual moral internalism proceeds from premises that Kant alleged are implicit in ordinary moral thought and experience. To us ordinary folk, Kant claimed, morality presents itself as a universal law that obligates all rational persons. Kant's argument for metaphysical moral internalism, on the other hand, makes no assumptions about morality. What it assumes is a conception of freedom or autonomy, one that Kant argued is implicit in the deliberative standpoint of a self-conscious, self-critical rational agent.

Each starting point sounds a central theme of **modern philosophy,** the thought of a period usually marked as beginning with René Descartes (1596–1641). As I mentioned in Chapter 10, seventeenth-century ethical philosophers like Hobbes (1588–1679) inherited the idea of morality to which Kant alluded in the **classical natural law** notion of a universal law transcending actual statutes and customs. Their problem, recall, was how to vindicate this idea philosophically without the classical theory's **teleological** metaphysics, which they believed to be inconsistent with what they were learning about the nature of reality from the emerging modern science. Kant's use of the deliberative standpoint of a free rational agent, on the other hand, is not unlike the stance Descartes took in his *Meditations* (1641), albeit for general epistemological purposes. What, Descartes there asked, can provide a firm foundation for belief for an individual self-conscious mind who assumes nothing?

And how necessary are these starting points? Even if Kant was right in thinking they would seem natural to eighteenth-century readers (or to us now), is that because they embody ideas that anyone thinking about ethics should take for granted? Or might there be some explanation of why these ideas would seem natural to certain people in certain times and places even though they are, in fact, defective or illusory?

A Genealogy of Morals

To consider the latter possibility, we would have to engage in what Friedrich Nietzsche (1844–1900) called a **genealogy** of notions like morality and freedom of the will. Rather than simply continuing to think with these ideas, we would have to step back from them and critically examine their histories. We would have to ask questions like, When and why did people begin to employ these notions? And what explains their continued use and development? These are not so much philosophical questions as empirical questions of historical anthropology or sociology of knowledge (or, as Michel Foucault called it, "archaeology of knowledge").[1]

The reason we tend not to pose these questions, Nietzsche believed, is the same reason we should: The answers are shocking! A suitably critical "genealogy of morals" will convince us that morality and freedom are the illusory projections of unconscious hostility and hatred.

"We are unknown to ourselves, we men of knowledge—and with good reason," Nietzsche proclaimed at the beginning of *On the Genealogy of Morals* (GM.Pref.1).[2] "We have never sought ourselves—how could it happen that we should ever find ourselves?" Nietzsche argued that this ignorance of ourselves extends to the sources of our ideas in our own psyches. We tend unthinkingly to take ideas like morality and freedom for granted, not bothering to ask whether we have them for good reason or whether they are result of *nonrational* psychic forces—for example, psychic needs for certain forms of illusion.

Ethics cannot help but presuppose *some* notion of value, but that doesn't mean it must assume the idea of *moral* value. A philosophical ethics must therefore include a "critique of moral values" (GM.Pref.6). And this requires a genealogy of morals: a critical study of the "conditions and circumstances" under which moral ideas arose, evolved, and are maintained (GM.Pref.6).

Nietzsche's genealogy of morals led him to conclusions diametrically opposed to Kant's. Nietzsche concluded that, far from morality's being inescapable for any rational agent, moral conceptions arose in specific historical circumstances through nonrational causes. For Nietzsche, morality is an **ideology**. It is a set of concepts and beliefs whose existence is explainable, not by any warrant or truth-making facts, but by their serving certain pragmatic interests. In particular, Nietzsche maintained that the idea of morality is a self-serving projection that enables those who are naturally weak or inferior to rationalize their repressed unconscious hatred for the strong. Worse, it is pathological. It is both a symptom and an aspect of an illness that devalues the lives of those who accept it—weak and strong. Nietzsche believed that its dominance of the culture of Western Europe had become the major obstacle to realizing human excellence.

Nietzsche's **historicism** is characteristic of nineteenth-century thought generally, especially when it is viewed in relation to that of the seventeenth and eighteenth centuries. Thus, whereas Kant may sometimes seem to have assumed that freedom and practical reason have no social or historical preconditions, Hegel (1770–1831) argued that they develop only historically, through a dialectical process. Marx (1818–1883) took this idea further, claiming that freedom and morality have underlying material conditions, and that development in the former is actually the consequence of historical, dialectical changes in the underlying economic base. Darwin (1809–1882) can be viewed as having taken this general approach further still, arguing that nothing less than the origin of species is explainable as the contingent historical result of an underlying biological process.

Although Nietzsche's historicism was typical of the nineteenth century, no thinker posed a sharper challenge to the "modern" idea of morality. Hegel agreed with Kant that morality has a deep connection to practical reason and freedom, even though he thought that these are realizable only through an historical process. And although there are places where Marx seems to debunk morality as a bourgeois preoccupation, his fundamental criticism that capitalism is exploitative evidently depends on a Kantian moral ideal of equal dignity. Finally, Darwin maintained that the existence of a moral sense is itself part of what evolution explains about the human species.

But Nietzsche tried to overturn a whole apple cart of notions that are absolutely central to modern moral philosophy—freedom, accountability, culpability, equal dignity, moral evil, and, finally, morality itself. He argued that all these ideas are ideological, fabricated in a "dark workshop" deep in the human psyche (GM.I.14.1). Nietzsche believed that once we have fully grasped moral ideas' origins and the psychic pathologies in which they are implicated, we will see that we must get "beyond good and evil" if we are to think about ethics in a healthy and fruitful way.[3]

This brief introduction may help us to glimpse why a contemporary commentator might remark that if Descartes is to be credited with beginning modern philosophy, then Nietzsche must "be credited with ending it."[4] And glimpse as well why Nietzsche has been such an important figure in what has come to be called "postmodern" thought.

Nietzsche's Critique of Morality: The Basic Idea

Because Nietzsche's ideas are so challenging, and because he wrote in a literary, often aphoristic way, it has taken a long while for other philosophers to come to terms with his thought. Ironically, then, we will begin with a parable that Nietzsche himself recounted, that of the lambs and birds of prey.

Nietzsche remarked that it "does not seem strange" that lambs might dislike great birds of prey, especially for "bearing off little lambs" (GM.I.13.2). But while this justifies the lambs' disliking the birds, it "gives [them] no grounds for *reproaching*" them. However, the lambs do reproach their predators. They see them as *evil* and "say among themselves . . . whoever is least like a bird of prey, but rather its opposite, a lamb—would he not be good?" The birds of prey respond, "'*We* don't dislike them at all, these good little lambs; we even love them: nothing is more tasty than a tender lamb" (GM.I.13.2).

Here we have a tale of two different forms of evaluation in conflict, along with a story about how one develops out of reaction to the other. The birds' values are entirely amoral. They have values, but not moral values. And the lambs, for their part, react to the birds' value scheme with a very different one. They see their predators' conduct not simply as bad but as morally *evil*.

Nietzsche's remark that the birds view the "good little lambs" as tasty morsels may mislead us to think that he believed nonmoral evaluation to be self-centered or hedonistic. But that is actually not what he had in mind. Rather, the birds accept an **ideal**. They have a *hierarchy* of values, some of which they look up to, esteem, and want to emulate, and others that they look down upon and scorn. Their core notion is the idea of a good of higher **worth** or **merit**, something that is superior or **noble**. And its contrary, the inferior or base, is simply the contrary of this good. It is what is *not noble*.

In this hierarchy, the lambs are the natural inferiors of the birds—they are meat. The birds have contempt for the lambs, but not in the sense that they bear them ill will. On the contrary, as they protest, they *love* the lambs—nothing tastes better. They have contempt for them in the sense that they don't take them seriously or respect them as peers. As they see it, the lambs are below them, not made of the same stuff, and it would be beneath a bird of prey to seem or act like a lamb.

The birds treat the lambs accordingly. And, naturally enough, the lambs do not like this. But there is nothing the lambs can do about it. Were one bird to treat another bird as they treat the lambs, the other wouldn't stand for it. He would retaliate and thereby vent his anger. But the lambs are in no position to retaliate, so their anger seeks another outlet. They experience what Nietzsche called **ressentiment**. They have an *unconscious* hatred of the birds arising from the frustration and repression of their hostility toward them. They cannot express their anger directly, but they are also unwilling to acknowledge their inferiority, which continuing conscious hostility would only confirm. So the lambs' hostility must be repressed. It must go underground to the "dark workshop" of the lambs' unconscious. And here, Nietzsche believed, begins the fashioning of moral concepts.

The lambs *reproach* the birds for preying on them. They *blame* them for it, but not just in the sense that they identify the birds as offending parties who are suitable targets for retaliation and vengeance. The lambs are in no position to express personal affront to the birds. Rather, the lambs' hostility appears in the disguised form of the thought that the birds of prey are *morally blameworthy,* that they are *culpable* or *guilty* for what they have done to the lambs—that they are *evil.* The lambs' personal hostility thus expresses itself in an objectified or depersonalized form. What they think and say is not "You have angered me." What would the birds care about that? They might agree but simply pay it no mind. Rather, what the lambs think and say is "You birds are, objectively, to be despised and held accountable for what you have done. You are morally culpable and evil." Unlike directly expressed personal hostility, this is a thought that, if it could be insinuated in the minds of the birds, would actually work to the retaliatory advantage of the lambs. If the lambs could get the birds to have *this* thought, they could use the birds' feelings of guilt to do the work they would not be able to accomplish through their own direct retaliation.

The lambs' valuational system inverts the birds' natural hierarchy of values. The birds' primary value notion was the naturally noble or **estimable,** with the **base** being whatever is below or the contrary of that. The initial impetus to moral values, however, is *denial*—quite literally, the lambs' psychological denial of their personal animus born of their unwillingness to recognize their natural inferiority to the birds. This denial takes the form of a negation and inversion of what the birds' values affirmed. What was reckoned noble and of high standing by the birds is accounted *morally* low or evil in the lambs' conception. And what the lambs reckon morally good is simply the contrary of these qualities—being "least like a bird of prey." Thus what was naturally superior becomes morally inferior. And what was naturally inferior becomes morally superior.

As Nietzsche related the parable, the birds merely laugh at the lambs' suggestion that they are somehow culpable for preying on the lambs. But that is not what Nietzsche thought actually happened in human history. Indeed, he bemoaned the fact that, from his perspective in nineteenth-century Europe, the weakest elements of humanity and their agents in the "priestly caste" appear to have been largely successful in promulgating the ideology of morality, much to the detriment of the species. This cunning on behalf of the weak did nothing less than turn the natural hierarchy of value on its head. It took what is naturally noble, beautiful, vigorous, and strong, and turned it into the embodiment of moral wrong and evil.

In addition to morality's questionable origins, the parable illustrates what Nietzsche believed to be morality's mistaken metaphysical presuppositions—most important, its necessary, but unwarranted, assumption of freedom of the will. It makes sense to blame someone, to regard her as morally accountable for a culpable action, only if we believe that she freely chose to do what she did and could have acted otherwise if she had chosen. But Nietzsche thought that freedom of the will, too, is an illusion. Although we differ from other animal species in various respects, we are no less part of the natural order. So human behavior, Nietzsche believed, must be just as explicable by natural causes as is any natural occurrence. (Question for thought: *Must* a **metaphysical naturalist**, like Nietzsche, reject freedom of the will?)

Morality requires us to hypothesize an agent or self behind every deed who freely chooses and so can be held accountable for her choices. But "'the doer' is merely a fiction added to the deed" (GM.I.13.3). The strong are no more "free to be weak" than is a bird of prey free to be a lamb. In behaving as they do, each simply expresses its respective nature.

We shouldn't conclude, however, that Nietzsche thought there is no place for notions like autonomy and responsibility. What he rejected are *moral* autonomy and responsibility—namely, the specific shape these notions take within morality. As we shall see, Nietzsche thought that autonomy and responsibility are possible, but not for everyone and not within morality. Only the few can be genuinely autonomous and responsible for themselves. And they can do so only by *rejecting* morality.

Natural Good and Bad (Noble and Base): The Ethics of Aristocracy

It is easy to be put off by Nietzsche's rhetoric in ways that can blind us to the depth of his insights. In particular, the image of natural predator and prey may occasion some such response as the following: "Maybe some species naturally prey on others, but ethics within the human species could not be based on such a 'natural' relationship. How could human values be based on natural subjugation?"

We miss Nietzsche's point, however, if we take him to be talking about features that give some human beings natural power *over* others. What Nietzsche was concerned with is not so much natural *domination* as a natural order of *esteem* and *respect*. Think of the qualities of people you find personally attractive or admirable—people you like to be with or would like to be like. If each of us were to list such qualities and to discuss our lists together, we might be able to achieve some consensus. Is it unreasonable to think that we might agree on some of the following: openness, cheerfulness, creativity, physical strength, agility, grace, beauty, vigor, health, wit, intelligence, charm, and friendliness?

If so, these might provide a basis for a natural order of esteem: natural *merit*. All these qualities admit of degree. A person may be more or less graceful, friendly, intelligent, healthy, and so on. Other things being equal, then, we are apt to esteem someone more or less depending on whether she has the qualities on this list to a higher or lower degree.

The same may hold true of respect. There may be something we might call *natural authority*. Quite apart from custom, convention, or law, some people seem to command respect simply through others' recognition of their wisdom, knowledge, judgment, credibility, and so on.

Thought of in these ways, respect and esteem establish a natural hierarchy of value or *worth*. They involve what Nietzsche called "rank-ordering, rank-defining value judgments" (GM.I.2.2). Nietzsche believed that this is the primary form that value takes in ethics. Ethics concerns what we should aspire to and avoid, not in the sense of what benefits us by making our lives happier but in the sense of what makes *us* better or more worthy human beings.

Because they define a natural hierarchy, Nietzsche described these original values as *aristocratic:* "The judgment 'good' did *not* originate with those to whom 'goodness' was shown! Rather it was 'the good' themselves, that is to say, the noble, powerful, high-stationed and high-minded, who felt and established themselves and their actions as good, that is, of the first rank, in contradistinction to all the low, low-minded, common and plebeian" (GM.I.2.2). What is noble is what is worthy or appropriately esteemed. And what is base is what those who are noble look down upon or have contempt for. But unlike the notion of evil, the base carries none of the connotations of what is to be hated or despised, which are part of what Nietzsche regarded as the pathology of morality.

In contrast with moral values, then, aristocratic values are inherently inegalitarian. But, again, that is not because Nietzsche was assuming the nobles should have power over or rule others. Rather, Nietzsche's inegalitarianism is built into the very idea of esteem or merit itself. All Nietzsche needed to be saying is that some qualities naturally deserve more esteem than others. Of course, there is also the metaethical question of what makes this true. Nietzsche didn't face this question directly, but we might try to fashion a naturalist explanation on his behalf. As Mill maintained concerning the relationship between desire and the desirable, so Nietzsche might argue concerning esteem and the estimable: Our best evidence for what is estimable is what people actually esteem. If there is a consensus that certain characteristics or individuals naturally elicit esteem, this gives us evidence of their natural merit or worth.

Nietzsche did not intend his natural hierarchy to be one of force. When people are naturally respected and admired, they do not have to coerce others. Nor, despite Nietzsche's occasional rhetorical excess, should we suppose that his nobles are concerned only with themselves as opposed to others. On the contrary, Nietzsche believed that they are good-natured, generous, "positive" people who are not given to defensiveness or mean-

spiritedness. They have what we might call Nietzschean rather than Kantian "good will." They express a spontaneous friendliness or warmth toward others that Nietzsche believed necessary for human nurturance and
growth. Good will of this sort, Nietzsche asserted, has "made much greater
contributions to culture" than such moralized motives as "pity, charity, or
self-sacrifice."[5]

Morality, Hatred, and the Herd

What is noble is what is healthy, vigorous, sensual, positive, nurturing, life-
affirming, strong, spontaneous, proactive, honest, creative, and clear. By contrast, Nietzsche maintained, morality is associated in its origins and tendency
with what is unhealthy, pathological, antisensual, unspontaneous, life-deny-
ing, illusory, secretive, reactive, weak, forced, destructive, and obscure.
Whereas aristocratic values have an essentially affirmative thrust, moral values derive from a self-deceptive denial that infects and stunts human growth.

The underlying psychological mechanism, again, is *ressentiment*. Those
lower in a natural hierarchy of merit are angered by the contempt with which
they are regarded by their natural superiors. In the parable of the lambs and
birds of prey, such contempt includes direct abuse. But this aspect may not be
essential to Nietzsche's genealogy. The nobles' monopoly on the natural
sources of esteem and respect may suffice. It may be enough, for Nietzsche,
that natural inferiors are angered by their inferiority and lack a direct outlet
for their anger and envy. (But what if they aren't angered?)

An aristocratic ethos denies that everyone has equal value or dignity simply because they are persons. Rather, dignity depends on merit, and merit
varies with the qualities that naturally elicit more or less esteem. Natural
inferiors are angered by their lower dignity, by their being treated as though
they have lesser worth. But they lack any means of redress. They cannot
change their own qualities into meritorious ones—or, at any rate, not all of
them can. It is of the very nature of merit that it establishes an ordering.
Moreover, like the lambs, the weak lack any means of taking out their
anger on the nobles. To the extent that they cannot avoid interaction with
the nobles and are unwilling to accept their own inferiority, they cannot
avoid anger. But since anger reminds them of its source and their inability
to alter it, it reminds them of the inferiority they cannot accept. Their anger
cannot be satisfied by a direct expression and is only intensified by continued consciousness. To have any release, it must be repressed and made unconscious. It must be disguised and made to present itself in another form
in the depersonalized, objectified projection of moral fault, guilt, and evil.

A strong person "shakes off with a single shrug much vermin that eats
deep into others" (GM.I.3.10). Slights to which the strong would not give a
second thought or directly retaliate against burrow deeply into the weak,

causing unconscious hatred that, to be satisfied, must be seen as occasioned not by *personal* affront but by a violation of some standing or dignity that *anyone* can claim and that *everyone* must respect. They must be seen as *moral* violations, to which the appropriate response is not personal anger but *impersonal* anger—that is, moral indignation or outrage on behalf of the victim and *guilt* on the part of the perpetrator.

No matter how these thoughts and feelings present themselves, Nietzsche argued that they are still only the conscious expression of unconscious, personal hostility and hatred. And his point, moreover, was that this is not just how these ideas originated but how they *continue* to be maintained. Moral ideas, he asserted, come from fundamentally negative forces in the human psyche—they grow "from the trunk of that tree of vengefulness and hatred" (GM.I.8.1). And, Nietzsche thought, that tree still grows.

From a different metaphorical perspective, however, Nietzsche also believed that the tree of morality is a cancer on the human species. Its growth impairs psychic health and stunts *human* growth. Morality's psychic mechanisms—guilt and fault finding—are negative. They chill human spontaneity and creativity and rein in the natural sources of human excellence.

How, then, did morality come to establish itself in human culture? If the strong are strong, and the weak, weak, then how did these growth-stunting ideas catch on even among the strong? Prominent in Nietzsche's historical narrative is an account of how religion and a Judeo-Christian "priestly caste" came to organize the weak and promulgate their projected hostility in a way that ultimately insinuated itself throughout Western culture. In Nietzsche's account, Judaism began a "slave revolt in morality ... which has a history of two thousand years behind it and which we no longer see because it—has been victorious" (GM.I.7). The supreme irony, by Nietzsche's lights, is that Christian love is actually the result of hatred: "Above the gateway to the Christian Paradise and its 'eternal 'bliss'" should be inscribed "I too was created by eternal *hate*" (GM.I.15.2).

An illustration of these ideas can be found in Nietzsche's discussion of punishment. Recall Mill's claim that punishment is central to the very idea of moral wrong: "We do not call anything wrong unless we mean to imply that a person ought to be punished in some way or other for doing it" (U.V.14). Nietzsche agreed completely. There are nonmoral notions that are in the neighborhood of the moral ideas of wrong and punishment, but that differ from them in crucial respects nonetheless. For example, Nietzsche believed there is a "pre-moral" idea of compensation for injury that need not involve the distinctive moral notion of culpability or guilt (GM.II.4). And a society can have practices that look much like penal institutions, and yet not have the moral practice of punishment, if their function is entirely one of deterrence and self-protection. What makes a restriction or sanction a punishment, in the relevant sense, is that it is thought to be *deserved* because of the person's *culpability* for some moral wrong. Being deserving of some form of punishment seems, as Mill said, to be part of the very idea of moral wrong and culpability. Similarly, to be strictly considered punishment, a sanction must involve the idea of being deserved by virtue of culpability.

The emotional experience of guilt is a case in point. Consider what it is like to feel guilty about something. What is the nature of these feelings? First, think about what we might call the content of your experience. What does your experience appear to you to be *as of*? Doesn't your experience appear to you to be as of your having done something wrong? Isn't its seeming to you as if you have done something wrong part of the experience? Now consider *how* you feel and what you feel like doing. Of course, you feel bad. But don't you also feel as though you *should* feel bad? As though your feeling bad is deserved? Indeed, don't you feel like punishing yourself? Or as though you *are* punishing yourself? Guilt feelings seem to be punitive in their very nature.

Nietzsche believed that punishment of this moral kind depends upon projected hostility. The distinctive character of morality cannot be understood apart from the repressed desire to get back at someone. "Throughout the greater part of human history," Nietzsche wrote, "punishment was *not* imposed . . . on the presupposition that only the guilty should be punished; rather, as parents still punish their children, [it was imposed] from [direct, conscious] anger at some harm or injury, vented on the one who caused it" (GM.II.4). What is distinctive about *moral* punishment is the thought that it is *deserved*— that, owing to the wrongdoer's free choice, she deserves to suffer. This suffering serves as a kind of compensation to the victim. But how can it? "To what extent can suffering balance debts or guilt? To the extent that to *make* suffer was in the highest degree pleasurable, to the extent that the injured party exchanged for the loss he had sustained . . . an extraordinary counterbalancing pleasure." (GM.II.6.1) Note that Nietzsche said that the victim's pleasure comes not just in the fact of the wrongdoer's suffering but in the fact of *making* the wrongdoer suffer. This is important. The victim takes pleasure in having power over the wrongdoer, in making her suffer just as he had suffered.

To serve its function, then, punishment must provide the occasion for pleasure in making another suffer. This conclusion confirms Nietzsche in his view that morality is the objectified projection of hostility: "The categorical imperative smells of cruelty" (GM.II.6.1).

A Perfectionist Ethics

At this point, it might seem reasonable to conclude that Nietzsche believed the cure for humankind's ills to be the overthrow of morality and a return to the ethics of aristocracy. True to his historicism, however, Nietzsche deemed this outcome neither possible nor desirable. For one thing, although the extraordinary few can flourish beyond morality, it is by no means clear that Nietzsche thought that the ordinary many would be much better off without their illusions. For another, Nietzsche believed that actually living through an historical stage of morality and then transcending it is necessary for humankind to reach its greatest excellence.

Before we consider why this is so, however, we should pause to note the overall **perfectionist** structure of Nietzsche's ethics. For a perfectionist view, such as Nietzsche's, the primary value is the realization of human excellence or *merit*. Unlike Mill (or Aristotle), Nietzsche did not claim that perfecting herself makes a person happier. (In fact, Nietzsche was not much interested in what will make people happy.) And unlike a **eudaimonist** such as Aristotle, Nietzsche did not hold that each person should seek his own greatest good or happiness. As we shall see, Aristotle's view was a **perfectionist eudaimonism.** He believed that each person should seek his own perfection since each should pursue his own good and the happiest, most flourishing human life involves higher, self-perfecting activities. And unlike Mill, Nietzsche certainly didn't believe that people should work to enable as many people as possible to realize their potential and thereby their greatest (and highest) happiness. Nietzsche was a perfectionist through and through. He believed that human excellence is of paramount importance *in itself*, not because it enriches human life and pays its way in happiness. "Mankind must work continually," he wrote, "to produce individual great human beings" in order to advance the achievement of human excellence.[6]

To feel the attraction of this view, consider what Nietzsche might have said to Mill. An important point for Mill was that some goods are higher or more worthy of human efforts than others. As against Bentham, Mill held that, for example, aesthetic activity requiring the cultivation of imaginative sensibilities is inherently more worthwhile and fulfilling than relatively mindless activities (Mill used the example of a child's game called "pushpin"). So even when human experiences are equally enjoyable or entertaining, they can vary in *depth*, in how profoundly they engage and realize us as human beings. Nietzsche agreed. But where he disagreed with Mill (and with Aristotle) was in the thought that higher goods are to be pursued or chosen because of the contribution they make to human happiness. The reason that we find poetry more fulfilling than pushpin, Nietzsche might have argued, is precisely that the enjoyment of poetry involves *an appreciation of the value of poetry itself* in a way that is relatively absent in activities that are merely pleasant pastimes. Think of experiences you regard as having genuine significance or depth. Isn't part of the depth of these experiences the appreciation of something that is seen as having value or worth in itself? Such experiences make extraordinary contributions to happiness and the value of life because they involve the appreciation of the intrinsic value of forms of human excellence. So their value, Nietzsche might have asserted, cannot itself derive from the contribution they make to human happiness.

However, if some activities are intrinsically more worthy of human efforts than others, then Nietzsche would seem to have been right that, at least other things being equal, we should work to realize those goods. Of course, it doesn't follow that this is the only thing worthy of our efforts. In particular, as Mill would have urged, it does not follow that we should not also be concerned about the quality of people's lives—both those of the ordinary many as well as those of the extraordinary few.

Beyond Morality?

Nietzsche insisted that morality's presupposition that every individual is a free, autonomous agent who can be held responsible for his deeds is an illusion. But he also believed that there is a form of autonomy and responsibility for self that human beings can achieve—one that, ironically, would have been impossible but for the role that morality itself played in human history. "The paradoxical task that nature has set itself in the case of man," he wrote, is "to breed an animal *with the right to make promises*" (GM.II.1.1). By this "right" Nietzsche meant the standing to take responsibility for oneself. Only persons able to "stand as their own guarantors" have the "extraordinary privilege of responsibility" (GM.II.2.2).

Before morality, human beings were insufficiently self-conscious or aware of the issue of responsibility to be responsible for themselves. In a sense, then, Nietzsche agreed with Kant that responsibility is impossible without the capacity to hold oneself accountable to a law that is represented in one's own will. Morality's error is an egalitarian fantasy born of envy and hatred of the meritorious. It assumes equal dignity—that all persons have a capacity for autonomy that makes them equally subject to a law requiring equal respect for this very capacity. But the truth, Nietzsche thought, is that everyone is not equally capable of autonomy and, indeed, that autonomy requires the *rejection* of morality.

Genuinely autonomous persons are "sovereign individuals" who are subject only to themselves and who see themselves as such. This is why, in Nietzsche's view, autonomy can be realized only by the few *after morality*. It is only in connection with the idea of morality and its pretension of a law that equally binds all human persons that the thought can arise that "I am not subject to this law. I am above it, subject only to a law of my own will." As Nietzsche wrote, "The ripest fruit is the *sovereign individual,* like only to himself, liberated again from morality of custom, autonomous and supramoral (for 'autonomous' and 'moral' are mutually exclusive)" (GM.II.2.2; original emphasis).

Morality Versus "Supramorality"

Of course, Kant agreed that, for the will to be autonomous, it cannot be bound by custom but only by its own law. However, his position was that morality itself *is* a custom-transcending law that springs equally from the will of each individual. What is ultimately at issue between Nietzsche and Kant is whether what Kant called **dignity** can be reduced to *merit*. For a perfectionist such as Nietzsche, human beings are worthy of respect; they have dignity, but in proportion to their excellence or merit. However, according to Kant (and the ideal of morality he espoused), there is a ground of respect that depends in no way on merit, not even on moral merit. Even a scoundrel is nonetheless a person and, hence, someone who cannot simply be used but whose dignity as a person must be respected. All persons have value *themselves* quite apart from the merit of anything they achieve or accomplish.

This brings us squarely back to what might be the warrant for the idea of morality. Nietzsche argued that it is a projective illusion caused by envy and hatred. He was no doubt right that the idea of morality has served as a cover for much cruelty and self-deception. But was he right that envy and hatred are the *source* of the idea of equal dignity? Indeed, do we have any reason to think that people whom Nietzsche himself would have described as extraordinary or meritorious are any less likely to see persons as valuable in themselves than are the many? On the contrary, the sort of positive openness to others that Nietzsche included within nobility may itself be linked to a receptivity to a value that any person may have in herself (leaving open the question of whether this value is to be interpreted in Kantian or utilitarian terms).

The challenge for those who would defend morality, of course, is to find a nonideological, philosophical account of the warrant for the moral ideal of equal dignity. On the other hand, the challenge for those who would follow Nietzsche is to avoid the charge of blindness to a distinctive kind of value—namely, the dignity represented by the moral equality of all persons. The Nietzschean looks at persons and sees someone who matters only to the extent of her excellence or merit. But this, it may be objected, is not all that matters about people: People matter in themselves.

Suggested Reading

Clark, Maudemarie. *Nietzsche on Truth and Philosophy.* Cambridge: Cambridge University Press, 1990.

Danto, Arthur C. *Nietzsche as Philosopher.* New York: Columbia University Press, 1980.

Kaufmann, Walter. *Nietzsche: Philosopher, Psychologist, Antichrist.* Princeton, N.J.: Princeton University Press, 1974.

Nietzsche, Friedrich. *Beyond Good and Evil* (1886). Walter Kaufmann, trans. New York: Vintage Books, 1989.

_____. *Human, All Too Human* (1878). Marion Faber, with Stephen Lehmann, trans. Lincoln: University of Nebraska Press, 1996.

_____. *On the Genealogy of Morals* (1887) and *Ecce Homo* (1888). Walter Kaufmann and R. J. Hollingdale, trans.; Walter Kaufmann, ed. New York: Vintage Books, 1989.

Nehamas, Alexander. *Nietzsche: Life as Literature.* Cambridge, Mass.: Harvard University Press, 1985.

Schacht, Richard. *Nietzsche.* London: Routledge & Kegan Paul, 1983.

Schacht, Richard, ed. Nietzsche, *Genealogy, Morality: Essays on Nietzsche's* On the Genealogy of Morals. Berkeley: University of California Press, 1994.

17

ARISTOTLE I

Philosophers who have been influenced by Nietzsche often spurn the ethical theories of philosophical moralists such as Mill and Kant. And when they do, it is frequently Aristotle (384–322 B.C.E.) to whom they turn. The "slave morality" that Nietzsche so bitterly complained had come to dominate Western Europe held no place in the thought of ancient Greece. We find in Aristotle no notion of a universal **moral law** requiring equal reciprocity and respect to which all are accountably subject. Aristotle's basic terms for evaluating conduct are **noble** and **base**, not **right** and **wrong**. He was concerned, not with questions of **guilt** or innocence, but with what gives cause for **shame** or proper pride. And in contrast to Mill, whose animating aim was to discover a "criterion" of right and wrong, Aristotle's project was to determine the "chief good" for human beings, the constituents of a valuable and flourishing human life.

Many thinkers who are not particularly skeptical about morality also find in Aristotle a subtler, richer, and, they argue, more realistic picture of the ethical life than they believe to have been provided by the philosophical moralists. Some believe moral theories like Mill's or Kant's to be unrealistically abstract. They agree with Aristotle's view that ethical knowledge involves a kind of wisdom or judgment that cannot be codified. Others believe that moral theories like Hobbes's or Kant's are excessively individualistic. They concur with the prominence that Aristotle gave to social connection and commonality over individual separation and conflict.

Other elements of Aristotle's ethics resonate in current thought as well. Many are persuaded by Aristotle's emphasis on the cultivation of character, including affect, perception, and emotion, in place of the inculcation of moral rules. And others are convinced by his account of friendship and other personal relationships as essential to virtue and a flourishing life. Indeed, despite the fact that Aristotle lived more than two millennia ago, his ethics are in some ways as fresh and lively as any we can consider.

The Chief Good

The Nicomachean Ethics begins with an argument for the existence of what will be its main object of inquiry: the chief good. Everything we do "aims at some good."[1] All action is purposive, involving some end or good for the sake of which we act. From this, Aristotle concluded that "the good has rightly been declared to be that at which all things aim" (1094a 1–3).

How should we understand this? Was Aristotle saying that whatever is desired is good simply by virtue of being desired (as **subjectivism** holds)? Or that it is the nature of desire to aim at objects we take to be good? In short, are things good because we desire them, or do we desire them because they are good?

Clearly, Aristotle meant the latter. If being good were the same as being desired, then it would be an uninformative tautology to say that we aim at the good. Worse, it would be false to the **phenomenology** of desire, as we discovered in our study of Hobbes in Chapter 10. When we desire something, we regard it favorably; we see *it* as good. And this is different from seeing that we desire it.

But neither did Aristotle agree with Hobbes that being good is a property that things just seem to have—that we project onto them—when we desire and pursue them. Our desires don't project value; they *reflect* value. Aristotle believed that we aim at and seek what we think to be good and, for reasons we shall begin to appreciate presently, that we tend to desire what actually is good.

So far, however, all we have is that every action aims at *some* good. Why did Aristotle think that there must be a single chief good at which every action ultimately aims? Why, as he also put it, must there be a "most final" good, an end that is uniquely desirable for itself with *all* other ends being desirable for the sake of it? (1097a 29). Aristotle gave one bad answer—namely, that if there were no chief good, then all desires would be instrumental. Without a chief good, he said, we would desire everything for the sake of something else, and this would make all our desires "empty and vain" (1094a 20). It makes no sense to desire one thing for the sake of another unless the latter, or something it will produce, is desirable in itself. But what this statement suggests is that every chain of desire must terminate in some "final end," not that there must be a single, most final end in which every chain terminates. There might be an irreducible plurality of intrinsic goods, a multiplicity of different kinds of things desirable for their own sakes.

In a sense, Aristotle agreed. Indeed, he makes this very point against the theory of his teacher Plato (427?–347 B.C.E.). Plato had held that there is a single "form" of the good, and that everything that is intrinsically desirable is so on account of its relation to this single "form." This would mean,

Aristotle said, that just as the "account" of why snow and white lead are both white is that there is an identical whiteness in them both, the same would be true for different intrinsic goods. But Aristotle insisted that this is not so. When we consider different intrinsically desirable things such as honor, wisdom, and pleasure, we see that "just in respect of their goodness, the accounts are distinct and diverse" (1096b 25). What we intrinsically value in wisdom is different from what we prize in honor. To put the point in terms of our familiar idea that value cannot be had "barely," honor's intrinsic-value-making properties are different from wisdom's intrinsic-value-making properties.

So why did Aristotle think there must be a chief good? A hint is provided by an analogy he made between archery and what thoughtful people seek in ethics: Only a chief good can give us "a mark to aim at" (1094a 24). Suppose that wisdom and honor are both intrinsically good and that you are forced to choose or make some trade-off between them. After all, it is physically (not to mention metaphysically) impossible to realize all intrinsic goods simultaneously (or perhaps to avoid all intrinsic evils), so we frequently face such choices and trade-offs. Indeed, which to choose is often the question that sets us thinking about ethics in the first place. Although which intrinsic goods and evils are at stake in our choices is often a straightforward and uncontroversial matter, which to choose when they conflict is frequently not.

Knowing only that both wisdom and honor are intrinsically good (or even what is distinctively good about each) cannot settle which to choose. But, by its very nature, deliberation seeks some basis for choice. It must be a working hypothesis of any deliberation between final ends, therefore, that there is some basis for choosing (or trading off) between them.

Now, we know that Aristotle believed that actions inherently aim at goods (ends). Whenever we choose some action, he said, we do so for the sake of some end or good that provides the reason for our choice. The problem is that what is, respectively, intrinsically good about distinctive intrinsic goods such as wisdom and honor provides no apparent basis for choice when they conflict. Accordingly, if there is some basis for choosing between intrinsic goods, and if such a basis can be given only by some end, it follows that this basis must be provided by some *further* end to which these two intrinsic goods can contribute. In any circumstance, therefore, there can be some reason to choose honor over wisdom, or vice versa, only if there is some further, *more* final end that is better realized by one of them than by the other.

This line of thought can be generalized. If we apply it to choices between intrinsic goods and evils generally, and follow it to its logical conclusion, we have an argument for the existence of a single end, desirable in itself, for the sake of which every other desirable thing is desirable. Or, rather, we have an argument that ethics must postulate such a chief good insofar as it is concerned with practical deliberation. (And Aristotle has told us that the end of ethics and "political science" is "not knowledge but action" [1095a 5].)

This argument may seem puzzling, however, for at least two different reasons. First, if we choose between intrinsic goods by considering their contribution to some further end, aren't we treating them as *instrumentally* valuable? Second, if everything's choiceworthiness ultimately depends on its relation to the chief good, doesn't this leave Aristotle with Plato's position, which he said he rejects?

Aristotelian Teleology.   Taking the second puzzle first, we find that Aristotle characterized his difference with Plato by saying that the chief good is a supreme good *for human beings,* not a value that exists independent of its relation to us. This point reveals a fundamental metaphysical difference between Plato and Aristotle and a key to the metaphysical underpinnings of Aristotle's philosophical ethics.

Aristotle believed that every natural thing has a purpose or "final cause" that simultaneously explains how it actually acts and provides a standard for evaluating its activity and development. Aristotelian science is **teleological** in the sense that it holds that how things actually behave can be explained by their inherent goal or *telos* (the Greek word for 'purpose' or 'end'). Thus acorns grow to become oak trees because this is their distinctive natural goal. And in addition to explaining a thing's actual action tendencies, its *telos* is evaluative or normative for it. It says how that thing *should* act. If a thing doesn't act or develop in accordance with its *telos,* something is wrong with it. It is a defective instance of its kind. Acorns that fail to grow into mature oaks do not develop as they should.

Recall the notion of **direction of fit** from Chapter 8. Ordinary beliefs and scientific hypotheses aim to fit the world: They attempt to represent things as they in fact are. And if there is a lack of fit, if the world is not as represented, then it is the representation that is faulty, not the world. Desires, intentions, plans, and normative propositions, on the other hand, have the reverse direction of fit. They aim for the world to fit them. An intention to feed the hungry, for example, aims to make the world such that the hungry are fed. If there is a lack of fit in this case, if the world fails to match the intention, then it is the world that is not as it should be (at least as judged from the perspective of the intention).

One way of explaining the Aristotelian notion of a *telos* is to say that the proposition that a natural species has a particular *telos* has both directions of fit. A *telos* aims, first, to describe and characterize that species, to truly represent it as an aspect of the natural world. If the facts about that species fail to match the representation, then the proposition is mistaken or false. But a *telos* is also normative for the species and its members, so the proposition has the reverse direction of fit as well. It says how members of that species *should* develop or act. If, consequently, a member of the species fails to match its *telos*, then there must be something wrong or defective with *it*. In short, there is no sharp line between Aristotelian science and ethics. Each is concerned with both facts and values. Value and purpose are thus inherent in the world, since everything has an end as part of what it is.

Teleological metaphysics and science have had few followers since the middle of the seventeenth century. Modern science is "value-free" in the sense that norms and values play no apparent role within its explanatory theories. From the modern perspective, the idea that there could be something like an Aristotelian *telos*, which can simultaneously explain both how things do behave *and* how they should behave, may seem virtually incoherent. From the scientific perspective, any claim about how something *properly* behaves is apt to seem beside the point. And from the perspective of ethics, any hypothesis about how things are seems, as Moore argued, to leave entirely open the question of how they should be.

Nevertheless, Aristotle's teleological metaphysics set the basic framework for his philosophical ethics. The chief good required to structure all human choice is an end inherent in our nature. What we should do, be, and become is implicit in what we are. Just as the young sapling does well or flourishes only if it is in the way of developing into a mature tree, we flourish and live as we should only if our growth is directed by our human *telos*.

Human Flourishing. Aristotle thought it was easy to give a platitudinous characterization of the chief good. It is happiness or *flourishing*. (The Greek word is *eudaimonia*, so we can refer to Aristotle's view that each person should seek his own happiness as **eudaimonism**.) When we develop as we should, we live *well*; we thrive, prosper, and flourish. And when we don't, we languish and suffer. This much Aristotle regarded as uncontroversial. Every human being is (and should be) aiming at a happy, flourishing life. What people disagreed about is what a flourishing human life involves.

Despite the hedonistic connotations that 'happy' has for us, Aristotle did not identify happiness with pleasure. He noted that some people think these are the same, but that they are misled by the fact that pleasure is the normal result or sign of a flourishing, happy life. It is not the substance of it. Flourishing consists rather in distinctively human *activity,* and pleasure "supervenes" on this activity much like "the bloom of youth does on those in the flower of their age" (1174b 34).

This argument helps to answer the first puzzle. The relation between other intrinsic goods and a flourishing life is not just an instrumental one. On the contrary, intrinsically good activities are parts of a flourishing life. They are what such a life consists of. If this idea sounds familiar, it should, since we encountered it before in Mill's work. Faced with the objection that if happiness is the only good, then virtue can be only extrinsically or instrumentally valuable, Mill replied that virtuous activity is an *ingredient* of a happy life, not a mere means to it. In doing so, he was embracing Aristotle's view of happiness (although, unlike Aristotle, he maintained that doing so was consistent with hedonism—and he also meant something different by 'virtue').

Teleology, Morality, and Normativity.   Before considering Aristotle's account of the chief good, we should briefly note features of his philosophical ethics that set his approach apart from that of the philosophical moralists. Here again, the comparison with Mill is illuminating. Mill substantially agreed with Aristotle about the constituents of a flourishing, happy life. But Mill believed that the **nonmoral** question of what a person can do to make her life happy is not the only ethical question she faces. After all, she is only one person among others. And when she views her life this way, from a **moral point of view,** her own flourishing seems to matter no more (but also no less) than any other person's. And so she can ask, What in light of this is it **morally right** to do?

Even if, as Aristotle and Mill both believed, human beings are profoundly social creatures whose happiness substantially includes the happiness of others, there can nonetheless be genuine conflicts of interest between them. At least in our imperfect circumstances, it can happen that a more flourishing life for some comes at the cost of a less flourishing life for others. When confronted with such a situation, we have to choose. We face the question, How should we balance our own flourishing against the happiness of others?

For philosophical moralists like Mill, this is the kind of situation that gives morality its point. Of course, one's own flourishing matters; but, morally, that of any other person matters the same. For Aristotle, however, the ultimate and unquestionable standpoint of practical deliberation is the agent's own flourishing, since it is the end that is inherent in her own metaphysical nature. By her very nature, living a flourishing human life is what any human being *is to do.* (Again, however, I should stress that Aristotle does not think that people can flourish without such virtues as justice.)

This is a natural view to take if one holds to a teleological metaphysics, since a teleological structure provides a metaphysical guarantee that individual interests will harmonize. A common *telos* ensures that human life does not present us with a fundamental collective action problem. It ensures that mutual disadvantage cannot result from everyone's acting for his own good. Consequently, no conception of another normative perspective (morality) that governs and overrides self-interest for mutual advantage is required. The flourishing of each is guaranteed to interlock with the flourishing of all. Without teleology, however, there is no such assurance. It is evidence of the depth of Aristotle's teleological presuppositions that he doesn't even consider a perspective from which everyone's flourishing matters equally.

Thus an important issue between Aristotelians and philosophical moralists concerns metaphysical teleology itself. The challenge that present-day Aristotelians face, then, is either to defend teleology or to exhibit some other basis for Aristotelian ethics. One promising idea has been to hold that evolution and natural selection can fund an appropriately naturalistic notion of natural function and purpose without appeal to metaphysics. According to the evolutionary theory of natural selection, it is *as if* natural species have implicit purposes, because they evolve to fit their ecological niche. But even here the philosophical moralist's challenge can be pressed. A philosophical moralist like Mill can agree that there are natural facts about what sort of life is most flourishing, yet hold that, unless the agent's own flourishing is somehow metaphysically given as her ultimate ethical standard (and how could that be?), she is still only one among others and from this (moral) standpoint her flourishing matters no more than anyone else's.

Of course, natural selection may also have fashioned us so that the goods of all *naturally* interlock—in which case problems of collective action may only be apparent and never real. But even were this true of human beings placed in the same auspicious natural circumstances (like oak saplings in equally fertile soil), or lacking, to the same degree, any history of exploitation, subjugation, or even just differential advantage, it can seem incredible that natural selection could guarantee a harmony of interests as humanity is actually distributed across the globe at this point in history.

Excellent, Distinctively Human Activity.   Aristotle's project, then, was to determine what the chief good is. What does a flourishing life consist in? Some say it is pleasure. Others identify it with status or honor, with having the esteem of others. Still others claim it consists in power and wealth. Finally, some identify it with excellence or virtue (*arete* in Greek). Aristotle's own view was squarely in agreement with this last group, and he gave various arguments to support it.

Some considerations spring from critically analyzing the alternatives. I have already mentioned Aristotle's reaction to the hedonist proposal: Pleasure is a sign of valuable activity rather than the substance of its value. Enjoyment can hardly be the whole of what is valuable about playing a musical instrument, for example, since appreciating musical activity's value is itself part of enjoying it. (Recall that this was also an important theme for Mill—although, as we saw in Chapter 12, he maintained its consistency with hedonism.)

Similarly, Aristotle argued that when we want others' esteem, it is not so much for its own sake but because it is a means to and a sign of other things we value. Most important, Aristotle claimed that we desire honor as evidence of our own **worth** (1095b 26). Consider the following. Do we desire the esteem of all people equally? Do we want the esteem of those we do not esteem as much as we want the esteem of those we admire? Obviously not. We care much more about being valued by those we esteem and respect than we do about being admired by those we do not. What explains this phenomenon? According to Aristotle's hypothesis, part of the explanation is that we want to *merit* the esteem of others, and that we regard esteem from others we esteem as evidence of our **merit** in a way that admiration from those we don't admire is not. But if we value the esteem of others for this reason, we cannot regard it as intrinsically valuable. Rather, what we intrinsically value is (our own) merit.

Of course, we don't desire the esteem of others only as evidence of our own worth. Even if we care more about the esteem of those we esteem, isn't that partly because we value relationships with them more highly? Aristotle agreed, but that is because he saw friendship of this kind as excellent (virtuous) activity, which itself involves the mutual sharing and appreciation of virtue.

Finally, there is power and wealth. But here again, Aristotle argued that these are only instrumentally valuable or treated by us as evidence of value, in the same way we treat status.

The Function Argument.   In addition to being able to explain ordinary beliefs about the chief good, Aristotle thought he had a general philosophical argument in support of the thesis that flourishing consists in virtuous activity. "For all things that have a function or activity," he said, "the good and the 'well' is thought to reside in the function" (1097b 26). Take Aristotle's example of lyre-playing. Lyre-players are defined (or define themselves) by a characteristic "function" or activity—playing the lyre. Not just anything counts as playing the lyre. Banging a lyre against a younger brother or using it to hang underwear to dry is not the same as playing it. The activity of playing an instrument has certain normative or evaluative standards built in, and to be engaged in that activity is to be guided by those norms. It is simply part of what it is to play the lyre to be making some attempt to do it well. And if one is able to and does, then one is a good lyre-player and one's lyre-playing flourishes—one flourishes as a lyre-player. Similarly, something can benefit or harm someone as a lyre-player insofar as it affects her ability to play.

Or consider an artifact that is designed for a certain purpose, such as a knife. Again, a knife's function determines what it is for the knife to perform well, for it to be a good knife, as well as what sorts of things can harm or benefit the knife (i.e., affect its ability to function well). The same is true of parts of the body that have functions. If an accident leaves my eyes a little itchy but does not affect my vision, then it has done them no harm.

In general, then, if something has a function, then its flourishing or good consists in its performing its function well.

Next, Aristotle argued that human beings have a function. This is a consequence of his teleological metaphysics. Every natural thing has a function by virtue of having a *telos*. For plants, such as an oak sapling, it is "a life of nutrition and growth"—each species in its distinctive way (1098a 1). For other animal species, it is what Aristotle called "a life of perception"—again, each in its characteristic way. Like all other natural beings, therefore, human beings have a function implicit in their *telos*. And, as with other natural beings, their distinctive function springs from what distinguishes them from other natural species.

But what *is* distinctively human activity? Aristotle said it is "an active life of the element that has a rational principle" (1098a 3). This "element" has two parts: "One part has [a rational] principle in the sense of being obedient to one, the other in the sense of possessing one and exercising thought" (1098a 4–5). Human beings can take thought and consciously deliberate about what we should do, think, be, and feel. In fact, it is this exercise of thought that leads us to frame the very questions with which Aristotle is concerned in the *Ethics*. But principles are also *implicit* in human life, even when we do not consciously reflect—namely, in the ways that I described at the beginning of this book. We choose and do things *for reasons* and, in so acting, commit ourselves to ethical conceptions, principles, and values. We also feel things *as for reasons*, and this, too, involves more general principle and thought. If, for example, you resent the way your boss treats you, it feels to you as if he does you an injustice, *as if* there is a reason warranting your response.

What is distinctive about human beings, therefore, are the ways in which reasons and ethical conceptions are woven throughout our thought, feeling, and action and the ways in which we can affect our feelings, thoughts, and choices by "exercising thought."

Aristotle concluded that "the function of man is an activity of soul which follows or implies a rational principle" (1098a 7). Now, if the flourishing of anything that has a function consists in its performing its function well, then human flourishing must also consist in performing its function well. "Human good," he wrote, "turns out to be activity of soul in accordance with virtue (excellence)" (1098a 17). A flourishing life is one of excellent, distinctively human (i.e., rational) activity. It is a life, as Aristotle also said, of *virtuous* activity, where virtue has connotations of excellence (*arete*) and virtuosity, not those it came to have within the Judeo-Christian tradition. 'Virtue' is the term translators typically use, but we should keep in mind what Aristotle meant by it (and what he didn't mean).

The hypothesis that a flourishing life consists in virtuous activity can explain many things that people believe about the chief good. Aristotle considered this further evidence of the correctness of his theory. First, as we've seen, it can explain why people want the esteem of people they admire: both because that provides evidence of their own merit and because the friendship of virtuous people itself involves virtuous activity. Second, virtuous activity is inherently enjoyable, thus explaining the appeal of the theory that the chief good consists in pleasure. Third, it explains the sense in which we think what is most valuable in life has a depth that does not overly depend on goods that are "easily taken from one" (1095b 26). Unlike honor, which depends on the vagaries of other people's attitudes, a life of virtuous activity depends primarily on the person herself. But, fourth, Aristotle's theory also explains why a flourishing life is thought to depend on "external goods" such as wealth and resources to some extent, inasmuch as Aristotle believed that some forms of virtuous activity are simply impossible without these.

Ethical Truth and Ethical Wisdom

Why, if Aristotle believed he had a general philosophical proof that a flourishing human life consists in virtuous activity, did he care about trying to show that this theory fits with what thoughtful people believe about the chief good? Why did he start the chapter just after the function argument by saying that "we must consider happiness in the light not only of our conclusion and our premises, but also of what is commonly said about it"? It is worth pausing here to reflect on the epistemological assumptions that underlie Aristotle's method.

"With a true view," Aristotle wrote, "all the data must harmonize" (1098b 11). By "data," Aristotle meant "respectable opinion." And he made clear that, to be taken seriously, an opinion must spring from the experience and maturity that, he believed, is necessary for judgment and wisdom. There are several important points here.

First, Aristotle believed that ethics is not like mathematics or physics, in which theoretical insight is possible with relatively little experience or maturity. Ethical knowledge is wisdom or judgment, not purely intellectual insight. And because ethics reflects on the stuff of life, ethical knowledge and wisdom are impossible if one has not lived through much and grown from it.

Second, since there is no pipeline to ethical truth other than through the judgments of mature, experienced human beings (note here a version of the ideal judgment theory), any ethical theory must be able to fit with and explain these judgments. That is why Aristotle undertook to show that his theory could explain them. This, however, is not to say that an adequate theory must be able to explain all such views exactly as they stand. A requirement like that would be excessively static and would not reflect the fact that philosophical thought is itself part of human growth and development. Rather, the touchstone of an adequate ethical theory is that it can make sense of the judgments of experienced judges when they ponder the theory's philosophical grounds together with its relation to the judgments they are inclined to make on the basis of their own experience.

Third, and finally, Aristotle cautioned that in any inquiry we must expect only as much clarity and precision "as the subject-matter admits of" (1094b 12). As we shall see, Aristotle believed that our best efforts in formulating general ethical ideals and principles are likely to be relatively unhelpful in providing specific practical guidance, especially to those who have not yet developed mature character and judgment. As he saw it, the role of the philosopher thinking about ethics is not to formulate and ground abstract rules that anyone can apply but, rather, to draw virtuous people into a process of reflection, much of the basis for which is their own experience and judgment, in order to further shape and develop their judgment. In the end, he believed, ethical knowledge involves a kind of perception, but one that, unlike that of the rational intuitionists, is tempered by experience, growth, and development in addition to philosophical reflection. Unlike, for example, the principle of utility, ethical knowledge cannot be formulated in rules and principles that people are able to understand and apply more or less independent of their own ethical development.

18

ARISTOTLE II

Virtue, Ideals, and the Noble

By the end of Book I, Aristotle had his general answer to *The Nicomachean Ethics'* fundamental question. The chief good consists of a life of excellent, distinctively human activity or, as he also said, virtuous activity. But although this answer is more informative than that the chief good is flourishing, it is still only a sketch. What actually *is* virtuous activity? And what, more specifically, are the human virtues? Also, how do we recognize virtues, and how do we become virtuous? These are the questions with which the rest of the *Ethics* is concerned.

Before considering how Aristotle approached them, we should note an issue that we will largely have to set aside. Readers of the *Ethics* frequently mark a tension between two apparently different descriptions that Aristotle gave of the good (virtuous) life. Up until Book X, Aristotle described an active and public ideal, emphasizing virtues such as courage, friendship, and justice. Starting in Book X, Chapter 7, however, Aristotle argued that, since human functioning distinctively involves rationality, and since the best life must be in accordance with the "highest virtue," pure rational contemplation must be the highest activity and the best life for human beings. And he suggested that the value of the other, more practical virtues depends on how they contribute to such a life. Contemplative activity involves the most "divine" element in us. When we imagine a god's happy life, we hardly imagine him "mak[ing] contracts" or engaging in other acts of justice, or acting like "a brave man . . . confronting dangers and running risks because it is noble to do so" (1178b 13–14). A divine being would lead a contemplative life. With our lesser powers, we cannot dispense with the practical virtues. Still, we can engage in contemplation also. Aristotle concluded that a human life is better to the extent that it involves contemplation and that the other virtues are ultimately valuable only to the extent that they permit us to engage in it.

Far be it from a philosopher to disagree with this last thought, but it does seem extreme and hard to fit with what Aristotle said in the rest of the *Ethics*. In any case, we shall have to set this fascinating interpretive issue aside and take Books I–IX of the *Ethics* at face value.

Action and Character.   What, then, is virtuous activity? Aristotle believed that it is impossible to answer this question simply by describing acts of some specific kind. You cannot tell whether someone's activity is excellent in the distinctively human way just by seeing what she does. Virtuous activity is rooted in *the person's virtue*, in her *character*, and this will be so only if she acts for certain reasons. For example, Aristotle believed that temperance is a virtue. Genuinely temperate activity arises from a temperate character, from a disposition to act for the reasons by which the temperate person is characteristically guided. If what explains my moderate intake of food and drink is spite for the cook, or anorexia, my eating manifests the vice of spitefulness or an eating disorder, not the virtue of temperance.

We can see how this follows from Aristotle's claim that distinctively human functioning involves guidance by reasons. No description of what someone does that leaves out her reasons can be sufficient to determine whether her activity involves the distinctive human excellence. Activity manifests human excellence on account of its temperance, therefore, only if the acting person does so for a temperate person's reasons.

Aristotle crystallized these considerations into a general characterization. In order for behavior to count as virtuous activity, "the agent . . . must be in a certain condition when he does them; . . . he must have knowledge; secondly he must choose the acts . . . for their own sakes, and thirdly his action must proceed from a firm and unchangeable character" (1105a 31–33). Thus, only if the temperate person chooses to eat moderately for its own sake is her moderation virtuous.

Ideals, Praxis, and the Noble.   But why did Aristotle say that the temperate person chooses moderation *for its own sake?* Isn't a temperate person moved by such considerations as whether more food or drink is desirable as a means to such further ends as health and well-being (or a flourishing life on the whole)?

Aristotle believed that moderation also matters to the virtuous person *intrinsically*, in the sense that she sees it *as a human excellence*, as something of worth that merits esteem and emulation in itself. Similarly, she sees gluttony and abstemiousness, the contraries of temperance on either side, as intrinsically deserving of disesteem.

In short, Aristotle believed that virtuous activity implies acceptance of an **ideal** and guidance by that ideal. Moderation is part of an ideal to which the temperate person aspires. In Aristotle's favorite term, it is **noble** (*kalon* in Greek), whereas gluttony is ignoble or **base**. Moderation is worthy of us and a proper source of pride, whereas gluttony is beneath us and an appropriate object of **shame**.

Excellence in exercising our distinctive human capacity for rational guidance thus entails that we act on the ideals we accept. For Aristotle, to put it simply, *excellent human activity is guided by an ideal of human excellence.*

This point is also reflected in a central distinction that Aristotle made between the sort of goal-directed activity that any intelligent being can engage in (*poiesis*, meaning "production" or "making") and distinctively human actions (*praxis*) that are chosen as instantiating an ideal of noble conduct. Only *praxis* is chosen for its own sake as *noble*. And only *praxis* is *distinctively* human. Figuring one's way out of a maze, no more, no less, is *poiesis*, whether one is a human or a rat. If, however, one does so in a pursuit one considers noble and intrinsically worthwhile, and does it for this reason, then this is *praxis*. So when Aristotle talked about a flourishing human life consisting in activities of a certain kind, it was *praxis* that he had in mind.

It is hard not to accept Aristotle's thesis that ideals figure centrally in the most significant goods of human life. Consider, for example, the importance we place on *narrative*. Why are we so gripped by stories and so prone to see our lives in narrative terms? Much of what interests us concerns ideals and character. We even refer to a story's main participants as "characters." We are inspired, intrigued, repelled, and disgusted by the traits that narratives reveal.

Our fascination with narrative extends to virtually all aspects of human life. A sports event, for example, is no mere contest of skill or prowess, but a drama in which noble opponents compete and an underdog may show courage or unexpected self-possession. Narratives sometimes even effect the events they are about, as when the press presents a political campaign as the story of a faltering front-runner or a dramatic comeback, thereby influencing public perceptions and, ultimately, how the story comes out.

"Self-narratives" are no less central. We are constantly constructing and reconstructing the story of our lives. And we are chagrined when forced to confront images of us that clash with those we have (or want to have) of ourselves. Anybody who claims not to accept ideals, or to care about whether he merits esteem or disdain in terms of any ideal, is thus virtually certain to be proven wrong at some point by his own red face.

Ethics Without Morality. This emphasis on ideals help us to see another basic difference between Aristotle and the philosophical moralists, in addition to his teleological metaphysics. To put the point in Nietzschean terms, Aristotle's is an ethics of good and *bad* rather than of good and *evil.* Its contraries are those of noble and base rather than of right and wrong.

What is ignoble and base gives cause for shame, not for guilt. Shame is the feeling we have when we see ourselves as worthy of disdain, scorn, or ridicule, whereas guilt is what we feel when we see what we have done as culpable or blameworthy. For Aristotle, the distinctively human ethical categories concern, not culpability, but what is worthy of or beneath one. Failing to meet this standard makes one subject to contempt or ridicule rather than accountable or worthy of blame or punishment. To refer to these differences, we might say that whereas the philosophical moralist's conception of ethics is **law-based,** Aristotle's is **ideal-based.**

Like Nietzsche's, Aristotle's ethics is a kind of **perfectionism.** But whereas Nietzsche held that the realization of the most perfect forms of humanity are what the species as a whole should be aiming at, Aristotle was a **eudaimonist.** He believed that each individual should pursue his own good and that a life of self-perfecting activity is what is good for each. More specifically, then, Aristotle was a **perfectionist eudaimonist,** whereas Nietzsche was a perfectionist through and through.

Ethical Education: Acquiring Virtue

We now have a number of ethical categories floating around in the air. Too many to proceed without clarifying their relations.

First, we have the chief good, the ultimate end of all practical deliberation. Second, there are virtue and the virtuous activity that Aristotle believed to constitute the chief good. And, third, we have the ideal of noble conduct to which, Aristotle said, the virtuous person is committed. In order for activity to be virtuous, it must be chosen as noble in itself. But how can conduct be choiceworthy both for its own sake *and* for the sake of its relation to the chief good? How can the temperate person choose temperance both because temperance is noble and because it contributes to a flourishing life? Such questions would have posed a problem for Aristotle if prizing the virtues for their relation to the chief good were to value them *instrumentally.* But this is clearly not what Aristotle intended. Virtuous activity is not a means to the chief good; it is what a flourishing life *consists in.* There is thus no inconsistency in valuing virtuous activity both for its own sake and on account of its relation to a flourishing life. It is part of what a good life is.

Human beings flourish through virtuous activity. But how do we become virtuous? How do we acquire the character necessary for us to enjoy what is best in life? Despite Aristotle's emphasis on the *internal,* character-based nature of virtue, his account of ethical education is notable for its stress on *practice.*

Acquiring virtue is like learning an art or craft. It includes a knack or "feel" that one can acquire only by doing.

The virtues we get by first exercising them, as also happens in the case of the arts as well. For the things we have to learn before we can do them, we learn by doing them; e.g., men become builders by building and lyre-players by playing the lyre; so too we become just by doing just acts, temperate by doing temperate acts, brave by doing brave acts. (1103a 30–1103b 1)

Consider how one learns to play a musical instrument. Theory is but little help in learning to play. For this one needs practical knowledge ("know-how") rather than theoretical knowledge ("know-that"). And to develop know-how, there is no substitute for practice. Practice both develops naturally based skills and inculcates the habits of good lyre-playing.

Likewise, with the virtues, "it makes no small difference, then, whether we form habits of one kind or of another from our very youth; it makes a very great difference, or rather *all* the difference" (1103b 22–25). People who have not been brought up well don't merely lack good habits, they usually have bad ones. And just as someone who has developed bad habits in a sport or art has to unlearn these before she can make any real progress in learning her craft, so someone with bad ethical habits—gluttony for example—is faced with the double challenge of unlearning what has become second nature to her before she can acquire the second nature of a temperate person.

There are really two points here. One concerns the importance of habit. We acquire the knack of virtuous activity only by practice. But how do we know what to practice? This is equivalent to the music student's question, How do I know what technique to practice? The answer in both cases is the same. This is not something you *can* know or discover by yourself. You need a teacher who can show you. In the case of the ethical virtues, you need to be shown by virtuous people. This is the second point. Ethical growth and development can be nurtured in the young only by mature adults who already have the practical knowledge that the virtues include. We glimpsed the same point at the end of Chapter 17. In ethics, it is *wisdom* that matters, not any formulae that can be grasped by someone whose upbringing has not already imbued him with values. Theoretical reflection in ethics presupposes virtuous character as a background. And we can acquire this only by emulating those who already have it.

Human beings naturally have the potential for the virtuous activity that their flourishing involves. But to develop this potential, they require a social environment in which they are mentored by the wise. So far, this is the same argument as would be made for any art or craft. But Aristotle believed there is an important difference between virtue and art. "The arts," he said, "have their goodness in themselves, so that it is enough that they should have a certain character" (1105a 27–28). Whether something is good art is largely independent of the motivations and character of the artist. Gaugin's paintings manifest artistic genius whether he was a rogue or not. But this is not true of virtuous activity, as we have seen. For conduct to be virtuous, it must spring from virtuous character. It follows that ethical education must instill a love of nobility and virtue no less than a sense of what to do. Maybe artists who do not love their art are less likely to produce good art than those who do. But the artists' attitude toward their art is no part of the artistic value of what they produce. The ethical value of virtuous activity, however, does depend on the virtuous person's character. So one cannot learn virtuous activity without learning to love nobility for its own sake.

As an example, consider the virtue of justice. In teaching justice to their children, parents may begin by pointing out opportunities to share. These may initially appear as invitations, commands, or cajolings. As the child's powers of comprehension develop, however, parental encouragements may begin to be accompanied by commentary that presents fairness as something worthy of their aspiration and emulation, on the one hand, and injustice and greed as unlovely traits worthy of disdain, on the other. Over time, external direction may give way to motivation that is at least partly internal as the child develops the desire for approval. Nonetheless, even if this desire were unfailingly to cause fair behavior, it would not yet manifest the virtue of justice. For this, the child must develop the desire to *merit* others' esteem by doing what is just for its own sake. And for that, she must internalize an ideal of justice that she accepts as her own. Finally, at this point, she wants to be, and can take pleasure in being, just for its own sake. Being just is now part of the kind of person she wants herself to be. In choosing just activity for this reason, she functions in a distinctively human way and, therefore, Aristotle believed, flourishes as a human being.

The Theory of the Mean

Aristotle is famous for the thesis that every virtue is a mean between opposing extreme vices. It is easy to misunderstand this idea, however. Despite appearances, it is not so much meant to tell us how to identify specific virtues or noble acts as to illustrate the fundamental structure of the virtues.

All ethical virtues concern "passions and actions," and these in turn always admit of "excess, defect, and the intermediate" (1106b 17). To see Aristotle's meaning, recall his core idea that distinctively human functioning is "an active life of the element that has a rational principle" (1098a 3), either explicitly, through rational thought, or implicitly, when we act and feel things *for reasons.*

Not even our emotions and passions assail us as completely irrational urges. We feel things *as for reasons,* reasons through which we make our feelings intelligible to ourselves. And this makes our emotions and desires subject to rational criticism. Fear, for example, presents itself as a response to danger. If danger really is present, then there is some reason to be afraid. But if no danger exists (or there is no reason to think so), then fear is unwarranted. There is no reason to be afraid.

Passions and emotions also admit of intensity. We can fear something more or less, be more or less angry about something, desire something more or less intensely, and so on. So Aristotle wrote that "fear and confidence and appetite and anger and pity and in general pleasure and pain can be felt both too much and too little" (1106b 17–19). In every case, the *appropriate* amount of passion or emotion to feel is some point between these extremes. Aristotle called this point the "intermediate": "To feel them at the right times, with reference to the right objects, towards the right people, with the right motive, and in the right way, is what is both intermediate and best" (1106b 20–23).

By the "intermediate," then, Aristotle just meant whatever degree and kind of passions and actions are appropriate to the specific situation in which the person finds himself, taking account also of the person's own characteristics. Six pounds, Aristotle told us, is too much food for "the beginner in athletic exercises," but too little for the athlete, Milo! (1106b 5). The relevant intermediate point is the "intermediate relative to us."

Aristotle used "mean" to refer to the character trait of "aiming at the intermediate" (1106b 15). Each virtue, then, is a mean. It is the trait that aims at the intermediate with respect to the passions and actions that are relevant to the virtues (and vices) of its specific kind.

The theory of the mean is thus no formula that can be used to determine virtues, as one might use a rule to bisect a line between two extreme points. Neither the mean nor the intermediate refers to a midpoint. The intermediate is simply whatever is the *appropriate* point, somewhere between the extremes of too much and too little. And the virtuous mean is the character trait that is targeted on that point.

What we do learn from the theory of the mean is something about the natural groupings of virtues and vices that Aristotle believed to be rooted in various natural passional contexts of human life. Why, for example, is temperance a virtue? By its very nature, temperance is concerned with the satisfaction, control, and regulation of certain natural *appetites*—specifically, those for the pleasures of "touch and taste" (1118a 26). If we lacked these appetites, if we were not subject to cravings of any sort or if their satisfaction did not affect health or other aspects of normal human life, then there would be no such human virtue as temperance. What sets the context for this virtue, then, is the fact that we are physically embodied creatures who are subject to certain distinctive natural pleasures and appetites, that our responses to these appetites affect our lives in various ways, and, therefore, that as rational creatures the question naturally arises for us how we *should* conduct ourselves with respect to these appetites and pleasures.

Appetites can be satisfied more or less, so the practical question confronting us is how much we should satisfy them—and which, when, and where. Simplifying, there would seem to be three possibilities: too much (self-indulgence), too little (abstemiousness or "insensibility"), or the intermediate, appropriate amount (the mean: temperance).

Or consider courage. Here the practical and passional context is set by fear and what Aristotle called "confidence" (our sense that we are equal to the dangers facing us). Again, were we not subject to these natural feelings, there would be no such virtue as courage. Because we are, however, and also rational, we can raise such questions as whether our fear or confidence is warranted, how we should act in light of these emotions, and so on. Again, both fear and confidence admit of degree. We can feel more or less fear or have more or less confidence in ourselves.

Both fear and confidence admit of extremes in both directions. We may feel more fear than the situation warrants, or less. "To fear some things is even right and noble, and it is base not to fear them—e.g.[,] disgrace" (1115a 13). The person who fears too much is a coward, and he who fears too little "a sort of madman or insensible person" (1115b 26). The courageous person "fears the right things and from the right motive, in the right way and at the right time" (1115b 17–18). Similarly, we may be overly confident or unjustifiably unconfident. We may rashly overestimate ourselves and underestimate risks, or be too easily discouraged and despairing of our own resources. Aristotle regarded all these as defects of character because they amount to a failure to regulate our feelings, thoughts, and actions as we should.

These are only two examples. Aristotle presented his entire catalogue of virtues in the same framework, although not without some heavy lifting. Liberality is the mean between being disposed to give too much and too little, justice the mean between taking too much and too little, and so on. In each case, the virtue/vice group is associated with a typical context in which any human being with normal emotions and desires naturally finds himself and with respect to which, as a rational creature, he asks how he should think, feel, and act.

Principles and Practical Wisdom

Aristotle summarized: "Virtue, then, is a state of character concerned with choice, lying in a mean, i.e., the mean relative to us, this being determined by a rational principle, and by that principle by which the man of practical wisdom would determine it" (1106b 36–1107a 2). How are we to understand this last part? Is Aristotle saying that there are, after all, principles that determinately identify virtuous activity? If the mean is determined by the principle by which the person of practical wisdom would determine it, we should ask what practical wisdom is.

Practical Wisdom. Aristotle discussed practical wisdom in Book VI of the *Ethics*. He began by rehearsing Book II's claim that "the intermediate is determined by the dictates of the right rule" and that "there is a mark to which the man who has the rule looks [the intermediate]" (1138b 21–22). To this Aristotle quickly added that "such a statement, though true, is by no means clear." Someone who understood only this much "would be none the wiser." He would be like a person who, wanting to know "what sort of medicines to apply," is told, "all those which the medical art prescribes, and which agree with the practice of one who possesses the art" (1138b 31). He would not yet have the "right rule" himself, so he would be unable to identify the intermediate. Perhaps, then, if we can identify practical wisdom, we can identify the "right rule" and the intermediate via it.

Practical wisdom is an intellectual virtue, but one that differs from the excellence involved in scientific theorizing. Rather, it entails excellence in practical thinking—specifically, in *deliberation* (1139a 12).

Now, as we know, Aristotle thought that deliberation is always guided by some end. So deliberative excellence must at least partly involve being able to work out the means to our ends. This ability, which Aristotle called "cleverness," is necessary for practical wisdom, but not sufficient. Cleverness enables us to hit the "mark" we set ourselves, but it is laudable only if the mark is noble (1144a 24–26).

That practical wisdom must be more than cleverness follows from Aristotle's distinction between *praxis* (distinctively human action) and *poiesis* (intelligent goal-directed behavior of the sort of which other animals are capable). Cleverness is sufficient for *poiesis* but not for *praxis*. Excellence in distinctively human deliberation requires that one deliberate well with respect to actions that are worth choosing for their own sake. Thus "practical wisdom is the quality of mind concerned with things just and noble and good for man" (1143b 21).

It follows that practical wisdom includes the ability not only to discern what to do to promote further ends but also to see which acts, on specific occasions, would be noble and which would be base—that is, the ability to see which specific act would *realize* the end of acting nobly on a given occasion. The practically wise person deliberates well with respect to the just and noble in the sense that she is able to see what justice, temperance, and courage specifically *call for*. So Aristotle said that practical wisdom can be thought of as a kind of insight or "perception" since it is concerned with an "ultimate particular fact . . . the thing to be done" (1142a 24–25).

But what enables the practically wise to know what particular marks to aim at? To this, Aristotle answered simply: virtue (1144a 7). It is impossible for a person to know what to aim at in deliberation unless she is already virtuous, unless her upbringing and personal development have brought her to a sense of what the appropriate passions and actions are and an acceptance of an ideal according to which these are noble and worth aiming at for their own sake.

A Virtuous or Vicious Circle?   But now we have completed a circle. Virtue is a mean determined by the principle by which the practically wise person would determine it. And the practically wise are thoughtful, perceptive people of virtue. If Aristotle was attempting to provide some sort of reductive definition of virtue—attempting, that is, to show how virtue could be defined in terms of other things that are definable without reference to it—he would be open to the charge of vicious circularity. How should we interpret him?

Much hangs on how we understand 'determine'. If Aristotle was asserting that the mean depends (metaphysically) on the rule used by the practically wise, and that whether someone is practically wise likewise depends, partly, on whether she is virtuous, then it looks as if we have a vicious circularity. Is a particular point the intermediate or not? Suppose it is according to a rule by which Jones guides herself. Then that point is an intermediate if, and only if, Jones is practically wise. But whether Jones is practically wise depends on whether she is virtuous. And whether she is virtuous depends on whether she aims at the intermediate. So there will be no fact about whether the point is an intermediate that is independent of a fact concerning whether the person who aims at it is virtuous. And there will be no fact about whether the person aiming at a point is virtuous independent of whether the point at which she aims is an intermediate.

It seems unlikely, however, that this is the way we should understand Aristotle. For one thing, he certainly didn't think that the chief good depends *metaphysically* on the aims of flourishing people. It is the other way around. Metaphysically, facts about the chief good depend on our function and *telos*. We desire the good because it is our good or *telos*. It is not our good because we desire it.

Facts about the good do not depend on the aims of the practically wise. But Aristotle believed that the chief human good just *is* virtuous activity that itself involves aiming at certain conduct and passion (the intermediates) for their own sake, being disposed to be proud of acting in these ways, ashamed of not doing so, and so on. It follows, then, from the fact that these forms of activity are our *telos* that this is how we *should* act and be.

So we should aim at just these forms of activity (and their respective inter-mediate points) for their own sake, be proud when we do so, ashamed when we do not, and so on. But if facts about the chief good make it true that we should aim at specific intermediate points for their own sake, be proud when we do, ashamed when we don't, and so on, then these facts make it the case that the relevant points determine what is noble, and their contraries, what is base. And if that is so, then there will be facts about which points define the mean virtuous traits (and the intermediate noble conduct at which these traits aim) independent of the fact that these are what the practically wise person aims at. Rather, whether someone is prac-tically wise will depend on whether she has aimed at these intermediate points.

Wise Seeing, Principles, and Ethical Reflection. So why did Aristotle say that the mean and intermediate are determined by "that principle by which the man of practical wisdom would determine it"? Actually, there are two puzzles here. First, if practical wisdom involves the ability to perceive *par-ticular* noble and base acts, why did Aristotle talk here about determination by a *principle*? And, second, if facts about the mean and intermediate de-pend on those concerning the chief good, which are metaphysically inde-pendent of the judgments of the practically wise, why did he say that the mean is determined by the practically wise at all?

Regarding the first puzzle, even if practical wisdom involves perception of particulars, it is not a perception of *bare* particulars that are unencum-bered by any universal properties but, rather, a perception of particular acts *as noble*. Being noble is an ethical property, moreover, and so if some par-ticular act has it, it must be by virtue of other properties it has, since noth-ing can have an ethical property barely. (Recall our old familiar point from Chapter 1.) There must be something about the act that *makes* it a noble thing to do. So there must be a universal principle implicit in the percep-tions of the practically wise even if they are not able to say what it is.

In addition, Aristotle believed that practical wisdom involves ethical re-flection. The practically wise deliberate well, and not just about what is good "in some particular respect" but also about "the good life in general" (1140a 27). They do not just take it as it comes. They step back from their activities and ethical thoughts to see what makes sense on reflection. And in doing this, they do ethical philosophy. They do what Aristotle himself did in the *Ethics*, beginning with ethical judgments that one can get only from upbringing and taking these as data for ethical and philosophical reflection. They make explicit the principles implicit in their particular judgments and critically reflect on their relation to each other and to the chief good. For example, finding herself disdainful of someone who seems oblivious to the risk of disgrace, a practically wise person will consider what underlies her judgment. And perhaps she will conclude, like Aristotle, that being fearless of disgrace is not noble but base.

We arrive at a similar conclusion if we think further about how Aristotle understood virtue and the chief good. Aristotle distinguished between two kinds of virtue, one that involves practical wisdom and one that does not. Someone who is virtuous in the "strict sense" has the explicit, reflective grasp of ethical conceptions and principles of the practically wise—the kind of ethical understanding that Aristotle imagined himself and his readers to be striving for in *The Nicomachean Ethics*. Virtue of this kind involves *contemplation*, the explicit exercise of our distinctive human rationality. So, for Aristotle, human life is *better* or more flourishing if it involves this kind of ethical reflection, since it involves more of the excellent exercise of distinctively human capacities. In this sense, then, it *is* of the nature of the best life *and* human virtue in the strict sense that these involve activity determined by the principles of the practically wise.

Conclusion

According to Aristotle and his followers, then, only an upbringing that nurtures natural maturation and growth and develops the right habits can get one inside the circle of ethical ideas and thought in the first place. Such an education is necessary to develop the full affective, conative, and cognitive complexity that is necessary to acquire ethical knowledge or even fully to understand ethical ideas and principles. Ethical knowledge is therefore not equally available to all. And it is impossible to formulate universal ethical principles in ways that can be understood by all those to whom they apply. In the end, there is no substitute for judgment and wisdom that can be acquired only by a process of human maturation and growth that is nurtured by the wisdom of the preceding generation.

This picture clashes profoundly with the conception of morality put forth by the philosophical moralists. Hobbes, Mill, and Kant aspire to formulations of the moral law that all who are subject to it can understand and apply. But perhaps we can now appreciate why Aristotle did not feel the same pressure in this direction that the philosophical moralists do. Their conception of morality is law-based, whereas Aristotle's ethical conception is ideal-based. Violation of the moral law involves culpability, the incurring of guilt and accountability for what one has done. And we can hardly be culpable for violating standards we can't know ourselves to be bound by. But culpability has nothing to do with the contrast between the noble and the base. What is base warrants disdain, not punishment. It is, quite simply, a less valuable or worthy way to live a human life—something to be shunned, not something to be punished. Nor does any doctrine of ethical equality play a significant role in Aristotle's thought (as is evident in Aristotle's views about women and natural slaves in the *Politics* [1252a 31–1252b 1; 1259b 18–12; 1260b 20]).

At the end of the last chapter, I suggested that the most important issues between Aristotle and the philosophical moralists may depend either on the plausibility of teleological metaphysics or on the question of whether some defensible alternative exists on which to ground Aristotle's ethics. However, it is quite possible to conclude that, although the philosophical moralists are right that the conception of morality is hardly dispensable in any setting that, like ours, raises profound issues of difference, conflict, and inequality, there are nonetheless many matters of ethical significance to which Aristotle speaks eloquently.

Some of these are included within the purview of orthodox moral theory. Thus, one might read *The Nicomachean Ethics* as providing an account of human good, which could then be fit within a moral theory of right and wrong. But other such matters are left largely unaddressed by the philosophical moralists. For example, Aristotle has shown us the myriad ways in which, quite apart from morality, ideals are central to a thoughtful human life. He has helped us to glimpse the subtle and complex place of the emotions in ethics, and reminded us that the ethical life concerns questions of feeling no less than those of practice. And he has spoken convincingly of how much of what matters in life cannot be comprehended without a process of personal growth that molds our habits and affectivity as well as our cognitive powers.

Finally, although we've been able to give friendship only scant attention, Aristotle devoted two of the *Ethics'* ten books to this issue. It seems indisputable that flourishing personal relationships are central to a valuable human life. Indeed, as we shall see in the next chapter, thinking about personal relationships arguably provides an alternative perspective on philosophical ethics.

Suggested Reading

Aristotle. *The Nicomachean Ethics*. W. D. Ross, trans.; revised by J. L. Ackrill and J. O. Urmson. Oxford: Oxford University Press, 1989.

Barnes, Jonathan. *Aristotle*. Oxford: Oxford University Press, 1983.

_____. *The Cambridge Companion to Aristotle*. Cambridge: Cambridge University Press, 1995.

Broadie, Sarah. *Ethics with Aristotle*. New York: Oxford University Press, 1991.

Burnyeat, Myles. "Aristotle on Learning to Be Good." In *Essays on Aristotle's Ethics*. Amelie Rorty, ed.

Irwin, T. H. *Aristotle's First Principles*. Oxford: Clarendon Press, 1988.

_____. "The Metaphysical and Psychological Basis of Aristotle's Ethics." In *Essays on Aristotle's Ethics*. Amelie Rorty, ed.

Kraut, Richard. *Aristotle on the Human Good*. Princeton, N.J.: Princeton University Press, 1989.

Rorty, Amelie, ed. *Essays on Aristotle's Ethics*. Berkeley: University of California Press, 1980.

Sherman, Nancy. *Making a Necessity of Virtue*. Cambridge: Cambridge University Press, 1997.

Urmson, J. O. *Aristotle's Ethics*. Oxford: Basil Blackwell, 1988.

19

ETHICS OF CARE

Consider what it is to care about someone, whether in a relatively short emotional engagement, as through **sympathy,** or in an ongoing relationship. Suppose, for example, that you see a child on the verge of falling into a well. You are gripped by the child's plight and moved to prevent the fall.[1] What would be your reason for acting?

You may, of course, hold some universal moral principle that counsels giving aid in such situations. This would give you a reason to help the child, since it would give you reason to help anyone who is in the same position the child is. It would, however, give you no reason that is essentially tied to this child *in particular,* only a reason to help him as someone who needs help in a situation like this.

But how do things seem from your perspective in feeling compassion? Isn't the object of your concern this particular child? Don't you have, through your sympathetic engagement, an interest in *his* plight? Imagine that years later your thoughts return to the scene. You might have a warm interest in the child's subsequent life path without caring similarly about the lives of all other children who had survived similar close calls.

Seeing the child in danger, you are moved to prevent the fall. But why? What is your reason? Don't you want to do so for *his* sake? Through sympathy, you have come to be concerned about him in particular. Your reason for acting is to prevent harm to *him,* not just to someone in need in a situation like his.

These points are reinforced by reference to more extended relationships. In a now-famous example, a man is in a position to save only his wife, Joan, or some stranger from drowning, but not both.[2] Presumably, morality requires the man to save one of the two, and, of the two, it presumably requires him to save his wife, given the importance of human relationships and the family. If, however, this is the man's full reason for acting, then his concern for his wife will be far from what we might expect in such relationships. He might have no concern for her at all and still have *this* reason. If, however, he cares about his wife in a way appropriate to relationships of mutual love and concern, his reason will be more like "*Joan* will drown unless I save her" than, say, "a person whom I am married to and consequently required to save will drown unless I save her."

Reflections like these have led in recent years to a critique of orthodox moral philosophy. For example, recall that for Mill, the central problem of ethics is to articulate universal principles or "criteria" of right and wrong; according to **particularist** critics, however, ethics begins with concerns like sympathy and love. Unlike motives resulting from the acceptance of universal principles, these concerns inevitably have particular individuals or groups as objects. They help define a web of relationships to others in which ethical questions apparently take the form, not of What is a person to do in a situation like this, but of What am I to do for this particular person, in light of her situation and our relationship?

Moral Development: From the Perspectives of Kohlberg and Gilligan

It will be useful to discuss these themes in relation to work on moral development presented by the psychologist Carol Gilligan in her influential *In a Different Voice*.[3] To establish a sense of context, let's begin with a recent history of psychological theorizing about moral development.

Gilligan began as a co-worker of Lawrence Kohlberg, whose theory of moral development was the leading paradigm during the 1970s and early 1980s. Kohlberg's "structuralist" approach was itself a reaction against behaviorist and Freudian theories, which held that moral development consists entirely in socialization rather than the development of inherent potential. According to behaviorist learning theorists, moral beliefs and attitudes are the product of positive and negative social reinforcements. And according to Freudians, they result from internalized parental directives fueled by powerful unconscious motives, such as fear of the loss of parental love. In either case, moral development has no specific inherent tendency. What people end up approving and disapproving, the content of their moral opinions, depends entirely on how they are "educated."

Kohlberg.   In 1932, the Swiss psychologist Jean Piaget published *The Moral Judgment of the Child*, in which he argued that moral thinking undergoes developmental stages and that these correspond to stages of cognitive development. Kohlberg pursued this theory experimentally in a series of papers beginning in the late 1950s, arriving at an elaborate and influential three-level/six-stage theory of moral development. Specifically, according to Kohlberg, moral development proceeds through three levels—preconventional, conventional, and postconventional—with each level involving two stages.[4]

In Stage 1 (punishment and obedience), children identify being good and bad solely in terms of avoiding punishment. Then, in Stage 2 (instrumental-relativist), they come to see their own needs and interests as having ethical standing and accept a rudimentary conception of fairness as advantageous reciprocity ("Scratch my back and I'll scratch yours").

These first two stages are preconventional in the sense that social rules are given no intrinsic ethical status; their salience depends entirely upon avoiding punishment or advancing egoistic aims. In the second, conventional level, children begin to see morality as having authority apart from their own needs and identify it with social expectations and rules. Stage 3 (interpersonal concordance) identifies good conduct with what others will approve or be pleased by. And in Stage 4 (law and order), individuals see the social order as a source of authority.

In the third, postconventional level, individuals begin to conceive of morality as a standard that is independent of social rules and that provides a standpoint from which to criticize social custom. Stage 5 (social contract) identifies this standard with values and ideals that have resulted from a society's own critical reflection. And Stage 6 (universal ethical principle) distinguishes between any actual consensus and the universal principles at which such a consensus aims, identifying morality with the latter abstract standard.

Kohlberg argued that these stages amount to a developmental sequence whose underlying mechanism is fundamentally cognitive. As human beings develop more sophisticated capacities for abstract reflective thought, he said, we come to increasingly adequate moral conceptions, culminating in the idea of a universal standard of conduct that is distinct from any actual social rule or custom or even from any standard on which people happen to agree.

Gilligan. As she worked within Kohlberg's theory, Carol Gilligan became increasingly troubled by implications it appeared to have concerning moral development and gender. For one thing, all the original experimental evidence for Kohlberg's theory came from studies of boys. For another, girls and young women tended to be less represented among Kohlberg's higher stages than were males. In particular, they were much likelier than boys to cluster in Stage 3, which emphasizes the pleasing of others (DV.18). Finally, when Gilligan conducted her own studies of both boys and girls, she began to notice what seemed to her two quite different ways of thinking about ethics, two different "themes" or "voices," which she found differently represented in males and females, respectively. The one more highly represented among males fits comfortably in Kohlberg's categories. She called this the "ethics of rights." The "different voice," represented more highly among females, and which did not fit well in Kohlberg's categories, she called the "ethics of care."

As Gilligan is careful to point out, she is not saying that there is anything essentially male or female about these respective ethical "voices" (DV.2). That the "ethics of care" tends to be associated with females and the "ethics of rights" with males is only a tendency and "an empirical observation." Gilligan's project has been to listen to the different voice of the ethics of care that she heard more frequently from girls and women in order to understand it in its own terms and to try to comprehend how ethical thought might develop within it. Even though her explicit aims are psychological, it is this element that makes her project interesting for philosophical ethics. It offers the potential to explore a different, particularist approach to ethics that might be either supplementary or alternative to the philosophical conceptions of "universalist" morality that we have previously considered.

Ethics of Rights Versus Ethics of Care

What exactly are these two different voices? Gilligan tells us that the ethics of rights

(a) constitutes a fair or just "system of rules for resolving disputes" (DV.10),
(b) conceives of self and other in universal or general terms (DV.11),
(c) aims to be impartial (DV.18),
(d) treats all as separate but equal individuals (DV.27), and
(e) recognizes the primacy of universal individual rights (DV.21).

With the possible exception of (e), this characterization corresponds to the conceptions of morality advanced by Hobbes, Mill, and Kant. If the problem of collective action was the issue to which the "modern" conception of morality was the solution, as I suggested in the discussion of Hobbes in Chapters 10 and 11, then Gilligan's characterization of the ethics of rights is close enough to morality as it has been conceived by the moderns. Not all consequentialists have been prepared to give primacy to universal human rights, of course, but some, like Mill, have. And virtually all consequentialists have felt the need to accept the doctrine of universal human rights in some form.

At the most fundamental level, morality assumes no particular connections between individuals other than equal membership in the moral community. Of course, other forms of relationship affect what is morally proper, as in the case of Joan and her husband above. But working out what morality calls for is not *fundamentally* a matter of figuring out what to do within these more specific relations. What morality requires of me is what it would require of any person in a situation like mine.

By contrast, Gilligan tells us, the ethics of care sees caring for others as primarily "an activity of relationship" (DV.62). It is concerned with responsibility and responsiveness *within* relationships—that is, with how we are to respond to the particular people to whom we are related.

Each of us enters into a complex web of relationships, including family, friends, neighbors, colleagues, fellow community members, fellow citizens, and so on. Relationships of these different kinds involve different forms of care and concern. What it is for a parent to care for a child is different from the kind of concern that friends or colleagues have. Our place in the network of relations is thus also a locus in a network of different forms of care.

As we saw illustrated earlier, care is particularistic. Its object is some *particular* individual(s) or group. My love for my children is for the particular individuals who are my children, not for anyone who might happen to be my child. My concern for my colleagues is for the particular people to whom I bear that relationship, and so on. The ethics of care sees ethics as fundamentally concerned with how properly to care for the particular others to whom we are related *within* the various different relations of care and concern we share with them. The form in which ethical issues present themselves is thus not a matter of what someone should do in a situation like mine where a person to whom I am related in such-and-such a way will be affected in such-and-such a manner. Rather, ethical issues will appear in particularistic form: What am I to do to respond adequately to *Joan's* need? What is my responsibility to *Harold?*

Given the ethics of care's focus on relationships, we can perhaps see why, if Gilligan is right about its being more representative of the thinking of girls and women, this might explain an overrepresentation of females in Kohlberg's Stage 3. As noted, this stage is the initial conventional stage, in which acting morally is identified primarily with pleasing others. From the perspective of Kohlberg's scheme, these traits seem to amount to a relatively immature confusion of the approval of others with being *worthy* of their approval—similar to what Aristotle said about the confusion of honor with genuine virtue. From the perspective of the ethics of care, however, relating to others in a way that elicits their continuing acceptance and affirmation is essential to maintaining connection.

An Example

I can illustrate some of these differences by noting what Gilligan says about the responses of two children, Jake and Amy, to an example she posed to them. The example, which also figured in Kohlberg's experiments, concerns what a man, Heinz, should do when his ill wife needs a certain drug to survive, Heinz cannot afford to buy the drug at the druggist's price, and the druggist will not lower his price. Specifically, the children are asked whether Heinz should steal the drug, and they are asked also to discuss the reasons for their response.

Eleven-year-old Jake is clear that Heinz should steal the drug, saying, "a human life is worth more than money" (DV.26). Although the druggist will continue to live if he loses money, Heinz's wife will die if she does not have the drug. Amy, also eleven, is less clear when asked whether Heinz should steal the drug. "I don't think so," she responds. "There might be other ways besides stealing it, like if he could borrow the money, . . . but he shouldn't steal the drug—but his wife shouldn't die either" (DV.28). Amy suggests that Heinz might work out a solution with the druggist by making his wife's condition more salient to him. "If Heinz and the druggist had talked it out long enough, they could reach something besides stealing" (DV.29).

What are we to make of these two different responses? Jake describes the issue as "sort of like a math problem with humans" (DV.26). For him, the problem is the relative value of life and property. Settling that determines whether, in a case of this kind, the prohibition against theft is weightier than the obligation to save lives or, more specifically, to save the life of one's spouse. Gilligan points out that Amy sees the situation in very different terms. For her, the issue is primarily how to maintain relationships—between husband and wife, customer and druggist, and so on. What may appear as a feeling of powerlessness or passivity in Amy, an inability to think systematically about moral questions, or an unwillingness to challenge authority, Gilligan suggests, may actually be a reluctance to think about the issue from a perspective outside the respective relationships involved or to "impose" a solution on the individuals in those relationships.

Jake's perspective on the situation is as from outside it. He adopts a **moral point of view**—a perspective that is impartial as between all persons. The problem as he conceives it is What, considered from that perspective, should *someone* do in a situation like this? But Amy is evidently reluctant to think about the issue in these terms. The problem as she conceives it occurs within a web of relationships and can be solved only within them—only, that is, if some solution is found by the *participants* that is mutually acceptable and maintains their respective relationships. For Amy, the problem is, as Gilligan puts it, "a fracture of human relationship that must be mended with its own thread" (DV.31). Since different relationships are structured by different forms of particularistic concern, a solution must be found by the people involved in a way that is consistent with or that expresses the respective relation-defining forms of care for each other as particular individuals.

The foregoing suggests two important apparent differences between the ethics of care and the ethics of rights: (1) the ethics of care is particularistic, whereas the ethics of rights is universalistic. And (2) the ethics of care conceives of ethical issues as tears in a fabric of relationship that "must be mended with its own thread," whereas, according to the ethics of rights, the solution to moral problems can be found only from an impartial perspective that transcends personal relationships.

Later we shall consider how real these differences are and, if they are real, how deeply they run. For now, however, we should note that neither depends essentially on the idea of universal *rights*. With respect to these two features, a utilitarian or consequentialist moral conception giving rights no intrinsic standing whatsoever would apparently still contrast with an ethics of care. Indeed, we might imagine a "consequentialism of relationships" which held that flourishing relationships are the only valuable thing in the world, and that the rightness of acts is reckoned by their promotion of this value. Would this be an ethics of care? It seems that it would not, since it would still reckon what to do from a perspective of impartial concern for this value, not from a perspective of particularistic concern within specific relationships themselves.

What Is at Issue?

What really is at issue between an ethics of care and the conception of morality defended by Hobbes, Mill, or Kant? I have indicated two apparent issues—one concerning the perspective of ethical thought and one concerning particularity versus universality. But how real are these disagreements?

Recall Amy's response to Heinz's dilemma: that what Heinz should do is to attempt to work out a solution with the various parties that will be mutually acceptable. Is this in unalterable conflict with Jake's response? Jake treats the parameters of the problem as fixed so that there is no option of convincing the druggist to lower his price or of taking out a loan. Were Jake to think either option a genuine possibility, there is no reason to conclude that he wouldn't think them morally preferable to theft. Similarly, it is not clear from Gilligan's reports what Amy thinks Heinz should do if all attempts to work out a mutually acceptable solution fail. Amy says both that Heinz shouldn't steal the drug and that his wife shouldn't die. Of course, her position may be that Heinz shouldn't steal the drug even if it is absolutely necessary to keep his wife alive. But it's hard to see how that position would be grounded in an unalterable conflict with orthodox conceptions of morality as opposed to springing from some idea within a moral conception—for example, that direct harm or theft is always wrong.

What seems undeniable is a difference of *approach* between Amy and Jake. Whereas Amy's instinct is to think about a *process* of ethical thought and discussion involving the participants, Jake's is either to confront directly the issues that such a process would itself address or to say what

Heinz should do if such a process were to break down. For his part, Jake is relatively blind to procedural questions concerning how Heinz should involve others in thinking through their respective problems and how their input is itself relevant to what he should do. And Amy, for her part, is relatively blind to the issue of what Heinz should do if such a process were not to yield a mutually acceptable solution. For all that Jake and Amy say, however, it may be that they would *agree* that Heinz should first attempt to find a mutually agreeable solution that will honor his various relationships and, only if such an attempt fails, that he should then steal the drug.

Amy's concern for process is rooted in her seeing the ethical landscape as a network of relationships. The idea is not that we should involve others in our deliberations because they will help us come to the right decision. Rather, because the question is always what to do in light of the various relationships we have to others, there is no way of specifying the right decision independent of others' input. And since the relevant relationships are often reciprocal, appropriate deliberation must often be *collective*. But here again, it seems that this point could have been fully acknowledged by Mill or Kant. Both could have agreed, for example, that friends have a duty to consult each other, if possible, on matters bearing on their friendship.

Particularism

Even so, there may remain a difference. For a utilitarian like Mill, such a duty would be grounded in the fact that social recognition of the duty is likeliest to promote the general happiness, especially when we take account of the important role that personal relationships play in human happiness. And for Kant, it would derive from the fact that, from the perspective of one rational person among others, anyone would will that friends consult one another. However, although Mill and Kant could have acknowledged a sense in which such a duty is owed to the individual friend, the individual-regarding character of this duty would itself derive from more fundamental universal considerations—utilitarian or Kantian, respectively. Each would owe it to the other, because friends having such a claim on each other in cases like this is recommended from an impartial, moral point of view.

Now, in one way, at least, an ethics of care is bound to agree with this thought. After all, someone who advances or even sympathetically describes an ethics of care, as Gilligan does, is herself thinking or writing not from the perspective of the friends themselves but from a reflective critical standpoint that anyone could adopt. So, although the form of concern that the ethics of care recommends is individual-regarding (defining a perspective of care for, say, Jack, in particular), the ethics of care recommends this concern not from that same point of view (a concern for Jack's welfare in particular) but as an ethical or moral ideal from a standpoint transcending any particular personal relationship.

But even so, the ethics of care recommends particularistic, individual-regarding care in itself. Its recommendation is not derivative. Utilitarianism and Kantianism, on the other hand, would seem to have a place for particularistic care only to the extent that it can be derived from equal concern and respect for all.

Morality as Derivable from Individual-Regarding Care and Respect

This way of viewing things may be somewhat superficial, however. It may be that both utilitarianism and Kantianism can themselves be seen as deriving from forms of concern and respect that, at their deepest levels, are also individual-regarding.

Utilitarianism. For example, sympathy plays an important role in one traditional route to utilitarianism. Utilitarianism can be seen as the extension to all of the kind of concern we feel for a particular individual through sympathy. Begin with the kind of sympathetic concern for a person that we considered in the example of the child on the verge of falling into a well. In experiencing sympathetic concern, we care about the child himself. We are concerned for *his* plight, for his sake. What happens to him matters to us because *he* has come to matter to us. We see his welfare as valuable because we see *him* as valuable.

Note, first, how this way of seeing the child's welfare as valuable differs from other forms that this thought might take. For example, I might generate an abstract or impersonal interest in the welfare of human or other living beings without genuinely caring about *them*. I might just think the improvement of their lives would make the world better in some abstract, impersonal way. Sympathy, however, is an individual-regarding concern. In having sympathy for the child, I care about *him*. And because I am emotionally engaged with him, and on his behalf, I care about what happens to him. I *therefore* see his welfare as valuable and important. Through sympathy, I come to value the child's welfare for *his sake* by coming to value *him*.

But sympathy is repeatable, of course. Although it can be overridden or stifled in all sorts of ways, sympathy is, by its very nature, a sensitivity that can be engaged by anyone. (Maybe even by any sentient being whose behavior we can interpret as expressing pleasure and pain—but we will confine ourselves to human beings in this discussion.) After all, I described a hypothetical example: a child about to fall into a well. Did it occur to you then that it would matter which *particular* child I was talking about? I doubt it. So although sympathy is a form of concern for a particular individual and a way of valuing that individual in himself, it is nonetheless implicitly general or universal. Although it is *this particular* child who has engaged our sympathy and who, through sympathy, we value in himself, there may be nothing about him in particular that has engaged us. Although he and no other child exactly like him is the particular object of our concern, another child just like him would equally have engaged us or, more accurately, would have been equally *apt* to do so. When, consequently, we reflect on what it is about the individual child we find valuable and warranting our concern, we must admit that it is nothing over and above the fact that he is *a* child, or even a human or sentient being—someone with a conscious life that can be affected for good or ill.

We can thus arrive at the foundational idea of utilitarianism, that everyone's welfare matters and matters equally, by reflecting on the particularistic, individual-regarding experience of sympathy. Although sympathy involves an experience as of some *individual's* value in himself, it is based on nothing that distinguishes him from any other sentient being. As we might then say, it is because each individual sentient human being (and so her welfare) matters intrinsically that the general happiness matters. In acting for the sake of the general happiness, therefore, we should think of ourselves as acting for *every individual's* sake.

Kantianism.   A similar line of thought, but featuring respect rather than sympathy, might be seen as underlying Kantianism. Because Kant spoke of respecting "humanity" or "rational nature" *in* persons, it might seem that he was calling us to the respecting of the feature of personhood or rational agency in persons rather than to the respecting of individual persons *in particular* (G.429). But as with sympathy, this appearance may be deceiving.

First, notice that the kind of respect we are talking about is one that consists in recognizing or acknowledging someone's **dignity** or standing (**recognition respect**) rather than esteeming their character or accomplishments (appraisal respect).[5] For Kant, all persons have dignity just by virtue of their moral agency, even scoundrels. Thus all are entitled to respect (recognition respect), even those whose character and conduct are not worthy of moral esteem (appraisal respect). Wrongdoing may involve the forfeiture of certain rights to, say, freedom, but wrongdoers do not forfeit their moral status as persons. Even criminals must be treated as ends in themselves.

When he spoke of valuing rational nature *in* someone, however, Kant did not intend any contrast with valuing the individual *herself*. For Kant, there is no distinction between the individual herself and the individual, a rational being. Valuing rational nature in someone is not like valuing her for the gold that is in her teeth. It *is* valuing the person herself.

As an illustration, consider what it is like to have a vivid experience of someone *as a person* whose dignity demands respect. Suppose you are a parent who, complacent in your authority, have become overbearing and self-righteous toward your emerging adolescent. For a while, your child has just been taking it; but this time you've gone too far, and your child upbraids you, saying something like "You treat me as if I were an irresponsible boob. But the fact is that I'm just like you, and you don't like it. I'm just as responsible as you are, and you're a hypocrite to pretend otherwise. You wouldn't stand for me to treat you the way you treat me. And you have no right to do so." You might be brought up short by such a remonstrance. Indeed, the blood might rush to your face as you recognize the justice of your child's charge.

In feeling shame, you also feel respect for your child.[6] Your shame consists in recognizing yourself through the eyes of your child. And to do that you have to acknowledge the authority of your child's view. You have to see him as having the standing to evaluate you, as someone whose view of you is to be taken seriously. Moreover, in recognizing the justice of his charge, you must be seeing your child as having the standing to lodge the claim he makes against you. This is different from the evaluative authority you see the child as having when you credit his evaluation of you as a hypocrite. In seeing him as having the standing to make the claim to respectful treatment, you see him as someone who can demand respect.

As with sympathy, there should be no doubt that your attitude is directed at an individual person, your child. It is *him*, in particular, whom you are experiencing as having a dignity deserving respect. And if you are moved by what he says to reflect on and change your conduct toward him, your changed conduct will express respect for him *individually*. At the same time, however, what it is in or about him that warrants your respect is nothing unique to him in particular but, rather, something he shares with any rational agent. So, although respect is individual-regarding, it is also implicitly general or universal. When you reflect on your respect for your child, you must admit that it is based on nothing that distinguishes him in particular. (A complication might be that you now respect him partly because he was willing to confront you. But even if this feature is part of the ground for your respect, it is a feature had by anyone who has been likewise willing.)

In this way, then, respect involves recognizing an *individual's* dignity or value in himself, but it is grounded in features that a person shares with any other moral agent. So just as utilitarianism can be seen as extending to all sentient beings (as equally warranted) a sympathetic concern that is directed at particular individuals, so likewise can Kant's ethics be viewed as extending to all persons a kind of respect that is directed at particular individuals also.

Conclusion

If we view them in this way, the conceptions of morality advanced by Mill and Kant are far from being in irresolvable conflict with the ethics of care. Indeed, Gilligan herself sees the ethics of care as involving a developmental process in the direction of "a responsibility to discern and alleviate the 'real and recognizable trouble' of this world," balancing needs of self and others (DV.100). This project seems entirely consistent with Mill or Kant, if not also with Hobbes.

In the end, the ethics of care may not be a radically opposed alternative to morality as conceived by the moderns, so much as an important supplement as well as a different path to some of the same ideas. In the former vein, it brings into the forefront of ethical reflection issues of relationship that, although they provide much of the stuff of our lives, have been relatively neglected by moral theorists. And in the latter, the ethics of care provides a way of seeing equal concern and respect as themselves rooted in ways of relating to others as particular individuals.

Suggested Reading

Baier, Annette. *Moral Prejudices.* Cambridge, Mass.: Harvard University Press, 1994.

Blum, Lawrence A. *Moral Perception and Particularity.* Cambridge: Cambridge University Press, 1994.

Gilligan, Carol. *In a Different Voice.* Reissued with a new "Letter to Readers." Cambridge, Mass.: Harvard University Press, 1993.

Meyers, Diana T. *Women and Moral Theory.* Totowa, N.J.: Rowman & Littlefield, 1987.

Noddings, Nel. *Caring.* Berkeley: University of California Press, 1984.

Williams, Bernard. "Persons, Character, and Morality." In *Moral Luck.* Cambridge: Cambridge University Press, 1981.

NOTES

Chapter One

1. Definitions for boldfaced terms are provided in a glossary at the end of the book.

2. Immanuel Kant, *Groundwork of the Metaphysics of Morals* (1785), H. J. Paton, trans. (New York: Harper & Row, 1964), p. 80 (p. 412 of the standard *Preussische Akademie* edition of Kant's works).

3. John Locke, *An Essay Concerning Human Understanding,* P. H. Nidditch, ed. (Oxford: Clarendon Press, 1985), p. 68.

4. Actually, what Locke says is stronger—namely, that we can also always ask for a justification of a moral *rule.* Any moral rule already includes a reference to universal features that (it claims) provide reasons for the moral status of particular actions.

Chapter Two

1. "Letters to Deng, From the Pit of Repression," *New York Times,* February 18, 1996, p. E7.

2. David Hume, *A Treatise of Human Nature* (1740). Second edition edited by L. A. Selby-Bigge, with text revised and variant readings by P. H. Nidditch (Oxford: Clarendon Press, 1978), p. 468.

3. Hume continued: "You never can find it, till you turn your reflexion into your own breast, and find a sentiment of disapprobation, which arises in you, towards this action. . . . It lies in yourself, not in the object" (ibid., p. 469). Taken literally, this passage means that what presents itself, in ethical experience and conviction, as genuinely external to oneself—as part of objective reality—is actually subjective.

4. Gilbert Harman, *The Nature of Morality* (New York: Oxford University Press, 1977), pp. 3–10.

Chapter Three

1. Aristotle believed that every natural being had an end or *telos* that is part of its very being; hence the term *teleological naturalism.*

2. See Allan Gibbard, *Wise Choices, Apt Feelings* (Cambridge: Harvard University Press, 1990), pp. 12–18.

Chapter Nine

1. But theological voluntarism by no means entails deontology. As I mentioned in Chapter 2, Locke was only one example of a theological voluntarist who was a consequentialist.

2. Carol Gilligan, *In a Different Voice,* reissued with a new "Letter to Readers" (Cambridge, Mass.: Harvard University Press, 1993).

Chapter Ten

1. Thomas Hobbes, *Leviathan* (1651). Edwin Curley, ed. Indianapolis, Ind.: Hackett Publishing Company, 1994. References in the text are to chapter and paragraph numbers, and 'L' denotes the title *Leviathan.*

2. Galileo, *The Assayer* (as translated by A. C. Danto).

Chapter Twelve

1. John Stuart Mill, *Utilitarianism* (1861), George Sher, ed. (Indianapolis, Ind.: Hackett Publishing Company, 1979). References in the text are to chapter and paragraph numbers, and 'U' denotes the title *Utilitarianism.*

Chapter Thirteen

1. John Rawls, *A Theory of Justice* (Cambridge, Mass.: Harvard University Press, 1971), pp. 28–29.

2. On this point, see Maria H. Morales's excellent *Perfect Equality: John Stuart Mill on Well-Constituted Communities* (Lanham, Md.: Rowman & Littlefield Publishers, 1996).

3. For an excellent discussion of the difference between the structuring social practices conceived by RU and the "summary rules" or "rules of thumb" of AU, see John Rawls, "Two Concepts of Rules," *Philosophical Review* 64 (1955): 3–32.

Chapter Fourteen

1. In the next two chapters I will be giving an interpretation of Kant's *Groundwork* that, to my mind, makes most sense as a philosophical ethics. I should emphasize, however, that Kant's views are complex, and that the interpretation I shall offer is only one of many that are possible. For some others, see the sources listed under "Suggested Reading" at the end of Chapter 15.

2. Immanuel Kant, *Groundwork of the Metaphysics of Morals* (1785), H. J. Paton, trans. (New York: Harper & Row, 1964). References in the text are to page numbers in the *Preussische Akademie* edition, and 'G' denotes the title *Groundwork.*

3. David Hume, *A Treatise of Human Nature* (1740). Second edition edited by L. A. Selby-Bigge, with text revised and variant readings by P. H. Nidditch (Oxford: Clarendon Press, 1978), pp. 155–173.

Chapter Fifteen

1. John Rawls, "Two Concepts of Rules," *Philosophical Review* 64 (1955): 11.
2. To forestall a fussy objection, suppose that it is intrinsic to the idea of nullishing that it can occur only when there is a going practice of telishment.
3. John Rawls, *A Theory of Justice* (Cambridge, Mass.: Harvard University Press, 1971), pp. 136–142, 251–257.
4. Immanuel Kant, *Critique of Practical Reason* (1788), Lewis White Beck, trans. (New York: Macmillan Publishing Company, 1985), p. 97 (p. 93 of the standard *Preussische Akademie* edition of Kant's works).

Chapter Sixteen

1. Michel Foucault, *The Archaeology of Knowledge* (New York: Pantheon Books, 1972).
2. Friedrich Nietzsche, *On the Genealogy of Morals* (1887) and *Ecce Homo* (1888), Walter Kaufmann and R. J. Hollingdale, trans.; Walter Kaufmann, ed. (New York: Vintage Books, 1989). References in the text are to essay, section, and (where necessary) paragraph numbers, and 'GM' denotes the title *On the Genealogy of Morals*.
3. Friedrich Nietzsche, *Beyond Good and Evil* (1886), Walter Kaufmann, trans. (New York: Vintage Books, 1989).
4. Arthur C. Danto, introduction to Nietzsche's *Human, All Too Human* (1878), Marion Faber, with Stephen Lehmann, trans. (Lincoln: University of Nebraska Press, 1996), p. xv.
5. Nietzsche, *Human, All Too Human,* sec. 49, p. 48.
6. Friedrich Nietzsche, *Untimely Meditations: Third Essay: Schopenhauer as Educator* (1874), sec. 6; cited in R. J. Hollingdale, *Nietzsche: The Man and His Philosophy* (Baton Rouge: Louisiana State University Press, 1965), p. 127.

Chapter Seventeen

1. Aristotle, *The Nicomachean Ethics,* W. D. Ross, trans.; revised by J. L. Ackrill and J. O. Urmson (Oxford: Oxford University Press, 1989). References in the text are to the canonical pages and line numbers of the Bekker Berlin Academy edition of Aristotle's works.

Chapter Nineteen

1. This example comes from the Chinese philosopher Mencius (4th century B.C.E.), who used it to illustrate the universality of compassion. *Mencius,* D. C. Lau, trans. (London: Penguin Classics, 1970), p. 82.
2. This example was originally provided by Charles Fried, although it has been most influentially discussed by Bernard Williams in "Persons, Character, and Morality," in Williams's *Moral Luck* (Cambridge: Cambridge University Press, 1981), pp. 17–18.

3. Carol Gilligan, *In a Different Voice*, reissued with a new "Letter to Readers" (Cambridge, Mass.: Harvard University Press, 1993). References in the text are to page numbers, and 'DV' denotes the title *In a Different Voice*.

4. See, for example, Lawrence Kohlberg's *The Psychology of Moral Development: The Nature and Validity of Moral Stages* (San Francisco: Harper & Row, 1984); *Essays on Moral Development* (San Francisco: Harper & Row, 1981); and *The Philosophy of Moral Development* (San Francisco: Harper & Row, 1981). See also his "The Claim to Moral Adequacy of a Highest Stage of Moral Development," *Journal of Philosophy* 70 (1973): 630–646.

5. For further discussion of this distinction, see Stephen Darwall, "Two Kinds of Respect," *Ethics* 88 (1977): 36–49.

6. In what follows, I am indebted to Sarah Buss.

GLOSSARY

act-consequentialism The view that an act is morally right if, and only if, of the acts available to the agent, it would produce the greatest total net good. (See also *rule-consequentialism*.)

actions Conduct undertaken for reasons—specifically, for the agent's reasons for acting. (See also *agency, agent*.)

act-utilitarianism The view that an act is morally right if, and only if, of the acts available to the agent, it would produce the greatest total net happiness or utility. (See also *rule-utilitarianism*.)

agency The capacity to act, to be an agent. (See also *actions, agent*.)

agent The subject who acts. (See also *actions, agency*.)

agent's perspective The first-person point of view of someone deliberating about what to do; also, the practical perspective. (See also *agency, agent, deliberation, practical perspective, practical reasoning, practical thinking*.)

agent's reasons for action Considerations that an agent regards as normative reasons for action and chooses to act on. (See also *normative reasons for action*.)

analytic Pertaining to a proposition whose truth or falsity is determined by the meanings of the terms in which it is expressed. (See also *synthetic*.)

analytically In an *analytic* way.

a posteriori Pertaining to a proposition whose truth value can be known only through experience. (See also *a priori*.)

a priori Pertaining to a proposition that is capable of being known or that is valid independent of experience—specifically, to a proposition whose evidence does not depend on experience. (See also *a posteriori*.)

authority A status from which the fact that one should do, think, be, or feel something can derive. For example, a moral rule is said to have authority if it generates normative reasons for acting as it requires, a political figure is said to have authority if his pronouncements generate normative reasons, and so on. (See also *normative, normativity*.)

autonomous Independent, as an autonomous subject area.

autonomy Self-determination; for Kant, the property of the will of being a "law to itself." (See also *free moral agent*.)

base That which is worthy of disesteem, contempt, or shame—the contrary of having worth or being noble. (See also *esteem, guilt, ideal, shame, worth*.)

categorical Pertaining to a reason, imperative, or requirement that is unconditional on the agent's current aims and desires in the way that hypothetical reasons, imperatives, or requirements are. (See also *hypothetical*.)

categorical imperative Any practical or moral requirement that is unconditional on the agent's current aims or desires. (See also *Categorical Imperative*.)

Categorical Imperative According to Kant, the fundamental principle of morality. (See also *categorical imperative*.)

character-consequentialism The view that the moral goodness of character is determined by its relation to the promotion of good consequences, and that an act is morally right if it is the one that would result from the morally best character, so determined. (See also *consequentialism*.)

classical natural law theory The view that there exist universal norms of conduct that reflect goods or ends that are inherent in the metaphysical structure of human nature.

cognitive content Something that can be true or false (like a proposition), that is expressed by a statement or opinion. Also called *propositional content*.

cognitivism The view that ethical thought and language express states of mind or propositions that are either true or false. (See also *noncognitivism*.)

collective action problem The phenomenon that occurs when, if each person acts to promote his or her own individual interest, everyone's interest is less well promoted. (See also *prisoner's dilemma*.)

conceptual moral internalism The thesis that it follows from the concept of morality that moral obligations are rationally binding.

conceptual thesis A proposition whose truth conditions are determined entirely by the concepts involved.

consequentialism Any moral theory that bases the moral rightness of conduct or the moral goodness of character or motives on the production of good consequences, directly or indirectly. (See also *act-consequentialism, rule-consequentialism, utilitarianism*.)

consequentialist Pertaining to *consequentialism*.

contingency Something that is *contingent*.

contingent If true, not necessarily true; if false, not necessarily false; pertaining to something whose truth or falsity is determined by what the facts happen to be, something that might have been otherwise. (See also *necessary*.)

contingently In a *contingent* way.

deliberation An agent's considering (reasoning about) what to do. (See also *agent's perspective, practical perspective, practical reasoning, practical thinking*.)

deliberative standpoint The standpoint of an agent deliberating about what to do.

deontological Pertaining to any theory of right and wrong that denies consequentialism—holding, for example, that the kind of action some act is is intrinsically right- or wrong-making. (See also *consequentialism*.)

desirability The property of being desirable.

desirable Valuable in the sense of being worthy of desire. (See also *value*.)

dignity A moral status or standing that is the appropriate object of (recognition) respect. (See also *esteem, recognition respect, worth*.)

direction of fit The characterization of states of mind in terms of whether, like belief, they aim to fit the world, which they attempt to represent, or whether, like desire, they aim for the world to fit them. Beliefs are "world-corrected"; they have a mind-to-world direction of fit. Desires are "world-correcting"; they have a world-to-mind direction of fit.

dispassionate Not influenced by moods or emotions that are irrelevant to the object of evaluation, as posited by the ideal judgment theory.

divine command theory The view that ethical propositions are made true or false by facts concerning what God desires or commands; also called *theological voluntarism*.

emotivism The noncognitivist view that ethical judgments express emotions or feelings rather than anything that can be literally true or false, like a belief. (See also *noncognitivism*.)

empirical Relating to sense experience.

empirical naturalism The metaphysical view that nothing exists beyond what is open to empirical investigation.

empirical naturalist Adherent of *empirical naturalism*.

epistemic Pertaining to *epistemology*.

epistemological Pertaining to *epistemology*.

epistemology The inquiry into the nature and possibility of knowledge and the justification of belief.

error theory The view that ethical thought and language express genuine beliefs and propositions (as with *cognitivism*), but that these are invariably false.

esteem The evaluative attitude we have toward things of merit, related to ideals of the noble or estimable and to shame rather than to guilt. (See also *guilt, ideal, noble, shame, worth*.)

estimable Worthy of esteem. (See also *esteem*.)

ethical naturalism The view that ethical propositions are made true or false by their correspondence to facts about the natural realm (including human beings and human society). (See also *nonreductive ethical naturalism, reductive ethical naturalism*.)

ethical naturalist Adherent of *ethical naturalism*.

ethical relativism The view that conflicting ethical judgments can be equally correct since they are made from different contexts.

ethical skepticism Strictly speaking, the view that ethical knowledge is impossible, although often another name for *nihilism*.

ethical supernaturalism The view that ethical propositions are made true or false by their correspondence to facts concerning some supernatural metaphysical realm. (See also *nonreductive ethical supernaturalism, reductive ethical supernaturalism*.)

ethics The inquiry into what we ought to desire, feel, be, or do. (See also *morality, normative, normativity*.)

eudaimonism The view that each person should seek his own good or happiness (after *eudaimonia*, Greek for happiness or flourishing). (See also *perfectionist eudaimonism*.)

eudaimonist Adherent of *eudaimonism*.

externalism The view that ethical judgments, and their truth conditions, are independent of motivation.

externalists Adherents of *externalism*.

extrinsic Pertaining to features concerning something's relations to other things. (See also *intrinsic*.)

first-order questions Issues that are not themselves philosophical about which second-order (philosophical) questions can be raised. In ethics, the first-order questions are issues of normative ethics and the second-order questions are questions of metaethics. (See also *metaethics, normative ethics, second-order questions*.)

free moral agent An autonomous agent who is able to take a self-critical perspective on his own reasons for acting, and to guide himself by his self-critical judgment. (See also *autonomous, autonomy*.)

fundamental dilemma of metaethics The dilemma whereby either the *objective purport* of ethical thoughts, opinions, and feelings reflects reality (but, then, What reality is there for ethical thoughts and feelings to reflect?) or it does not (but, then, What explains our thinking and speaking as though it does?).

genealogy The study of something's origins. For example, Nietzsche's genealogy of morals is a study of the origins of the idea of morality.

good for Pertaining to something that benefits a person or promotes her good or welfare. (See also *person's good*.)

good-making Pertaining to properties that provide the reasons why something is good or delimit what its goodness consists in.

guilt The feeling or emotion as of having done something wrong; also, culpability for violating the moral law.

hedonism The view that pleasure is the only intrinsic good. (See also *qualitative hedonism, quantitative hedonism*.)

historicism The view according to which things can be known only within their historical contexts.

hypothetical Pertaining to a reason, requirement, or imperative that is conditional on the agent's current aims or desires, rationally requiring her either to take some means to her end or to give the end up.

hypothetical imperative A practical or moral imperative that is conditional on the agent's current aims or desires, rationally requiring her either to take means to her end or to give the end up.

ideal A conception or standard of worth, of the noble, or of the estimable—that is, of what is worthy of esteem, human aspiration, and emulation, related to shame rather than to guilt (as in Aristotle and Nietzsche). (See also *esteem, guilt, noble, shame, worth*.)

ideal agent theory Another name for the *ideal deliberative judgment theory* or *ideal practical judgment theory*.

ideal-based Based on an *ideal*.

ideal deliberative judgment theory The view that propositions about what one should do are made true or false by whether they would issue from an ideal process of deliberation or practical judgment. Also called *practical reason theory*.

ideal judgment A judgment made under ideal conditions.

ideal judgment theory The view that ethical propositions are made true or false by whether they would issue from an ideal judge under ideal conditions of judgment.

ideal moral agent theory The view that an act's moral right or wrongness is determined by whether it would be chosen by an ideal moral agent.

ideal observer theory Another name for *ideal judgment theory.*

ideal practical judgment theory The view that propositions about what one should do are made true or false by whether they would issue from an ideal process of deliberation or practical judgment. Also called *practical reason theory.*

ideology A set of beliefs that result and are supported not by evidence but by pragmatic interests and, consequently, can be maintained only through ignorance of their real causes.

impartial Uninfluenced by personal bias, either in one's own favor or in favor of some other person to whom one has a personal connection, as posited by the ideal judgment theory.

impartiality The state of being *impartial.*

internalism A family of views according to which normative reasons for acting or motives are internal to ethical or moral facts or to ethical or moral judgments. (See also *conceptual moral internalism, metaphysical moral internalism, moral internalism.*)

intersubjective The property of being able to be perceived, judged, or appreciated from some shared, first-person-plural ("we") perspective.

intrinsic Pertaining to features that concern only what makes something what it is, not its relations to other things. (See also *extrinsic.*)

intuitionists Adherents of the view that ethical propositions (e.g., those concerning right and wrong) can be known by direct inspection and perception. (See also *rational intuitionists.*)

justice The aspect of morality that is concerned with rights and what people deserve. (See also *right.*)

law-based Based on a moral law—that is, on a universal moral requirement that all moral agents are accountable for not violating.

logical positivism A radical form of empiricist naturalism that accepts the verifiability criterion of significance. (See also *verifiability criterion.*)

logical positivists Adherents of *logical positivism.*

merit A kind of value that consists in warranting esteem, admiration, and emulation. (See also *esteem, ideal, noble, shame, worth.*)

metaethical Pertaining to *metaethics.*

metaethical naturalist (See *ethical naturalist.*)

metaethics Philosophical inquiry into metaphysical issues concerning the nature and status of (normative) ethics (e.g., the nature of value), epistemological questions about the possibility of ethical knowledge or the justification of ethical opinion, and issues in the philosophies of language and mind concerning ethical language and thought. (See also *normative ethics, philosophical ethics, second-order questions.*)

metaphysical Pertaining to *metaphysics.*

metaphysical moral internalism The view that there are moral obligations that bind all rational agents, giving them conclusive reasons for acting. (See also *conceptual moral internalism, moral internalism.*)

metaphysical naturalism Another name for naturalism, making it explicit that naturalism is a metaphysical doctrine.

metaphysical naturalist Adherent of *metaphysical naturalism.*

metaphysics The inquiry into what things exist and their fundamental natures.

modern conception of morality (When contrasted with ethics taken broadly), a set of universal norms of conduct that all moral agents are accountable for following and that express concern and respect for all as equals.

modern philosophy The philosophy of the period usually marked as beginning in the seventeenth century with Descartes.

moral externalism The view that moral obligations do not imply conclusive reasons for acting on them (see *conceptual moral externalism*) and that there exist no moral obligations, understood as the conceptual moral internalist understands them (see *metaphysical moral externalism*).

moral goodness What is good from the moral point of view.

moral internalism The view that for something to be a moral obligation it must provide conclusive reasons for those subject to it (see *conceptual moral internalism*) and that there are such moral obligations (see *metaphysical moral internalism*).

moral internalist Adherent of *moral internalism*.

morality The part of ethics that is concerned with right and wrong.

moral law A universal moral requirement that all moral agents are accountable for not violating.

morally desirable Desirable from the moral point of view. (See *moral point of view*.)

morally good Either desirable (appropriately desired) or estimable (appropriately esteemed) from the moral point of view—in the latter sense, predicable of moral agents, motives, and characters. (See also *moral point of view*.)

morally right Predicable of actions; either morally permitted or morally required.

moral point of view The perspective of morality, one of equal concern and respect for all as equal members of the moral community. (See also *morality*.)

moral value Value from the moral point of view.

naturalism The view that only what is natural exists, as opposed to the idea that there are supernatural substances or properties.

natural law Either a descriptive universal generalization used to explain natural phenomena (e.g., the laws of physics) or a prescriptive universal norm to which all persons are subject. (See also *classical natural law theory, moral law*.)

necessary Pertaining to a *necessity*. (See also *contingent*.)

necessity Something that couldn't have been otherwise; that, if true, couldn't possibly have been false and, if false, couldn't possibly have been true. Necessity contrasts with *contingency*.

nihilism The view that nothing matters, that there is no good and bad, right and wrong.

nihilists Adherents of *nihilism*.

noble Having a value worthy of esteem and aspiration, related to ideals of the estimable and to shame rather than to guilt. (See also *esteem, guilt, ideal, shame*.)

noncognitivism The view that ethical thought and language express not beliefs or propositions that are literally true or false but, rather, other states of mind (e.g., feelings, attitudes, intentions, or motives) that lack truth value. (See also *cognitivism*.)

noncognitivists Adherents of *noncognitivism*.

nonmoral Without reference to morality.

nonmoral goodness Value that is not moral value.

nonreductive ethical naturalism The view that ethical properties and facts are natural properties and facts, even if they may not be able to be "reduced to" properties and facts referred to by the vocabulary of the empirical natural and social sciences or naturalistic "folk theory." (See also *empirical naturalism, reductive ethical naturalism.*)

nonreductive ethical naturalists Adherents of *nonreductive ethical naturalism.*

nonreductive ethical supernaturalism The view that ethical properties and facts concern some supernatural metaphysical realm, although they may not be able to be "reduced to" those referred to by the terms of some other metaphysical inquiry (e.g., theology). (See also *reductive ethical supernaturalism.*)

normative Relating to what one ought to be, do, think, choose, feel, and so on. (See also *authority, normativity.*)

normative ethical theory Another name for *normative ethics.*

normative ethics The inquiry into, and systematic theorizing about, what, substantively, one should desire, be, feel, or do, either in particular cases or in general; as opposed to metaethics. (See also *metaethics, philosophical ethics.*)

normative reasons for action Considerations that favor or oppose an action, that recommend it or disrecommend it.

normativity The property of relating to what one ought to be, do, think, choose, feel, and so on. (See also *authority, normative.*)

norm expressivism The noncognitivist view that ethical judgments express the motivational state of accepting a norm, which state is held to lack cognitive or propositional content. (See also *noncognitivism.*)

objectively right (or prudent) Pertaining to the morally right act in light of the objective features of a situation, as contrasted with what is right in light of what the agent believes or has reason to believe (i.e., what is *subjectively right [or prudent]*).

objective purport Seeming to be of something objective and independent of the perceiver (e.g., some objective fact or an objective property of some substance).

obligation Something that is morally required, which it would be wrong not to do. (See also *categorical, wrong.*)

observer's theoretical perspective The third-personal perspective of someone who can grasp and contemplate goings on as part of an objective world, contrasting with the *agent's* or *practical perspective.*

open question G. E. Moore's argument that ethical properties cannot be identified with any natural or metaphysical properties, since, for any such latter property, it is an open question whether something, X, having that property has some ethical property (e.g., is good).

particularism The view that ethical attitudes are directed, irreducibly, at particular individuals or groups.

particularist Adherent of *particularism.*

perfectionism The view that the fundamental ethical value or standard is the promotion of excellence, worth, or merit.

perfectionist Adherent of *perfectionism.*

perfectionist eudaimonism The view that each person should seek his own happiness or good (eudaimonism) and that this consists in self-perfection. (See also *eudaimonism.*)

perfectionist eudaimonist Adherent of *perfectionist eudaimonism.*

person's good That which is promoted when someone is benefited. (See also *good for.*)

phenomenology Thought and experience, as from inside the perspective of the person undergoing it—"what it's like" to have a certain thought or experience. Also, the study of phenomenology, so defined.

philosophical ethics The systematic attempt to integrate metaethics and normative ethics. (See also *metaethics, normative ethics.*)

philosophical moralists Philosophers who attempt to provide a philosophical vindication and explication of morality. (See also *morality.*)

practical perspective The first-person point of view of someone deliberating about what to do; also called the *agent's perspective.* (See also *agency, agent, deliberation, practical thinking, reasons for action.*)

practical reason Critical thought on the question of what to do, also called practical thinking, or the faculty of such thought. (See also *agent's perspective, deliberation, practical perspective, practical thinking.*)

practical reasoning Critical thought on the question of what to do; also called *practical thinking.* (See also *agent's perspective, deliberation, practical perspective.*)

practical reason theory The view that propositions about what someone should do are made true or false by whether they would issue from proper practical reasoning; also called *ideal agent theory, ideal deliberative judgment theory,* or *ideal practical judgment theory.*

practical thinking Critical thought on the question of what to do; also called *practical reasoning.* (See also *agent's perspective, deliberation, practical perspective.*)

practice Social activity structured by rules defining roles and social expectations.

prescriptivism The noncognitivist view that ethical judgments express states of the will (e.g., intentions) and are more like grammatical imperatives than like declaratory sentences. (See also *noncognitivism.*)

prisoner's dilemma A game theory situation, usually involving two persons, in which if each does what is best individually, both end up worse off; an example of a *collective action problem.*

projection The psychological phenomenon of being caused by some subjective state (e.g., an emotion) to regard something as having some objective property. The objective property is said to be a projection of the subjective state.

propositional content The meaning or semantic content of a statement; the proposition it expresses. For example, "Snow is white" expresses the proposition that snow is white (the latter, then, is the propositional content of the sentence). Also called *cognitive content.*

prudent Pertaining to what would actually promote the agent's interest (be objectively prudent) or would be likeliest to do so in light of his beliefs or what he reasonably believes.

qualitative hedonism The view that pleasure is the only good and that value varies directly with the kind of (quality of) pleasure as well as with its amount. (See also *hedonism, quantitative hedonism.*)

quantitative hedonism The view that pleasure is the only good and that value varies directly only with the amount of pleasure. (See also *hedonism, quantitative hedonism.*)

radical choice theory The view that there are no ethical facts independent of the actual choices of agents, that agents' choices create values.

rational human need (See *rational need*.)

rational intuitionism The view that ethical truths are necessary, *a priori*, and open to direct perception by reason. (See also *a priori, necessary*.)

rational intuitionists Adherents of *rational intuitionism*.

rational need Something that any rational human agent can be presumed to need regardless of his specific individual ends.

reasons for action (See *agent's reasons for action, normative reasons for action*.)

reciprocity Cooperation involving a willingness of each to act as he would have the other act if the other is similarly willing as well.

recognition respect The attitude of recognizing someone's dignity. (See also *dignity*.)

reductive ethical naturalism The view that ethical properties can be identified with ("reduced to") properties referred to in some empirical natural or social science or in naturalistic "folk theory." (See also *empirical naturalism, nonreductive ethical naturalism*.)

reductive ethical naturalists Adherents of *reductive ethical naturalism*.

reductive ethical supernaturalism The view that ethical properties and facts can be identified with those referred to by the vocabulary of some supernatural metaphysical form of inquiry (e.g., theology). (See also *nonreductive ethical supernaturalism*.)

respect See *recognition respect*.

ressentiment A state of unconscious hatred in those who feel injured or diminished by others and are unable directly to seek compensation or satisfaction.

right (As in 'morally right' or as predicable of actions), either not morally prohibited ("all right") or morally required (morally prohibited not to do). (See also *wrong*.)

right (As in 'having a right'), a morally justified claim to, or liberty to do, something.

right-making Pertaining to properties that are the reasons why something is right.

rule-consequentialism The view that an act is morally right if, and only if, it is required by a rule the establishment of which in a social practice would promote the greatest total net good. (See also *act-consequentialism*.)

rule-utilitarianism The view that an act is morally right if, and only if, it is required by a rule the establishment of which in a social practice would promote the greatest total net happiness or utility. (See also *act-utilitarianism*.)

second-order desire A desire that has as its object the satisfaction of some first-order desire (e.g., the desire that one's present and future desire be satisfied).

second-order questions Philosophical issues that arise concerning the status of first-order questions. In ethics, the second-order questions are issues of metaethics. (See also *first-order questions, metaethics, normative ethics*.)

shame The emotion or feeling that presents itself as of one's disvalue in some respect—frequently, as one imagines oneself seeming when (correctly) viewed by another. (See also *base, esteem, guilt, ideal, noble, worth*.)

social contract theory The view that political obligation derives from a social contract (whether explicit or implicit, actual or hypothetical), made in a state of nature. (See also *state of nature*.)

state of nature A state of affairs, possibly hypothetical, in which there exists no political authority. (See also *social contract theory.*)

subjectively right (or prudent) The morally right act in light of the agent's beliefs or what she has reason to believe, in contrast with what is right in light of the objective situation (i.e., what is *objectively right [or prudent]*).

subjectivism The view that the content of an ethical judgment concerns the subjective state of the person making the judgment (e.g., that "*x* is good" means "I approve of *x*").

supernatural Pertaining to a realm of properties or facts that is thought to exist in addition to or beyond the natural realm. (See also *natural.*)

sympathy The emotion of concern for someone for his own sake, prompted by an emotional engagement with his plight.

synthetic Pertaining to a proposition whose truth or falsity is not determined by the meanings of the terms in which it is expressed. (See also *analytic.*)

teleological Relating to the idea that things have natural ends or purposes (from the Greek *telos*).

teleological naturalism Aristotle's view that natural substances include inherent goals or purposes (e.g., a 'final cause' or *telos*) that both explain their behavior and provide a standard for their evaluation.

theological voluntarism The view that ethical propositions are made true or false by facts concerning what God desires or commands; also called the *divine command theory.*

universality The property of applying exceptionlessly to all cases of a certain kind.

utilitarian Pertaining to *utilitarianism.*

utilitarianism Any moral theory that bases the moral rightness of acts or the moral goodness of character or motive directly, or indirectly, on the promotion of happiness. (See also *act-utilitarianism, consequentialism, rule-utilitarianism.*)

value Desirability, worth, or dignity. (See also *desirable, desirability, dignity, value-making, worth.*)

value-making Pertaining to features that provide reasons why something is valuable or define what something's value consists in.

verifiability criterion The criterion whereby a sentence or judgment has cognitive or propositional content only if its truth conditions can be verified by sense experience. (See also *logical positivism.*)

virtue Most generally, excellence; more specifically, excellence of character.

weakness of will The condition exhibited when one does other than what one thinks best.

will The capacity or faculty involved in agency and action for reasons. (See also *agency.*)

world-corrected The direction of fit that belief is said to have, since it aims to represent or "fit" the world and is to be corrected if it misrepresents (fails to fit) it. (See also *direction of fit.*)

world-correcting The direction of fit that desire is said to have, since it aims to have the world "fit" it; and if it doesn't, then, with respect to the desire, there will seem to be a fault or error in the world that is to be corrected. (See also *direction of fit.*)

worth A kind of value consisting in being worthy of esteem or emulation, related to ideals of the estimable or noble and to shame rather than to guilt. (See also *esteem, guilt, ideal, merit, noble, shame.*)

wrong (As in 'morally wrong'), pertaining to morally prohibited conduct, to what one morally must not do. (See also *obligation, right.*)

INDEX